T0330307

The Propagation of Misinformation in Social Media

The Propagation of Misinformation in Social Media

A Cross-platform Analysis

Edited by Richard Rogers

Amsterdam University Press

The publication of this book is made possible by grants from First Draft and SoBigData++ which received funding from the European Union's Horizon 2020 research and innovation programme under grant agreement nr. 871042.

Cover illustration: Kurt Schwitters, Merz #1, 1920.

Cover design: Coördesign, Leiden
Lay-out: Crius Group, Hulshout

ISBN	978 94 6372 076 2
e-ISBN	978 90 4855 424 9
DOI	10.5117/9789463720762
NUR	670

Every effort has been made to obtain permission to use all copyrighted illustrations reproduced in this book. Nonetheless, whosoever believes to have rights to this material is advised to contact the publisher.

Printed and bound by CPI Group (UK) Ltd, Croydon, CR0 4YY

Table of Contents

Preface

This book is a product of a collaboration of media researchers at the University of Amsterdam, working together with colleagues in Belgium, Canada, Italy, the U.K. and the U.S. and supported by First Draft, the journalist training network concerned with misinformation. As a group we set out to study the "misinformation problem" in the areas where social media platforms were seemingly working with great ardor to address it: elections and the pandemic. How are they contending with misinformation in the areas that have their special focus, some years on from the seminal "fake news" crisis? In preliminary work we had found that platforms such as Facebook appeared active in retarding the spread of extreme viewpoints and sources that directly related to elections and the pandemic but less successful in immediately adjacent areas such as election-related social issues and vaccines.

What have platform efforts to curb the misinformation problem yielded? The findings we report here are both generalizable as well as platform-specific, which are the two sides of our cross-platform analysis. Generally, social media platforms are mainstreaming the fringe and marginalizing the mainstream. As others have found, extreme viewpoints and sources, particularly from one side of the political spectrum, are receiving disproportionate engagement compared to other sources. But we made the additional, broad observation that even in issue areas deemed serious—elections and the pandemic—mainstream media are less referenced or otherwise marginalized.

More specifically, the manner in which the platforms decenter the mainstream differs. Twitter, for example, has high percentages of "hyper-partisan" sources present in tweets concerning politics, and while not in the majority, many of Facebook's most engaged-with sources would be classified as "fake news," if one deploys the original definition by Craig Silverman in the seminal 2016 *Buzzfeed News* article ushering in the term. Where other platforms are concerned, Instagram users prefer influencers over experts, and rely on their social responsibility in debunking falsehoods. TikTok users parody mainstream media, and Reddit and 4chan (at least their leading forums and boards) dismiss it and send users to alternative influence networks and YouTube videos with extreme cultural commentary. Google Web Search, whose results for political queries we also studied, returns more quality than alternative media but the presence of these sources decline as the election nears, owing to the preponderance of what the researchers call special interest sites. Incidentally, we also found that in election-related Google returns the sources are politically imbalanced.

As I note in the opening chapter, the social media platforms have introduced "editorial epistemologies" for elections and the pandemic, authoring lists of authoritative sources that appear when one queries core election-related or pandemic-related keywords or making other manual interventions beyond commercial content moderation, the outsourced, low-wage work of removing offensive content. They also have had to assume the role of "accidental authorities," developing rapidly evolving source and information adjudication policy that at the same time invites backlash for heavy-handedness as well as competition from "alt-tech" platforms that moderate with a lighter touch. The extent of the platforms' editing, and particularly where it ends, is on display in each of the studies.

Each of the chapters benefits from techniques developed to capture the data necessary to exhibit the current state of the misinformation problem. Some rely on platform-supplied data (Twitter, Instagram), another on a repurposed marketing data dashboard (Facebook) and others on scraping (Google Web Search, Reddit, 4chan, TikTok). There is also a study that uses one platform (4chan) to analyze another (YouTube), given the copious referencing of YouTube videos by "alternative influencers" and later to vernacular newcomers. Many of the studies also classify sources as mainstream or alternative (to varying degrees) as well as evincing a political bent, relying on (and triangulating) external classification schemes developed by journalists and other media analysts.

The platform studies were undertaken twice (and on occasion three times), first in the early run-up to the U.S. presidential elections and the pandemic (March, 2020) and again after the elections and deeper into the pandemic (January, 2021 and/or March, 2021). One of the Twitter studies takes advantage of the data spanning the Capitol riots of January 6, 2021 in Washington, DC, allowing for the analysis of how the platform's subsequent purge of accounts had an impact on the quality of the sources encountered.

The studies have been written up in the format of the *Harvard Kennedy School Misinformation Review*, where earlier versions of the Facebook and 4chan/Reddit chapters were published. It is a format that leads with the research questions and is followed by an essay summary, the implications and the findings. The methods section comes last. To us the format highlights the relevance of the work to journalists and thus also serves well the collaboration with First Draft.

Richard Rogers
November, 2022

1   "Serious queries" and "editorial epistemologies"

How social media are contending with misinformation

Richard Rogers

Abstract
The following concerns the "misinformation problem" on social media during the run-up to the 2020 U.S. presidential election. Employing data journalism techniques, it develops a form of cross-platform analysis that is attuned to both commensurability as well as platform specificity. It analyses the top-ranked political content on seven platforms and finds that each marginalizes mainstream media and mainstreams the fringe. TikTok parodies mainstream media, while 4chan and Reddit dismiss it and direct users to alternative influence networks and extreme YouTube content. Twitter prefers the hyperpartisan over it. Facebook's "fake news" problem concerns declining amounts of mainstream media referenced. Instagram has influencers dominating user engagement. By comparison, Google Web Search buoys special interest sites. It concludes with a discussion of how platforms filter the content through increasing editorial intervention.

Keywords: Problematic information, content moderation, cross-platform analysis, platform criticism, fringe media

Introduction: The politics of problematic information and its cross-platform study

While scholars of hearsay, rumor and conspiracism would point to the history of its staying power (Olmsted, 2009), the spread of misinformation and other problematic information is said to be "supercharged" by contemporary social media (Bounegru et al., 2018; Daniels, 2018). The following examines

Rogers. R. (ed.), *The Propagation of Misinformation in Social Media: A Cross-platform Analysis.*
Amsterdam: Amsterdam University Press 2023
DOI: 10.5117/9789463720762_CH01

that thesis through an analysis of the current state of what globally could be called the "misinformation problem" (Allcott et al., 2019) across seven online platforms: TikTok, 4chan, Reddit, Twitter, Facebook, Instagram and Google Web Search. The part played by YouTube is viewed by way of the videos referenced on 4chan. The case in question is the political information environment in the run-up to the U.S. presidential elections, or what may be dubbed U.S.-based, "political Facebook," "political Twitter," "political Instagram," etc. Borrowing a technique from data journalism, and examining the most interacted-with content around the candidates, political parties and election-related issues, the work reported here found that stricter definitions of misinformation (imposter sites, pseudo-science, conspiracy, extremism only) lessen the scale of the problem, while roomier ones (adding "hyperpartisan" and "junk" sites serving clickbait) increase it, albeit rarely to the point where it outperforms mainstream media.

The misinformation problem differs per platform. On such youthful platforms as TikTok and to a lesser extent Instagram, misinformation may be delivered sarcastically or insincerely, making it difficult to characterize intent (Phillips and Milner, 2017). On the masked or anonymized political boards and communities of 4chan and Reddit, problematic sources are not as copiously referenced as mainstream ones, but that finding does not mean to suggest the absence of a problem, as the most referenced collection of sources (on 4chan) are extreme YouTube videos, many of which end up being deleted from the platform. The users of mainstream social media as Twitter and Facebook continue to point in great proportions to hyperpartisan sources, originally defined as "openly ideological web operations" (Herrman, 2016). Political spaces on Instagram, however, were found to be the "cleanest," where most election-related content is non-divisive and earnestly posted, and influencers, with some exceptions, were found to be responsible information providers, debunking rather than spreading 5G coronavirus conspiracy theories.

The research provides a technique for "cross-platform analysis," or the examination of a single phenomenon (through engagement analysis) across a variety of social media. It thereby addresses critiques of "single platform studies," where societal trends or phenomena are seen through one social media lens without the benefit of a comparative perspective that would furnish a baseline (Rogers, 2019). Engagement analysis of a single subject matter (election-related information, in this case) is considered one robust cross-platform approach since it captures each platform's top content, which refers to the posts or web URLs that receive the most interactions (directly or indirectly). It has the benefit of being more global in its outlook compared to other cross-platform approaches that rely on seeking one or more digital objects shared across platforms (e.g., a hyperlink) and comparing resonance (Rogers, 2017).

But the cross-platform approach put forward here is not blind to platform specificities. It seeks to account for differing platform metrics, vernaculars of use and user subcultures. Accounting for this "medium specificity" is performed in at least three ways. The first is that engagement is measured distinctively per platform, as discussed in some detail below. Second, social media manipulation (such as artificially amplifying misinformation so that it appears to be engaged-with content) also differs per platform. One is interested in fake followers on Instagram and bots on Twitter, for example. Being attuned to platform vernaculars, finally, rests on the study of cultures of use. For example, certain sound effects or facial gestures on TikTok suggest disbelief or mistrust. In all, commensurability thereby relies on both the cross-platform study of engagement as well as individual platform analyses imbued with a medium-specific approach.

In the following I first introduce the current misinformation problem online as bearing some resemblance to the quality of information debates from early web history. The contemporary concerns, however, flow from the "fake news" crisis of 2016, together with the continual study of the extent to which the platforms have addressed the issue (and how they have done so). Moreover, these debates have not escaped the politicization of "big tech" and its supposed "liberal bias" (Vaidhyanathan, 2019), a claim that is also a source of empirical study in the Google Web Search analysis below.

Indeed, designating certain information as problematic may be political (and increasingly politicized), because, as others before us also have found (Benkler et al., 2018; Rogers and Hagen, 2020), it is more prevalent on the right side of the political spectrum, as are problematic or "inauthentic" users, though they are not alone there. Making a case for balancing the partisanship of sources outputted by social media and search engines (rather than serving filter bubbles through personalization, for example) is among the emerging source adjudication methods under consideration, as I will discuss. The piece concludes with a discussion of source criticism on social media, including the recent rise of "editorial epistemologies" alongside crowdsourced ones associated with the (early) web.

Uncertainty online renewed

The web historically has been thought of as a space for the unsubstanti-ated, authored by rumormongers, conspiracy theorists and all manner of self-publishers and fringe contributors. Indeed, one could argue, as it was put in 1994, that on the web "the eminent and the crackpot" stand side-by-side, a feature once celebrated as a productive collision (Rheingold, 1994; Rogers, 2004). Indeed, in early internet studies, next to the blurring of the real and the virtual, conspiracy theory in particular but also the production and circulation of rumor were subjects of study, before notions as the "wisdom of the crowd" and projects as Wikipedia appeared to place the web on a less shaky epistemological footing (Dean, 1998; Shirky, 2008). Arguably, social media have put paid to that brief period of relative stability. Conspiracists or at least those who discuss such phenomena as the link between 5G and the coronavirus are among some of the high-profile influencers or microcelebrities found there (Bruns et al., 2020).[1] In turn, scholars now write, as they did two decades earlier, that the internet is "mainstreaming the fringe" (Barkun, 2016).

The recent uptick in attention to the study of problematic content online could be attributed as well to the "fake news crisis" of 2016, where it was found that so-called fake news outperformed mainstream news on Facebook in the run-up to the U.S. presidential elections that year (Silverman, 2016). That finding also set in motion the subsequent struggle around the occupation of the term from a type of news originating from imposter media organizations or other dubious sources to a "populist" charge against mainstream and "elite" media that seeks to delegitimate sources found publishing inconvenient or displeasing stories (van der Linden et al., 2020).

In its recent study we have had calls to cease using the term, fake news (Pepp et al., 2019). There also has been a series of classification moves. Both the expansion as well as contraction of the notion may be seen in its reconceptualization by scholars as well as by the platforms themselves (Venturini, 2019). The definitional evolution is embodied in such phrasings as "junk news" and "problematic information," which are broader in their classification, while the platforms appear to prefer terms such as "false" (Facebook), which is narrower (Rogers, 2020a).

On the back end the platform companies also develop responses to these activities. They would like to automate as well as outsource its detection and policing, be it through low-wage, outsourced content moderators, (volunteer) fact-checking outfits or user-centered collaborative filtering such as Twitter's "birdwatchers," an initiative they say born of societal distaste for a central decision-making authority, as found through qualitative interviews (Gillespie, 2018; Roberts, 2019; Coleman, 2021). They also take major decisions to label content by world leaders (and indeed have world

---

1   5G is the "fifth generation" technology standard for mobile phone networks.

leader content policies), which subsequently land platform governance and decision-making in the spotlight (Twitter, 2019).

More broadly there has been a rise in the study of "computational propaganda" and "artificial amplification" which the platforms refer to as "inauthentic behavior" (Woolley and Howard, 2016; Colombo and De Gaetano, 2020). These may take the form of bots or trolls; they may be "coordinated" by "troll armies," which has been outlined in Facebook's regular "coordinated inauthentic behavior reports" (Facebook, 2021a). As its head of security policy puts it, Facebook defines it (in a plain speak manner) as "people or pages working together to mislead others about who they are or what they are doing" (Facebook, 2018). Occasionally datasets become available (by Twitter or other researchers) that purport to be collections of tweets by these inauthentic, coordinated campaigners, whereupon scholars (among other efforts) seek to make sense of which signals can be employed to detect them (Roeder, 2018).

Other types of individuals online have caught the attention of the platforms as "dangerous" (Facebook), and have been deplatformed, a somewhat drastic step that follows (repeated) violations of platform rules and presumably temporary suspensions (Rogers, 2020b). "Demonetization" also is among the platforms' repertoire of actions, should these individuals, such as extreme internet celebrities, be turning vitriol into revenue, though there is also the question of which advertisers attach themselves (knowingly or not) to such content (Wilkinson and Berry, 2020). Moreover, there are questions about why certain channels have been demonetized for being "extremist." Others ask, is "counter-speech" an alternative to counter-action (Bartlett and Krasodomski-Jones, 2015; Gagliardone, 2019)?

On the interface, where the metrics are concerned, there may be follower factories behind high follower and like counts (Lindquist, 2019). The marketing industry dedicated to social listening as well as computational researchers have arrived at a series of rules of thumb as well as signal processing that aid in the flagging or detection of the inauthentic. Just as sudden rises in follower counts might indicate bought followers, a sudden decline suggests a platform "purge" of them (Confessore et al., 2018). Perhaps more expensive followers gradually populate an account, making it appear natural. Indeed, there is the question of which kinds of (purchased) followers are "good enough" to count and be counted. What is the minimum amount of grooming? Can it be automated, or is there always some human touch? Finally, there is a hierarchy in the industry, where Instagram followers are the most sought after, but "influencers" (who market wares there) are often contractually bound to promise that they have not "participated in comment pods (group 'liking' pacts), botting (automated interactions), or purchasing fake followers" (Ellis, 2019).

Having touched upon the current state of uncertainty online, I would like to turn to how problematic information manifests itself in social media platforms around specific social issues as well as election-related keywords. The following recounts a cross-platform analysis into the "misinformation problem" in the run-up to the 2020 U.S. presidential election. As noted above, the overall approach is to study most engaged-with content with a sensitivity to platform metrics, vernaculars of use and user subcultures. It relates a set of empirical studies that enquire into the extent to which platforms are again mainstreaming the fringe, examining more specifically those spaces conjured through "serious queries" that contain election-related as well as COVID-19 information. When querying political hashtags, candidate and party names as well as issues, and sifting through the content most interacted with on the platforms, how do more mainstream sources fare in comparison to those characterized as problematic? More to the point, is social media marginalizing the mainstream?

Here I take the most salient findings per platform in turn, before concluding with a discussion of the emergence of editorial epistemologies put into use by social media platforms as well as search engines. Editorial source adjudication is a remarkable transformation in how these platforms sift and filter sources, indicating an exceptional information state, a point upon which I conclude.

TikTok: Instilling doubt in mainstream accounts

TikTok is not usually considered a site for political encounter, but recently the short video sharing platform, used predominantly by youth, has posted rules about political content, indicating its growing presence there. It also warns against "misleading information" and urges users to "verify facts using trusted sources," suggesting that misinformation could be worthy of investigation on the platform (TikTok, 2020). Apart from how to think about TikTok's place in political discourse, we asked, how do TikTok users express themselves politically? How may forms of creative expression on TikTok manifest themselves as misinformation?

On TikTok the most engaged-with videos (returned through platform queries of hashtags) are fresh and topical, which implies that the platform can be regarded as an event-commentary medium, where users may encounter political "news" first through its parody. Political parody in media has a long history, though here the argument is that rather than specialized magazines such as *Punch*, the British weekly satirical magazine (1841–2002), or *The Onion*, an American one (1988–), it is a regular or "mainstream mode" of election engagement for users of the platform.

How are they expressing themselves? The singing and dancing users demonstrate a form of civic engagement by making, tagging and uploading videos that are characterized as forms of "playful political performances" as well as "remixing as ambivalent critique." The playful performances include "giving a speech" as well as "staging an opinion" such as when a man speculates that he hears "thank God for Donald Trump" in the song, Da Da Da. The remixing of news clips and other video that is typical on TikTok satirize candidates, their supporters as well as their viewpoints by introducing sounds that sew mistrust or ridicule, though it is not always clear whether the critique is sincere or ironic, thereby meriting the description "ambivalent critique" (Philips and Milner, 2017).

These sounds are networked objects in the sense that one can select and follow the sound to other videos that have embedded it. The sounds are often deployed in analogous manners, meaning that the audio pathway will lead to more remixed videos that satirize the candidates and their supporters, or videos that have stitched into the another with the sound in order to comment on it (e.g., by commenting on it or mocking it). For instance, "Ride It" by Regard is a viral sound that is often paired with finger dancing to relate stories of cultural misunderstanding. TikTokers have used it when dealing with accusations of being a Trump supporter, such as "get called racist 24/7" (sound), "get yelled at for presenting facts" (sound), and "accused of not respecting women" (sound). The viral sound denotes being misunderstood, eliciting sympathy but also a knowing smile.

TikTokers employ a range of creative expression such as singing, dancing, duet, lip-syncing, mimicking, finger dancing, viral sounds and facial expressions. Some have specific connotations for TikTok insiders and make for trends. Having queried election related hashtags, such as #trump2020 and #biden2020, it was found first that TikTokers make copious use of political hashtags, attaching both Trump and Biden-related hashtags to the same video, thereby striving to maximize the audience and view counts, rather than identify with one candidate or another. In the analysis, the researchers undertook a format and content analysis of the top 30 videos per hashtag query, examining which forms of creative expression are used in political videos and where misinformation may be imparted.

Apart from viral sounds, two other forms of creative expression stand out: lip-synching and facial expressions. TikTokers match the lip movements of the candidates, often sarcastically, for example when the comedian, Sarah Cooper, lip-synched Trump's remarks during a White House briefing on using ultraviolet light and detergent to thwart the coronavirus (2020). Finally, the facial expression that approximates the doubtful emoji is another creative expression often encountered. In these videos news footage may be cut into the shots, such as multiple clips of Joseph Biden hugging women, with the intention to sew doubt about his fitness for presidential office. Here we found many of the political videos instilling mistrust in news clips through sarcastic and doubtful facial expressions. Such a finding prompted consideration of adding "instilling mistrust" as a category of misinformation types developed by Wardle (2017), which ranges from parody (least intent to deceive) through misleading content and false context to fabricated (most intent). Alternatively, one could argue that on TikTok all categories of misinformation could be hybridized, for TikTokers are employing parody when simultaneously introducing misleading content, false context or other misinformation types.

4chan and Reddit: Referencing extreme YouTube content

Unlike public-facing platforms such as Facebook and Twitter, where users cultivate an online self, 4chan and Reddit are so-called masked spaces of anonymous users (De Zeeuw and Tuters, 2020). Particularly the board, 4chan/pol, and the subreddit, r/TheDonald, have been associated with election politics, and especially the 2016 Trump campaign, where support for his candidacy took the form of "the great meme war," which comprised the deployment of vernacular language, image macros and other tactical media to support the candidate's cause (Donovan, 2019). Previous research into misinformation in 4chan/pol and across Reddit found little reference to outwardly problematic sources, such as imposter news sites or (Russian) disinformation, but rather numerous links to extreme videos on YouTube that were later removed (Hagen and Jokubauskaitė, 2020). Thus, while not necessarily a space that links to disinformation sources, it is problematic for other reasons.

Here, in the context of the run-up to the U.S. presidential elections of 2020, the research enquired into the extent to which U.S.-based political boards and forums on 4chan and Reddit share misinformation and "junk" content, and more specifically imposter news and other types of "pink slime" websites, termed as such for the use of low-cost, newspaper-like sites often publishing repurposed content (Tarkov, 2012; Bengani, 2019). We also were questioning the interest these boards and communities might have in what has been termed an "alternative influence network," a group of extreme social media influencers that "facilitates radicalization" (Lewis, 2018). The research employed the so-called "needle-to-haystack" technique, querying 4chan/pol and all of Reddit for the URLs of the pink slime websites, and the "haystack-to-needle" technique which queries an expert list of problematic sources (hosts) in the same platform datasets (Hagen and Jokubauskaitė, 2020).

There are two separate sub-studies, one covering the period from January 11, 2019 to March 25, 2020 and the second picks up where the first ended and runs to December 31, 2021. Throughout no pink slime sites were encountered, suggesting either their lack of significance (despite returning high in Google queries) or the media literacy of the users on the boards and communities (or both). Modest amounts of problematic sources were found but like in previous research copious YouTube links were identified, which led to the inquiry into whether YouTubers from the alternative influence network are significantly present in those online cultures. The alternative influence network (AIN) is described here as a set of YouTube channels fluctuating between "news and personality-centric vlogging, spreading misinformation-laden commentary" (Burton and Koehorst, 2020). Indeed, in the first period, many of these channels were found between the boards and subreddits under study, though their presence was unequally distributed. 4chan/pol and Reddit are rather different in their media consumption, with political Reddit preferring to reference videos using the "alternative debate style" and /pol electing more for the "toxic vox populist" style of single person, direct-to-audience (Tuters and Burton, 2020). Indicating their extreme speech, a significant percentage of the YouTube videos referenced on 4chan has been removed by the platform. In the second period in the run-up to the elections, however, the alternative influence network's presence declined significantly. It should be noted that in June 2020 Reddit closed r/TheDonald as well as other extreme subreddits for breaking platform rules. The decline in links to the AIN coincided with the deplatforming as well as the decline in "junk news" referenced in political Reddit. But given the AIN's decline on 4chan (where no analogous deplatforming took place) one could speculate that they were no longer considered "alternative" for the fringe space.

Twitter: Hyperpartisan sources in ascendancy

Like Facebook and to a lesser extent Instagram, Twitter also has been the focus of public attention concerning misinformation around the 2016 U.S.

presidential elections and beyond. Twitter, rather unlike the other two platforms, has aided researchers in its study through providing curated datasets of Russian and alleged Iranian trolls and influence campaigners, or what are referred to as inauthentic users (Gadde and Roth, 2018). Thus, in the study of misinformation on Twitter, there are generally two strands of analysis to consider—problematic content as well as users. During the 2016 election campaigning and running through to at least late 2019, much of that content and those users, described as "sprawling inauthentic operation[s]" were promoting "pro-Trump messages" (Romm and Stanley-Becker, 2019).

Here we revisit these claims through a study of the content and users on "political Twitter" in the early run up to the 2020 U.S. presidential elections and its aftermath, where we examine result sets of queries for election-related hashtags and keywords, together with the users most active in deploying them (Groen and Geboers, this volume). How much problematic information is present in the most interacted-with content on political Twitter? Are problematic users among the most active? Are they generally of a particular political persuasion?

The content under study are the URLs (hosts) that are referenced in the tweets, and the most active users defined as those who tweet the most. In a three-week timeframe prior to and just after Super Tuesday (March, 2020), when a cluster of election primaries and caucuses were held, in the aftermath (December, 2020 / January, 2021) and after the dust had settled on the Capitol building riots (March 2021), we compared the hosts found in the tweets to a list of problematic sources curated by combining pre-existing labeling sites, including Allsides.com, Media Bias/Fact Check, "the Chart," and NewsGuard. We also consulted Wikipedia and other news sources mentioning the sources in question. With one exception (related to the query DACA, the immigration issue), we found little reference to disinformation, imposter news sources, pseudo-science, conspiracy theory sources or extreme sites. When expanding the definition of problematic information to include hyperpartisan sites, however, in the first period nearly half would fall into that category, with the implication that social media (or at least a goodly share of users of political Twitter) appear to marginalize mainstream sources. Put differently, if we were to employ Craig Silverman's original definition of "fake news," it could be said to challenge mainstream sources anew, as it had in the immediate run-up to the 2016 U.S. elections (on Facebook) (2016). In December 2020 / January 2021 the proportion of hyperpartisan hosts in the examined tweets decreased slightly, but by March, 2021, after Twitter removed users breaking platform rules (e.g., of glorification of violence) that figure was significantly lower, suggesting a "deplatforming effect."

For the study of the most active users, we analyzed "authenticity" with the aid of SparkToro, which employs indicators (abnormal tweeting activity, unusual combinations of followers/following, etc.) to make a determination. We also studied user partisanship or side-taking through qualitative profile analysis. Our findings are not dissimilar to others in that there is far more inauthenticity in the pro-Trump user base, but we also found that there are a few flagged users on the other side of the political spectrum, too.

Facebook: The seminal "fake news" problem persists

Journalists began calling Facebook the seminal "fake news machine" (Gallucci, 2016) just after the finding made by *Buzzfeed News* that so-called fake news was liked and shared more than mainstream news on the social media platform in the three months prior to 2016 U.S. presidential elections (Silverman, 2016). Since then, there has been a steady stream of stories from Facebook's corporate blog concerning both its crackdowns on "inauthentic coordinated behavior," or influence campaigning, as well as its initiatives to curb misinformation and "false news," which is a narrow definition including pseudo-science and conspiracy sites though excluding hyperpartisan ones (Mosseri, 2017). The measures began in at least April 2017 with among other plans to economically disincentivize such sources as the infamous Macedonian fake news factory that chose divisive pro-Trump messaging (over pro-Sanders') because it brought in far more revenue (Silverman and Alexander, 2016; Tynan, 2016). Has much changed in how well "fake news" is consumed on the platform since 2016?

A team of researchers and I revisited the original *Buzzfeed News* story and its data journalism method in order to investigate the state of the "fake news" problem in January–March, 2020 (Rogers, 2020a), which is roughly the first of the three timeframes under consideration in the original *Buzzfeed News* piece entitled, "viral fake election news stories outperformed real news on Facebook" (Silverman, 2016). We investigated again in January 2021, looking into the run-up to the election as well as its aftermath, from March 2020 until the end of December, 2020.

Silverman defined "fake news" as sources ranging from "hoax sites [to] hyperpartisan blogs" (Silverman, 2016). Akin to his method, we ran election-related queries in BuzzSumo, the social media research and monitoring tool. From the results we compiled a list of sources and characterized them with the aid of a series pre-existing "bias" labeling sites, as in both Twitter and Google studies in this volume, so that we had a rough indication of their quality and partisanship. Sources are categorized as problematic or non-problematic (which more colloquially could be called "mainstream"), and those falling into the latter category were subcategorized as (hyper) partisan-conservative, (hyper)partisan-progressive or neither of the two, again with the aid of the existing labeling sites. Problematic sources included imposter news (and so-called "pink slime" sites), pseudo-science, conspiracy theory and extreme sites, as was done in the Twitter study above (Bengani, 2019).

When using Silverman's "fake news" definition (that includes hyperpartisan sites) Facebook's fake news problem has worsened slightly. In the seven timeframes under study (from March 2019 to December 2020) the proportion of engagement of "fake news" to mainstream was on average 1:1.8 compared to 1:2.6 in 2016. If, however, we tighten the definition, as Facebook has done, to "false news" and include in that category only the sources or stories flagged as "problematic" the scale of the problem drops substantially to 1 in 12 on average per quarter. It should be noted that we encountered one imposter news site, which may suggest that they are well targeted by Facebook or that they are not significantly resonating among users.

Nonetheless, in the last period under study in 2016, when Silverman found that "fake news" performed well, imposter sites (as the Denver Guardian) comprised a majority of those most interacted-with. One implication of the finding is that efforts to identify imposter sites (and other "pink slime") continue to have value, despite the fact that they are not yet well consumed. Another implication is that if the problem remains of a smaller scale, scaled-up fact-checking may continue to find its place amongst the counter-initiatives, rather than only mass content moderation and automation.

Instagram: Influencers as responsible information sources?

Instagram had been one of the more understudied and under-appreciated social media platforms when it came to misinformation. That changed with the release of two major reports on the Russian disinformation campaigning surrounding the 2016 U.S. presidential elections (Howard et al., 2018; DiResta et al., 2018). In fact, in one study, it was noted that unlike the other social media platforms Instagram actually saw a rise in disinformation activity in the period just after the elections (Howard et al., 2018). Many of the posts, including memes, were openly divisive, but others were sarcastic and more difficult to decode with respect to stance or side-taking. As scholars have found, over the past few years more and more content online could be described as equivocal or ambivalent, where the sincerity of the post and the sender is unclear (Phillips and Milner, 2017; Hedrick et al., 2018).

In the study of election-related Instagram posts in the early run-up to the 2020 U.S. presidential elections (January–April, 2020) and in the run-up to the election and its aftermath (September, 2020–January, 2021), we enquired into the amount of divisive and ambivalent posts, compared to non-divisive and earnest ones (Colombo and Niederer, this volume). How sarcastic and "edgy" are the top election-related posts on Instagram? Does it form the dominant mode of political discourse on the platform? We also are interested in whether misinformation is spread in this divisive, ambivalent style. To begin to answer these questions, we queried CrowdTangle, Facebook's content monitoring tool, for the names of the candidates and select social issues (healthcare, gun control, COVID-19 and 5G), and coded the top 50 posts for divisiveness (or non-divisiveness) and ambivalence (or earnestness), whereby each post is ultimately given a hybrid label, e.g., divisive-ambivalent. We scrutinized the candidate- or issue-related posts by influencers that had particularly high engagement scores, often at the top of the rankings. We also sought misinformation.

Perhaps counter-intuitively, we found Instagram to be a rather healthy platform. The vast majority of the top posts concerning the candidates as well as the social issues are earnest and non-divisive. Virtually no posts were found to be divisive and ambivalent. Indeed, most posts were sincere expressions of support. Of the few divisive posts which the coders addition-ally found to be earnest, half were by Donald Trump or Donald Trump, Jr., and most of the rest concern Trump or gun control. Apart from a few posts pushing a conspiracy theory surrounding 5G and COVID-19 (including one post that ranked second in engagement), no other misinformation was encountered. The top 5G related post, by an influencer, debunked the conspiracy. Indeed, with a few exceptions we also found that the influencers were posting responsibly and earnestly.

In a separate exercise we studied the authenticity of the followers as well as the political parties, employing the HypeAuditor tool. While, in both timeframes, the Republican Party's account had over 25% of suspect follow-ers, and Trump's had 25%, Biden was not far behind at about 20%. His party also had 25% of suspect followers. It should be noted that when separating the two categories that make up inauthentic followers—"mass follower" accounts and "suspect" accounts—in the first period the Republican Party and Trump tally higher on suspicious followers, defined as "Instagram bots and people who use specific services for likes, comments and followers purchase" (Komok, 2020), while in the second period the candidates and parties grow closer together in their suspect counts.

Google Web Search: Liberal sources outnumber conservative ones

While Google Web Search could be considered the dominant information machine online, among the major platforms and online services it has been one of the least studied for misinformation. Recognizing the potential for its spread during the pandemic, or what the head of the WHO called the "infodemic" (UN DGC, 2020), Google has been curating the results for queries concerning the COVID-19 pandemic, with side bars ordering the official information served, and results geo-tailored to provide local and national resources. Such information curation is rather unprecedented, unless one counts Google's disclaimer notice on top of the results page for the query "Jew" (Sullivan, 2004), or the cleaning up of autosuggested queries to remove ethnic, homosexual and other slurs (Gibbs, 2016). Another contemporary context behind the study of election-related Google results concerns the debate surrounding "liberal tech bias" (Schwartz, 2018). Could Google results be thought to exhibit a bias towards or against particular types of sites? How to characterize the sites returned for political queries?

In order to start to answer these questions, we queried candidate names, political parties and a host of election-related issues in Google, with results from the "U.S. region" from January 12, 2019 to March 23, 2020 and again from March 24, 2020 to January 5, 2021 (Torres, this volume). In an examination of the top 20 results per query, we ask, how to characterize the sources returned? Are problematic sources present and even highly ranked? How could the results be characterized politically? To do the analysis, we curated a source list of problematic and non-problematic sources, largely news and cultural commentary, combining a set of media labeling sources, as in the Twitter and Facebook projects discussed above. We also consulted Wikipedia and online news mentions of potentially problematic sources. The categorization is considered rough and is meant to give an indication rather than a determination. With the aid of the labeling sites, we also assigned political leanings. There are two distinctive political categorization schemes, one "ample" and one "narrow," with the former merging center-left and left and center-right and right, and the latter only including left (liberal) or right (conservative) labels, according to the sites that sort sources in such a fashion. (When there was disagreement among the labeling sites, we went with the majority.) We also labeled the sites returned that fell outside the categories, such as "special interest," "local news" and "official."

In all we found that the Google results for our nearly 120 queries resulted in scant problematic information returned. Hardly present as well were official sources that we defined as federal or local government, intergovernmental agencies, politicians, or campaign websites. Special interest sites, a broad category ranging from think tanks to advocacy groups, have an outsized presence in the results, however, especially in the run-up to the elections. These sites tend to specialize in an issue or industry, which is also an indication of how Google values information sources. Most significantly, when considering the political leanings of sources, it is striking that Google could be said not to seek "balance." That is, liberal sources outnumber conservative ones in the results for all queries made. Employing the "ample" categorization, for the first period, the results were 6:1 in favor of liberal sources, and 3:1 when employing the narrower scheme, and for the second period they jumped to 12:1 and 14:1.

Marginalizing the mainstream

At the outset the question to be addressed concerned the extent to which social media is "mainstreaming the fringe," not so unlike the early web, prior to the development of epistemologies that placed it on firmer ground. Among those mentioned were the wisdom of the crowd such as Wikipedia's collaborative editing, but there were others. For instance, Yahoo! and DMOZ employed librarianship in their directory-making, Google used hyperlink analysis scientometrically, and the early U.S. blogosphere constituted a kind of fact-checking, epistemic community, most famously uncovering faked documents held up as authentic by an authoritative TV news program (60 Minutes), in what has become known as the "Killian documents controversy" (Callery and Proulx, 1997; Langville and Meyer, 2006; Wikipedia contributors, 2020). Here we now ask the same of social media. How to characterize the current epistemological foundations of online platforms?

In order to grapple with that question, I briefly sum up the findings with respect to the relationship between the mainstream and the fringe per platform and draw conclusions from our cross-platform approach. Generally speaking, social media and its users appear to be marginalizing the mainstream. Subsequently, I discuss the prospects of source adjudication in terms of results curation or otherwise managing which content is allowed to remain on social media platforms. It is a form of "platform criticism" that speaks to the various emerging epistemologies on offer to stabilize social media.

The social media platforms under study have varied relationships with mainstream media, at least with respect to those sources or posts most interacted with in the run-up to the 2020 U.S. presidential elections and its aftermath. Broadly speaking, TikTok parodies it, 4chan and Reddit dismiss it and direct users to alternative influence networks and extreme as well as conspiratorial YouTube content. Twitter nearly prefers the hyperpartisan over it. Facebook's "fake news" problem also concerns declining amounts of mainstream media referenced. Instagram has influencers (rather than, say, experts) dominating user engagement, though is a rather healthy space. By comparison, Google Web Search buoys the liberal mainstream (and sinks conservative sites), but generally gives special interest sources, as they were termed in the study, the privilege to provide information rather than official sources.

These findings were made on the basis of cross-platform approach that seeks to attain commensurability of the findings through employing engagement analysis on each platform. At the same time, it remains sensitive to the platforms' specificities by remaining attuned to each of their differing metrics, vernaculars of use and user subcultures, as related above.

Overall, we found that social media marginalize the mainstream, albeit in manners specific to each platform. Given the decline of what one could call "mainstream authority" online, how to characterize the contemporary approaches to source adjudication, when considering problematic information? That platforms are manually editing results (for certain queries) indicates what I would call an "exceptional information state."

Recently, social media platforms and Google web search have begun to curate the results of such "serious queries" as coronavirus, COVID-19 and similar terms related to the global pandemic. Such filtering may explain the scant amount of outwardly problematic information such as conspiracy websites encountered in the top results for coronavirus queries across the platforms. It does, however, raise the question of the epistemology behind the authority that is being applied, and whether it puts paid (for example) to the signals approach of algorithms, and instead puts forward "editing in" official sources as the top content recommended.

Editorial epistemologies and serious queries

Source list or results curation is laborious work and fell into decline with the overall demise of the human editing of the web and the rise of the back end, and algorithmic signals, taking over from the editors (Rogers, 2013). COVID-19 and the coronavirus are thus exceptional for they have marked the return of the editors and raise the question of whether their work should extend beyond pandemic sources to election-related information, as discussed above. Maintaining COVID-19 and the coronavirus as an exceptional information state would draw the line there, though cases could be made to extend the adjudicative practice to the democratic process, where policymakers especially in Europe have directed their efforts. France's false news legislation comes to mind, as does Germany's extension of its hate speech act. There are also Facebook's efforts to maintain a political ad archive tool. Each is (partially) a response to concerns of a repeat, in Europe and beyond, of the "fake news" crisis of 2016.

So far, the pandemic and (for some) election-related matters are "serious queries" in the sense that the information returned should not be fully in the hands of current trends in algorithmic culture but returned to editors. With content reviewers and moderators, there is currently a blurring (and in a sense cheapening) of editors, however. Their low-wage, outsourced work to date has had to do with violent and pornographic content rather than the "quality of information" (Roberts, 2019). There is the question of the journalistic training and qualifications for the editing work (Parks, 2019). The professional fact-checking editors, as mentioned above, would struggle with volume.

There are advocates of an editorial recovery online. Source adjudication techniques on offer these days for results curation are, among others, journalistic balance, the absence of biased sources, fact-checked stories, and "longue durée" expertise, be it official and/or established. Crowd-sourcing users to flag inappropriate content or only checking trending content are also available approaches. All mark the return of qualitatively determining the worthiness of source appearance and could be dubbed editorial epistemologies. Each requires judgements in advance of the moment of gaveling the A/B or ignore/delete decision, as platforms are wont to decide to allow a post or not. (For world leaders, as mentioned, the posts may be labeled.) There is also the question of handling the volume of posts to be scrutinized

When curating results or otherwise managing outputs, to undertake "balanced list" work implies making political or partisan source distinctions, and continually returning to the outputs to check the weight of each side per substantive query. An approach seeking an "absence of biased sources" presupposes classification and monitoring and likely relying on official, institutionalized information. Fact-checking, rather than on a source level, switches the efforts to the individual story, and subsequently researches, archives and labels them. At least as it has been performed on Facebook posts by DPA and AFP, the German and French news agencies respectively, it is such meticulous work that it outputs a total of about four fact-checks per day, if their production prior to the 2021 Dutch elections is exemplary (AFP, 2021; DPA, 2021). Relying on "longue durée" expertise could be another means of offering high-quality sources, as organizations working in the same terrain for many years would have accrued credibility, but to official sources it would add non-governmental and other specialized organizations with an established track record (and perhaps a noticeable political leaning).

Another starting point is to take an active audience approach, and assume that another, perhaps more significant instance of filtering lies with the user or what was once known as the "wisdom of the crowd." Users can "flag" or report content on various platforms and label it as inappropriate, misleading, etc. Taking such user reporting practices a step further, as mentioned above, Twitter's "Birdwatch" program seeks dedicated users (not so unlike Wikipedians, albeit without the non-profit spirit) to sift content and enforce platform rules.

As demonstrated in the empirical research reported above, engagement measures that consider rating (liking), circulating (sharing) and commenting (reading) are another means to determine the activity of audiences. On Facebook, but also on Twitter (retweeting), one may inquire into the stories about the coronavirus and other issues making audiences active. Adjudicating only those posts with the highest engagement would allow liking and sharing to trigger editorial interest.

Finally, one also could argue for an "anything goes" approach to misinformation, returning to a pre-pandemic algorithmic signals method operated in tandem with standard content moderation, editing out violence, pornography, terrorism and hate. Such a return would appear unlikely as it would imply a regress in content review standards on mainstream platforms. For example, since 2019, Twitter policies cover not *just* violence but its "glorification" (Twitter, 2019a), as publicized in a case of the labeling a Donald Trump tweet as such. Indeed, more content types are scrutinized these days. Specifically, since the coronavirus pandemic, the types have been expanded to include "misleading" information.

With respect to identifying such information, Twitter writes, "moving forward, we may use these labels ... in situations where the risks of harm ... are less severe but where people may still be confused or misled by the content" (Roth and Pickles, 2020). Setting aside for a moment the question of taking social media company utterances at face value (John, 2019), the statement raises the prospect that the new editorial epistemologies, together with the contestation that accompanies their fundaments, may abide beyond the current exceptional information state.

Note

An earlier version of the article appeared in the journal, *Frontiers in Big Data* (Rogers, 2021).

References

AFP (2021). AFP Factcheck Nederland, Agence France-Presse. https://factchecknederland.afp.com/list.

Allcott, H., Gentzkow, M. and Yu, C. (2019). Trends in the diffusion of misinformation on social media. *Research & Politics*, April–June 2019: 1–8. https://doi.org/10.1177/2053168019848554.

AllSides (2020). Media Bias Ratings. https://www.allsides.com/media-bias/media-bias-ratings#ratings.

Barkun, M. (2016). Conspiracy theories as stigmatized knowledge. *Diogenes*, 62(3–4). https://doi.org/10.1177/0392192116669288.

Bartlett, J. and Krasodomski-Jones, A. (2015). Counter-speech: Examining content that challenges extremism online. Demos. http://www.demos.co.uk/wp-content/uploads/2015/10/Counter-speech.pdf.

Bengani, P. (2019, December 18) Hundreds of "pink slime" local news outlets are distributing algorithmic stories and conservative talking points, Tow Center for Journalism, Columbia University. https://www.cjr.org/tow_center_reports/hundreds-of-pink-slime-local-news-outlets-are-distributing-algorithmic-stories-conservative-talking-points.php.

Benkler, Y., Faris, R. and Roberts, H. (2018). *Network propaganda: Manipulation, disinformation, and radicalization in American politics*. Oxford University Press.

Bounegru, L., Gray, J., Venturini, T. and Michele, M. (2018). *A field guide to fake news*. Public Data Lab.

Bruns, A., Harrington, S. and Hurcombe, E. (2020) "Corona? 5G? or both?": The dynamics of COVID-19/5G conspiracy theories on Facebook. *Media International Australia*, 177(1). https://doi.org/10.1177/1329878X20946113.

Burton, A. and Koehorst, D. (2020). The spread of political misinformation on online subcultural platforms. *Harvard Kennedy School Misinformation Review*, 1(6). https://doi.org/10.37016/mr-2020-40.

BuzzSumo (2020). Buzzsumo media monitoring. https://buzzsumo.com.

Callery, A. and Proulx, D.T. (1997) Yahoo! Cataloging the web. *Journal of Internet Cataloging*, *1*(1). https://doi.org/10.1300/J141v01n01_06.

Coleman, K. (2021). Introducing Birdwatch, a community-based approach to misinformation. https://blog.twitter.com/en_us/topics/product/2021/introducing-birdwatch-a-community-based-approach-to-misinformation.html.

Colombo, G. and De Gaetano, C. (2020). Dutch political Instagram: Junk news, follower ecologies and artificial amplification, In R. Rogers and S. Niederer (Eds.) *The politics of social media manipulation* (pp. 147–168). Amsterdam University Press.

Cooper, Sara (2020). How to medical, TikTok video. https://www.tiktok.com/@whatchugotforme/video/6819061413877763334.

Daniels, J. (2018). The algorithmic rise of the "alt-right." *Contexts*, *17*(1). https://doi.org/10.1177/1536504218766547.

De Zeeuw, D. and Tuters, M. (2020). Teh Internet is serious business: On the deep vernacular web and its discontents. *Cultural Politics*, *16*(2), pp. 214–232. https://doi.org/10.1215/17432197-8233406.

Dean, J. (1998). *Aliens in America*. Cornell University Press.

DiResta, R., Shaffer, K., Ruppel, B., Sullivan, D., Matney, R., Fox, R., Albright, J. and Johnson, B. (2018). The tactics & tropes of the Internet Research Agency. New Knowledge. https://disinformationreport.blob.core.windows.net/disinformation-report/NewKnowledge- Disinformation-Report-Whitepaper.pdf.

Donovan, J. (2019). How memes got weaponized: A short history. *MIT Technology Review*. https://www.technologyreview.com/2019/10/24/132228/political-war-memes-disinformation/.

DPA (2021). DPA fact-checking. Deutsche Presse-Agentur. https://dpa-factchecking.com/netherlands/.

Ellis, E.G. (2019, September 10) Fighting Instagram's $1.3 billion problem—fake followers. *Wired*. https://www.wired.com/story/instagram-fake-followers/.

Facebook (2018, December 6). Coordinated inauthentic behavior. Facebook Newsroom. https://about.fb.com/news/2018/12/inside-feed-coordinated-inauthentic-behavior/.

Facebook (2021a, February 9). January 2021 coordinated inauthentic behavior report. Facebook Newsroom. https://about.fb.com/news/2021/02/january-2021-coordinated-inauthentic-behavior-report/.

Gadde, V. and Roth, Y. (2018, October 17). Enabling further research of information operations on Twitter. Twitter blog. https://blog.twitter.com/en_us/topics/company/2018/enabling-further-research-of-information-operations-on-twitter.html.

Gagliardone, I. (2019). Defining online hate and its "public lives": What is the place for "extreme speech"? *International Journal of Communication*, *13*. https://doi.org/1932–8036/20190005.

Gallucci, N. (2016, November 22). 8 ways to consume news without using Facebook. *Mashable*. https://mashable.com/2016/11/22/consume-news-without-facebook/.

Gibbs, S. (2016, December 5). Google alters search autocomplete to remove "are Jews evil" suggestion. *The Guardian*. https://www.theguardian.com/technology/2016/dec/05/google-alters-search-autocomplete-remove-are-jews-evil-suggestion.

Gillespie, T. (2018). *Custodians of the Internet: Platforms, content moderation, and the hidden decisions that shape social media*. Yale University Press.

Harris, S. (2019, February 5). #148 – Jack Dorsey. Sam Harris Podcast. https://samharris.org/podcasts/148-jack-dorsey/.

Hedrick, A., Karpf, D. and Kreiss, D. (2018). The earnest internet vs. the ambivalent internet. *International Journal of Communication*, 12(8). https://ijoc.org/index.php/ijoc/article/view/8736.

Herrman, J. (2016, August 24). Inside Facebook's (totally insane, unintentionally gigantic, hyperpartisan) political-media machine. *New York Times*. https://www.nytimes.com/2016/08/28/magazine/inside-facebooks-totally-insane-unintentionally-gigantic-hyperpartisan-political-media-machine.html.

Howard, P.N., Ganesh, B., Liotsiou, D., Kelly, J. and François, C. (2018). The IRA, social media and political polarization in the United States, 2012–2018, Computational Propaganda Research Project, Oxford Internet Institute.

HypeAuditor (2020). Instagram reports, https://hypeauditor.com/reports/instagram/.

John, N.A. (2019). Social media bullshit: What we don't know about facebook.com/peace and why we should care. *Social Media + Society*, January–March: 1–16. https://doi.org/10.1177/2056305119829863.

Komok, A. (2018). How to check Instagram account for fake followers. HypeAuditor. https://hypeauditor.com/blog/how-to-check-instagram-account-for-fake-followers/.

Langville, A.N. and Meyer, C.D. (2006). *Google's PageRank and beyond: The science of search engine rankings*. Princeton University Press.

Lewis, R. (2018). Alternative influence: Broadcasting the reactionary right on YouTube. Data & Society Research Institute. https://datasociety.net/output/alternative-influence/.

Lindquist, J. (2019). Illicit economies of the internet. *Made in China Journal*, 3(4), pp. 88–91. https://madeinchinajournal.com/2019/01/12/illicit-economies-of-the-internet-click-farming-in-indonesia-and-beyond/.

Mahendran, L. and Alsherif, N. (2020, January 8) Adding clarity to our Community Guidelines. TikTok newsroom. https://newsroom.tiktok.com/en-us/adding-clarity-to-our-community-guidelines.

Media Bias/Fact Check (2020). Filtered search. https://mediabiasfactcheck.com.

Mosseri, A. (2017, April 6). Working to stop misinformation and false news. Facebook Newsroom. https://about.fb.com/news/2017/04/working-to-stop-misinformation-and-false-news/.

NewsGuard (2020). NewsGuard Nutrition Label. https://www.newsguardtech.com.

Olmsted, K. (2009) *Real enemies: Conspiracy theories and American democracy, World War I to 9/11*. Oxford University Press.

Otero, V. (2017). The Chart. version 3.1. ad fontes media. https://www.adfontesmedia.com/the-chart-version-3-0-what-exactly-are-we-reading/.

Parks, L. (2019). Dirty data: Content moderation, regulatory outsourcing and The Cleaners. *Film Quarterly, 73*(1). https://doi.org/10.1525/fq.2019.73.1.11.

Pepp, J., Michaelson, E. and Sterken, R. (2019). Why we should keep talking about fake news. *Inquiry*. https://doi.org/10.1080/0020174X.2019.1685231.

Phillips, W. and Milner, R.M. (2017). *The ambivalent internet: Mischief, oddity, and antagonism online*. Polity.

Porter, J. (2020, May 29). Twitter restricts new Trump tweet for "glorifying violence." *The Verge*. https://www.theverge.com/2020/5/29/21274323/trump-twitter-glorifying-violence-minneapolis-shooting-looting-notice-restriction.

Rheingold, H. (1994). *The millennial whole earth catalog*. HarperCollins.

Roeder, O. (2018, August 8). We gave you 3 million Russian troll tweets. Here's what you've found so far. FiveThirtyEight. https://fivethirtyeight.com/features/what-you-found-in-3-million-russian-troll-tweets/.

Rogers, R. (2004). *Information politics on the web*. MIT Press.

Rogers, R. (2013). *Digital methods*. MIT Press.

Rogers, R. (2017). Digital methods for cross-platform analysis. In J. Burgess, A. Marwick and T. Poell (Eds.) *The SAGE handbook of social media* (pp. 91–108). Sage.

Rogers, R. (2019). *Doing digital methods*. Sage.

Rogers, R. (2020a). The scale of Facebook's problem depends upon how "fake news" is classified. *Harvard Kennedy School Misinformation Review, 1*(6). https://doi.org/10.37016/mr-2020-43.

Rogers, R. (2020b). Deplatforming: Following extreme internet celebrities to Telegram and alternative social media. *European Journal of Communication, 35*(3). https://doi.org/10.1177/0267323120922066.

Rogers, R. and Hagen, S. (2020). Epilogue: After the tweet storm. In R. Rogers and S. Niederer (Eds.) *The politics of social media manipulation* (pp. 253–256). Amsterdam University Press.

Romm, T. and Stanley-Becker, I. (2019, December 21). Facebook, Twitter disable sprawling inauthentic operation that used AI to make fake faces. *Washington Post*. https://www.washingtonpost.com/technology/2019/12/20/facebook-twitter-disable-sprawling-inauthentic-operation-that-used-ai-make-fake-faces/.

Roth, Y. and Pickles, N. (2020, May 11). Updating our approach to misleading information. Twitter Blog. https://blog.twitter.com/en_us/topics/product/2020/updating-our-approach-to-misleading-information.html.

Schwartz, O. (2018, December 4). Are Google and Facebook really suppressing conservative politics? *The Guardian*. https://www.theguardian.com/technology/2018/dec/04/google-facebook-anti-conservative-bias-claims.

Shirky, C. (2008). *Here comes everybody*. Penguin.

Silverman, C. (2016, November 16). This analysis shows how viral fake election news stories outperformed real news on Facebook. *Buzzfeed News*. https://www.buzzfeednews.com/article/craigsilverman/viral-fake-election-news-outperformed-real-news-on-facebook.

Silverman, C. and Alexander, L. (2016, November 3). How teens in the Balkans are duping Trump supporters with fake news. *Buzzfeed News*. https://www.buzzfeednews.com/article/craigsilverman/how-macedonia-became-a-global-hub-for-pro-trump-misinfo.

Sparktoro (2021). Audience intelligence. https://sparktoro.com.

Sullivan, D. (2004, April 24) Google in controversy over top-tanking for anti-Jewish site. *Search Engine Watch*. https://www.searchenginewatch.com/2004/04/24/google-in-controversy-over-top-ranking-for-anti-jewish-site/.

Tarkov, A. (2012, June 30). Journatic worker takes "This American Life" inside outsourced journalism. Poynter. https://www.poynter.org/reporting-editing/2012/journatic-staffer-takes-this-american-life-inside-outsourced-journalism/.

Tuters, M. and Burton, A. (2021). The rebel yell: Toxic vox populism on YouTube. *Canadian Journal of Communication*. forthcoming.

Twitter (2019a). Glorification of violence policy, Twitter help center. https://help.twitter.com/en/rules-and-policies/glorification-of-violence.

Tynan, D. (2016, August 24) How Facebook powers money machines for obscure political "news" sites. *The Guardian*. https://www.theguardian.com/technology/2016/aug/24/facebook-clickbait-political-news-sites-us-election-trump.

UN DGC. (2020, March 31). UN tackles "infodemic" of misinformation and cybercrime in COVID-19 crisis. UN Department of Global Communications. https://www.un.org/en/un-coronavirus-communications-team/un-tackling-'infodemic'-misinformation-and-cybercrime-covid-19.

Vaidhyanathan, S. (2019, July 28). Why conservatives allege big tech is muzzling them. *The Atlantic*. https://www.theatlantic.com/ideas/archive/2019/07/conservatives-pretend-big-tech-biased-against-them/594916/.

Van der Linden, S., Panagopoulos, C. and Roozenbeek, J. (2020). You are fake news: Political bias in perceptions of fake news. *Media, Culture & Society, 42*(3). https://doi.org/10.1177/0163443720906992.

Venturini, T. (2019). From fake to junk news: The data politics of online virality. In D. Bigo, E. Isin and E. Ruppert (Eds.) *Data politics: Worlds, subjects, rights* (pp. 123–144). Routledge.

Wardle, C. (2017, February 16). Fake news: It's complicated. First Draft. https://firstdraftnews.org/latest/fake-news-complicated/.

Wikipedia contributors (2020). Killian documents controversy. *Wikipedia: The Free Encyclopaedia*. https://en.wikipedia.org/w/index.php?title=Killian_documents_authenticity_issues&oldid=962589844.

Wilkinson, W.W. and Berry, S.D. (2020). Together they are Troy and Chase: Who supports demonetization of gay content on YouTube? *Psychology of Popular Media*, 9(2). https://doi.org/10.1037/ppm0000228.

About the author

Richard Rogers, PhD, is Professor of New Media & Digital Culture, Media Studies, University of Amsterdam, and Director of the Digital Methods Initiative. He is author of *Information Politics on the Web* and *Digital Methods* (both MIT Press) and *Doing Digital Methods* (SAGE).

2 Problematic information in Google Web Search?

Scrutinizing the results from U.S. election-related queries

Guillen Torres[1]

Abstract

The goal of this study is to analyze the type and ranking of information sources furnished by Google Web Search for queries related to the
2020 U.S. presidential election. Overall, we found that the presence of
problematic information in the returns is scant. In additionally studying
the diversity of sources, we found an asymmetry between liberal and
conservative websites in the top results. This imbalance is notable when
approaching it through the lens of an opposition or even competition for
high rankings between liberal and conservative media, broadly defined. A
more nuanced classification does not eliminate the imbalance given the
near absence (from March 2020 to January 2021) of explicitly conservative
outlets.

Keywords: Google, problematic information, digital methods, elections
research

Research questions

How are problematic sources positioned within the first 20 Google.com
results, when querying U.S. candidates and their most significant issues?
For issue-related queries, what are the predominant source types returned,
and how may their leanings be characterized politically?

[1] Parts of this research were carried out in collaboration with Varvara Boboc and Robert
Baciu.

Rogers. R. (ed.), *The Propagation of Misinformation in Social Media: A Cross-platform Analysis*.
Amsterdam: Amsterdam University Press 2023
DOI: 10.5117/9789463720762_CH02

Essay summary

The main finding is that within the top 20 Google results for election-related queries from February 2019 to January 2021 the presence of problematic information is low. We also find that when using either "ample" or "narrow" definitions of liberal and conservative sources to query Google Web Search in different moments in time, liberal outnumber conservative. Moreover, we find the predominance of mainstream news, a considerable presence of "special interest" websites and a fluctuating presence of official sources. "Special interest" is used as a broad category including professional associations, think tanks, and industry or community news sites, producing information mostly around one specific topic (e.g., farming or taxes), while "official sources" are largely governmental or the candidates' own campaign websites.

This study undertakes a source-distance analysis of Google.com results for the periods of February 12, 2019 to March 23, 2020 and March 24, 2020 to January 5, 2021, where one measures how far from the top of the returns are particular types of sources. To assign a rough political bias category to the search results, two classifications were devised, based on existing schemes. An "ample" classification combines center-left and left political orientations into left, and center-right and right into right. A "narrow" classification makes a stricter division and only considers explicitly left or right sources as liberal or conservative, while center-left and center-right outlets are considered mainstream.

Implications

The low presence of official institutional sources in the returns to our queries is not necessarily problematic, but the strategies Google implemented to fight problematic information related to SARS-CoV-2 beg the question about whether something similar may be justified for queries related specifically to elections, or more generally to public policies or governmental programs that have proven controversial or divisive in the past (e.g., DACA or foreign relations with China). Google already employs "featured snippets" that highlight certain sources for general searches (e.g., [Trump policies] bring up a Wikipedia page), but this is not the case for queries about specific policies. Whether it is desirable that Google privileges information produced by politically accountable institutions is a discussion that lies beyond the scope, but the fact that the company has decided to take a stance regarding SARS-CoV-2 suggests that there might be benefits to such a strategy.

Secondly, the near absence of such problematic sources as imposter, conspiracy, pseudo-science or extreme sites in the top twenty results suggests that Google's efforts to prevent such misinformation from rising to the top are succeeding (Google 2019a). This is the case at least for queries related to political issues and candidates. As other platforms are arguably losing the battle against problematic information, particularly in the context of the global pandemic and political unrest in the U.S. (Alba, 2020), Google's strategies could be considered by other actors.

Third, we found a preponderance of liberal sources over conservative ones using both an "ample" and a "narrow" classification of information sources. Although this result could be related to the wording of our queries (i.e., occasionally using more liberal keywords), we found that the imbalance still stands for those queries that could be considered more neutral (i.e., immigration). Considering that a perceived liberal media bias lingers in the U.S. political imaginary (Hassel et al., 2020), Google may find that clarifying anew why its algorithm privileges certain outlets over others could contribute to the debate about a "liberal tech bias" (Boxell et al., 2020). Although Google previously has openly stated that there is no bias affecting its results (Wakabayashi, 2018) and the platform's role in polarizing its users is still a heavily contested matter (Boxell et al., 2017; Sunstein, 2018; Bail et al., 2018), Google's reflection about the possibilities of implicit bias could be beneficial. The company often frames the production of its results as a process guided by objective measures of content quality and value (Google, 2019a, 2019b); however, reflections around these concepts (Kelemen, 2005; Heuts and Mol, 2013) as well as about the politics of search engine rankings (Introna and Nissenbaum, 2000; Noble 2018) could be matters for Google to discuss more explicitly.

Finally, the considerable presence of websites of special interest in our queries implies that these sources have the privilege of supplying election-related information. Considering how those voices are boosted over official sources, this finding calls for a more specific analysis into the politics of the information they produce. Although previous studies have also noted the presence of this type of source (Courtois et al., 2018; Unkel and Haim, 2019), they have not yet been the exclusive object of research. Such an analysis would pertain to the study of less obvious partisanship in search engine rankings (Robertson et al., 2018).

Findings

Finding 1: Official sources are hardly in evidence in Google Web Search results for queries related to the 2020 U.S. presidential candidates Joe Biden and Donald Trump. Overall, the presence of official sources, such as ".gov" sites or official campaign sites is quite low. For the first period under research (February 12, 2019 to March 23, 2020), official sources make up only 1% of the total. For the second (March 24, 2020 to January 5, 2021), which includes the official campaign season, the elections and the days prior to inauguration day, the presence of these sources increases considerably, making up 5% of the dataset. Queries related to Donald Trump produce the highest number of official sources, accounting for nearly 10% of that subset of the results. In fact, the whitehouse.gov website was the third most common top result for Trump-related queries. Given the scope of this chapter, it is not possible to identify whether this change is related to contextual factors such as current events or a change in the evaluation of source relevance by the Google Web Search service.

Finding 2: Problematic information is hardly present in Google Web Search results for queries related to the 2020 U.S. presidential candidates before the start of the pre-campaigning, and it is entirely absent afterwards. Problematic sources are only present in our dataset if this category is made to include hyperpartisan websites. No imposter, fake news or fly-by-night sources were identified. Only five sources classified as problematic were identified: *The World Tribune, National File, RedState, TheBL,* and *Breitbart,* all labeled as hyperpartisan. These sources were present exclusively during the period between the unofficial start of Trump's campaign and the suspension of in-person rallies due to the COVID pandemic. Table 2.1 displays the distribution of problematic sources among the results. There is no particular query that seems to be more likely to return problematic sources than others, although queries where hyperpartisan sources are present also seem to have more conservative sources than liberal, which is remarkable given the overall low presence of right-of-center sources. It is noteworthy that while the presence of this type of source is minimal, *The World Tribune, National File* and *RedState* show up as the first result for some queries. Queries related to Joe Biden produced the highest number of problematic sources.

Table 2.1   Problematic sources in Google Web Search results.

Source	Query	Candidate	Result ranking
World Tribune	K-12 Education	Donald Trump	1
TheBL	Reparations	Joe Biden	14

Source	Query	Candidate	Result ranking
National File	Charter Schools	Joe Biden	1
Breitbart	DACA	Joe Biden	19, 20
Red State	The Constitution	Joe Biden	1

Timeframe: February 12, 2019 to March 23, 2020. Data from Google.com.

Finding 3: Mainstream news websites dominate the top 20 Google Web Search Results. For both periods under review, the majority of the websites present in the first 20 results of our political queries are mainstream news and special interest sites. Table 2.2 summarizes the types of sources present in our queries for the first period under review. The ten most present sources are the following: *Politico, The New York Times, The Hill, Forbes, Common Dreams* (which we classified as a liberal source, rather than mainstream), *The Guardian, Reuters, USA Today, The Wall Street Journal* and *Wikipedia*. Together, they make up 28% of the total results.

Table 2.2 Occurrences of different types of sources in the results of Google Web Search to political queries.

Candidate	News (national)	Special interest	News (local)	Official	Platform	Academic	Problematic/ hyperpartisan	Other
Trump	73%	19.2%	6.2%	1%	0.9%	0.09%	0.04%	1.3%
Biden	71%	15.8%	9.34%	1.5%	1.2%	0.08%	0.2%	1.3%

Timeframe: February 12, 2019 to March 23, 2020. The category "other" includes websites that appeared in the results due to the keywords we used in connection with the names of the candidates, but that did not include political information. Data from Google.com.

Table 2.3 summarizes the types of sources returned by Google Web Search for the second period under review. The top positions this time are held by *The Washington Post*, followed by *CNBC, The New York Times, Reuters, Forbes, NPR, Politico, The White House, The Guardian* and *NBC News*. Together, these sources represent 34% of the total results, which implies an increase in the overall prominence of these ten mainstream sources (together with the one official source) in comparison to the period before. This result is noteworthy considering that the overall presence of mainstream sources is lower in this second dataset, since special interest websites increased their incidence. The stable presence of *The New York Times, Politico, Forbes, Reuters* and *The Guardian* suggests that Google Web Search assigns them a high relevance.

Table 2.3   Occurrences of different types of sources in the results of Google Web Search to political queries.

Candidate	News (national)	Special interest	News (local)	Official	Platform	Academic	Other
Trump	58%	20%	8%	9.3%	3%	0.7%	1%
Biden	53.4%	28.5%	11.4%	3%	2.3%	0.5%	0.7%

Timeframe: March 24, 2020 to January 5, 2021. The categories of "problematic" and "hyperpartisan" are not included given that no source was classified as such. Data from Google.com.

Finding 4: Overall, the presence of liberal sources is greater than that of conservative websites. Using news bias labeling sites as a rough indicator, we found a greater presence of liberal sources in comparison to conservative ones in all queries and for both periods under review, with a slight decrease in the presence of right-of-center sources in the second. This was the case both with "ample" and "narrow" definitions of what constitutes a liberal or conservative source. Imbalances within search results have been noted before by researchers, journalists and civil society organizations, and results have varied depending on geography and subject matter. For example, Haim et al. (2017) found an overrepresentation of conservative sources in Germany, while in the U.S. audits tend to find more liberal websites than conservative ones (Trielly and Diakopoulos, 2018). In our case, using the "ample" classification makes the imbalance grow to a proportion of 6:1 in favor of liberal sources for the first period under analysis and 12:1 for the second. Using the "narrow" scheme changes the imbalance to around 3:1 and 14:1, respectively. The increase in the ratio of liberal to conservative sources in the second period of analysis is credited to a considerable decrease in the number of conservative websites in the returns, rather than an increase of liberal ones. In fact, the data show an overall decrease of both types of sources, although the presence of conservative sources declined more. Tables 2.4 and 2.5 show the proportions using both classifications. The imbalance stands even for queries that deal with topics that would, intuitively, be connected to a higher presence of conservative sources (i.e., [Donald Trump] [Gun control] or [Donald Trump] [immigration]).

Table 2.4   Proportion of liberal and conservative news sources per candidate. Early campaigning period

Candidate	Liberal (ample)	Unbiased (ample)	Conservative (ample)	Liberal (narrow)	Unbiased (narrow)	Conservative (narrow)
Donald Trump	44.4%	24.2%	8%	11%	63%	3%
Joe Biden	39%	25%	14%	12%	59%	6%

"Special interest" websites are not considered, as their political orientation has not been defined. Timeframe: February 12, 2019 to March 23, 2020. Data from Google.com.

Table 2.5   Proportion of liberal and conservative news sources per candidate. Run-up to election and aftermath

Candidate	Liberal (ample)	Unbiased (ample)	Conservative (ample)	Liberal (narrow)	Unbiased (narrow)	Conservative (narrow)
Donald Trump	41%	22%	2%	4%	61%	0.3 %
Joe Biden	39%	22%	3%	5%	59%	1%

"Special interest" websites are not considered, as their political orientation has not been defined. Timeframe: March 24, 2020 to January 5, 2021. Data from Google.com.

The imbalance is also present when analyzing the diversity of unique URLs from which Google Web Search draws its results. Our dataset consists of 1,300 unique URLs. The proportion liberal/conservative of these sources using the ample scheme is around 3:1, whereas using the more restrictive criteria it is around 4:1. This difference suggests that, overall, Google seems to be drawing results from a more diverse pool of liberal sites than conservative. When only explicitly progressive/conservative websites are classified as such, the imbalance increases. Rather than implying a liberal bias, this result could be related to the existence of a higher number of liberal outlets (Trielli and Diakopoulos, 2019).

There is also a slight difference in the political composition of the unique sources in the two moments of data capture. For example, the five hyper-partisan conservative sources found in the first dataset did not appear in subsequent queries, despite the use of the same keywords. This could be related to current events during the dates of the queries rather than a bias in Google's service. Table 2.6 showcases the political composition of the two datasets in terms of unique sources. This table suggests a tendency towards the reduction of liberal and conservative sources in the search results over time.

Table 2.6   Number of unique sources in absolute numbers, by political orientation.

| | February 12, 2019–March 23, 2020 | | | March 24, 2020–January 5, 2021 | | |
	Left	Center	Right	Left	Center	Right
Narrow	60	290	28	40	265	7
Ample	235	80	78	201	79	36

Data from Google.com.

Table 2.7 digs further into the reduction in the presence of explicitly liberal or conservative sources by showcasing how their presence changed between the two periods under review. Common Dreams and *Jacobin Magazine* exhibit the biggest change, given that they were prominently featured in the first period, when they were even featured as the top result in 11 out of 114 queries.

Table 2.7   Top liberal and conservative sources in absolute numbers, for both periods under research.

| February 12, 2019–March 23, 2020 | | | | March 24, 2020–January 5, 2021 | | | |
Liberal		Conservative		Liberal		Conservative	
commondreams.com	96	washingtontimes.com	53	newsweek.com	21	Foxbusiness.com	10
jacobinmag.com	61	washingtonexaminer.com	45	newyorker.com	20	washingtonexaminer.com	3
newsweek.com	55	nationalreview.com	36	prospect.org	17	city-journal.org	1
nymag.com	49	thefederalist.com	7	vanityfair.com	13	washingtontimes.com	1
thenation.com	12	city-journal.org	1	nymag.com	9	nationalreview.com	1

Data from Google.com.

Finding 5: Special interest websites (and local news stations) have a considerable presence within top 20 Google results for election-related queries. Although national mainstream news outlets make up for the largest proportion of results to our queries, they are not in the majority when analyzing the diversity of unique sources. For the first period of analysis, special interest websites represent 40% of the pool of sources from which Google Web Search draws its results, whereas local news websites represent 20% and mainstream news websites represent only 19%. The presence of this type of source is higher when querying candidate names together with sensitive topics such as drugs, migration or gun control, but also for some less obviously contentious topics such as K-12 education and transportation.

Table 2.8 presents the distribution of unique sources in the results to our queries for both periods under review. Sites we have defined as special interest are the largest number in both cases, and the data shows an increase of 40% of this type of source in the latter queries. The considerable presence of special interest websites suggests that Google's understanding of relevance values specialization and expertise less than the journalistic qualities of established news outlets. Thus, although search results are drawn from a more diverse pool of special interest websites, they are featured less often. The top five special interest websites for the first period were Marijuana Moment (cannabis enthusiasts), *The Motley Fool* (investment), *EdWeek* (education), American for Tax Reform (policy), and The Tax Foundation (policy). For the second period, the top five sources were Marijuana Moment, The Tax Foundation, The Balance (real estate), KHN (public health), and The Tax Policy Center (policy). These sources tend to feature prominently and exclusively within their niche topics, rather than being spread over multiple issue-queries.

The presence of local news websites within our dataset can be characterized in similar terms to special interest websites with the difference that the numbers of the former did not increase from the first period of analysis to the second. In this case, we could argue that Google's understanding of relevance values the geographic proximity of content producers to the issues in question, but that this quality is less valued than the expertise of mainstream news outlets. Local news sources are usually confined to the second page of results, and although high in number in terms of source diversity, they have a low occurrence. The most prominent local news sites in both datasets are connected to large metropolitan areas, such as Los Angeles, Philadelphia, Miami or Chicago.

Table 2.8   Classification of unique sources in search results.

	National News	Local News	Special Interest	Academic	Platform	Official	Problematic	Other
First period	179	213	267	7	8	20	5	36
Second period	136	188	372	18	7	34	0	24

Data from Google.com.

Methods

We implemented a simple source-distance methodology (Rogers, 2019) whose objective is to locate the position of different types of sources within Google Web Search results, in order to find which ones are privileged by the search engine by assigning them positions close to the top. This method is employed to answer the following research questions: How are problematic sources positioned within the first 20 Google.com results for queries concerning U.S. candidates and their most significant issues? And for election-related queries, what are the predominant source types returned, and how may they be characterized politically? We followed Caroline Jack's conceptualization of problematic information as "inaccurate, misleading, inappropriately attributed, or altogether fabricated" (2017: 1).

The queries were designed on the basis of a list of political issues, triangulated from the two political parties' platforms, individual candidate's platforms, and three voter support services: Politico,[2] VoteSmart[3] and On the Issues.[4] The queries consisted of the following keywords: [candidate] AND [issue]. Donald Trump and Joe Biden were the candidates queried. The queries do not strive to replicate the search behavior by Google users, but rather to test the type of information returned generically in the United States by the search engine when querying political issues deemed relevant by voter support services.

Although research has shown that personalization is low in Google's Web Search (Haim et al. 2017, Robertson et al., 2018b), we still sought to reduce the prospects of individual (but not geographical) personalization in our results by performing queries on a clean Firefox Extended Support Release browser (with a fresh installation and with no prior use of any other Firefox version); Virtual Private Network (VPN) software was used to acquire a U.S. IP address. The queries were performed with the Search Engine Scraper (Search Engine Scraper, n.d.). Adjusting the parameters of the tool, we scraped the first 20 results provided by Google, in the U.S. region, for two different periods: February 12, 2019–March 23, 2020 and March 24, 2020–January 5, 2021. While the first period captures the unofficial start of the Trump campaign and up to the suspension of in-person rallies due to the COVID pandemic, the second period captures the official pre-campaigns, the elections, and up to a few days before Joe Biden's inauguration. We set

2   https://www.politico.com/2020-election/candidates-views-on-the-issues/
3   https://justfacts.votesmart.org/
4   https://www.ontheissues.org/Issues.htm

the number of results to 20 under the assumption that users tend not to look much further than that (Jansen and Spink, 2003; Dan and Davison, 2016). Our dataset consists of the results for searches of about 114 issues, each of which was queried two times (one for each candidate) on two different dates (March 23, 2020 and January 5, 2021). This "one shot" strategy introduces some limitations to the study given the known variability in the composition of Google results through time. This variability can be connected with breaking news (Curtois et al. 2018), or updates to the algorithm. Although results variability affects the position that each source holds in the results page (which would have been relevant for our second finding, had we found more problematic information), it seems to affect less the composition of the results in terms of source diversity. For example, in two studies conducted by Trielly and Diakopoulos (2019, 2020) source diversity seems to remain stable throughout the queries performed. Thus, our findings 1, 3 and 4 could be considered indicative despite ours not being a longitudinal study conducted through daily queries.

The resulting list of 9,120 links was compared against an expert list of known problematic sources, which was curated by fellow researchers, using a combination of labeling sites, AllSides.com, Media Bias/Fact Check, "the Chart," and NewsGuard. Wikipedia and news mentions of potentially problematic sources also were consulted. In the relatively few cases where sources had not been previously classified, two researchers independently classified them, following the guidelines of the labeling sites. When unla-beled sources reproduced the content created by larger outlets (as is the case with most local news), the resulting label was the same as assigned to the parent outlet (e.g., CBS, ABC, NPR). In cases where no affiliate was explicitly acknowledged (mostly local news editorial pieces), the coding attempted to locate politically laden opinions. If no bias was detected, the source was labeled as "least biased."

Two categorization schemes were devised, still following the existing labeling sites' overall viewpoints. The first, "ample" one, combines center-left and left political orientations, on the one hand, and center-right and right, on the other. As a result, mainstream sites such as *The Guardian* and *The New York Times* were labeled "liberal," while *The Wall Street Journal* was labeled "conservative." The second, "narrow" scheme makes a stricter division and only considers more explicitly liberal or conservative sources as either left or right, while most mainstream news outlets remain in the center. As a result, sites as *The New York Times*, *The Guardian* and *The Wall Street Journal* switched categories to "center" and sites as *The National Review* and *The Washington Times* were labeled as conservative. Furthermore, we also labeled certain websites as "special interest," "local news," "official," "academic," "platform" and "other." Special interest, the broad category of sources whose content is mostly oriented towards one particular topic, include such professional associations and think tanks whose ultimate goal is to advocate for public policy (e.g., Americans for Tax Reform or the Center for Immigration Studies), as well as industry or community news sites focusing on a particular audience (e.g., *Transport News*, *Agripulse* or the National Low Income Housing Coalition). We differentiated between local and national news outlets, since even if the first sometimes reproduce the content of the latter, we found considerable original local reporting and opinion columns in the results of our queries, prompting a further opportunity to classify partisanship. We considered as "official sources" those belonging to the U.S. federal or local government, inter-governmental agencies, politicians in office, or the official campaign websites of current and former candidates. Academic sources are those connected to a university (e.g., the University of Pennsylvania's Budget Model), while the platforms encountered are Wikipedia, Twitter, YouTube and Facebook. Finally, the category "other" includes all sources that bore no direct relation to the other types.

References

Alba, D. (2020, June 1). Misinformation about George Floyd protests surges on social media. *The New York Times.* https://www.nytimes.com/2020/06/01/technology/george-floyd-misinformation-online.html.

Bail, C.A., Argyle, L.P., Brown, T. W., Bumpus, J.P., Chen, H., Hunzaker, M.B.F., Lee, J., Mann, M., Merhout, F., and Volfovsky, A. (2018). Exposure to opposing views on social media can increase political polarization. *Proceedings of the National Academy of Sciences, 115*(37), pp. 9216–9221. https://doi.org/10.1073/pnas.1804840115.

Boxell, L., Gentzkow, M., and Shapiro, J. (2017). Is the internet causing political polarization? Evidence from demographics. National Bureau of Economic Research. http://www.nber.org/papers/w23258.

Boxell, L., Gentzkow, M., and Shapiro, J. M. (2020). Cross-country trends in affective polarization. National Bureau of Economic Research. https://www.nber.org/papers/w26669.

Courtois, C., Slechten, L., and Coenen, L. (2018). Challenging Google Search filter bubbles in social and political information: Disconforming evidence from a digital methods case study. *Telematics and Informatics, 35*(7), pp. 2006–2015. https://doi.org/10.1016/j.tele.2018.07.004.

Dan, O., and Davison, B. D. (2016). Measuring and predicting search engine users' satisfaction. *ACM Computing Surveys*, *49*(1), pp. 1–35. https://doi.org/10.1145/2893486.

Diakopoulos, N., Trielli, D., Stark, J., and Mussenden, S. (2018). I Vote For—How Search Informs Our Choice of Candidate. In M. Moore and D. Tambini (Eds.), *Digital dominance: The power of Google, Amazon, Facebook and Apple* (pp. 320–341). Oxford University Press.

Digital Methods Initiative. (n.d.). *Search Engine Scraper*. https://wiki.digitalmethods.net/Dmi/ToolSearchEngineScraper.

Google. (2019a). How Google Fights Misinformation. Google Blog. https://www.blog.google/documents/37/How_Google_Fights_Disinformation.pdf.

Google. (2019b). Search Quality Evaluator Guidelines. https://static.googleusercontent.com/media/guidelines.raterhub.com/en//searchqualityevaluatorguidelines.pdf.

Haim, M., Graefe, A., and Brosius, H.-B. (2018). Burst of the filter bubble?: Effects of personalization on the diversity of Google News. *Digital Journalism*, *6*(3), pp. 330–343. https://doi.org/10.1080/21670811.2017.1338145.

Hassell, H. J. G., Holbein, J. B., and Miles, M. R. (2020). There is no liberal media bias in which news stories political journalists choose to cover. *Science Advances*, *6*(14), eaay9344. https://doi.org/10.1126/sciadv.aay9344.

Heuts, F., and Mol, A. (2013). What is a good tomato? A case of valuing in practice. *Valuation Studies*, *1*(2), pp. 125–146. https://doi.org/10.3384/vs.2001-5992.1312125.

Introna, L., and Wood, D. (2004). Picturing algorithmic surveillance: The politics of facial recognition systems. *Surveillance & Society*, *2*(2/3), pp. 177–198.

Jack, C. (2017). Lexicon of Lies. Terms for Problematic Information. Data & Society Research Institute. https://datasociety.net/pubs/oh/DataAndSociety_LexiconofLies.pdf.

Jansen, B. J., and Spink, A. (2006). How are we searching the World Wide Web? A comparison of nine search engine transaction logs. *Information Processing & Management*, *42*(1), pp. 248–263. https://doi.org/10.1016/j.ipm.2004.10.007

Kelemen, M. (2005). *Managing Quality: Managerial and Critical Perspectives*. Sage. https://doi.org/10.4135/9781446220382.

NewsGuard (2020). NewsGuard Nutrition Label. https://www.newsguardtech.com.

Noble, S. U. (2018). *Algorithms of oppression: How search engines reinforce racism*. New York University Press.

Otero, V. (2017). The Chart. version 3.1. ad fontes media. https://www.adfontesmedia.com/the-chart-version-3-0-what-exactly-are-we-reading/.

Robertson, R. E., Lazer, D., and Wilson, C. (2018). Auditing the personalization and composition of politically related search engine results pages. *Proceedings of the 2018 World Wide Web Conference on World Wide Web – WWW '18*, pp. 955–965. https://doi.org/10.1145/3178876.3186143.

Rogers, R. (2019). *Doing digital methods*. Sage.

Sunstein, C. R. (2018). *#Republic: Divided democracy in the age of social media*. Princeton University Press. https://doi.org/10.2307/j.ctv8xnhtd.

Trielli, D., and Diakopoulos, N. (2019). Search as news curator: The role of Google in shaping attention to news information. *Proceedings of the 2019 CHI Conference on Human Factors in Computing Systems – CHI '19*, 1–15. https://doi.org/10.1145/3290605.3300683

Unkel, J., and Haim, M. (2019). Googling politics: Parties, sources, and issue ownerships on Google in the 2017 German federal election campaign. *Social Science Computer Review, 39*(5), pp. 844–861. https://doi.org/10.1177/0894439319881634.

Wakabayashi, D. (2018, September 5). Trump says Google is rigged, despite its denials. What do we know about how it works? *The New York Times*. https://www.nytimes.com/2018/09/05/technology/google-trump-bias.html.

Data availability

Data available at: https://bit.ly/2Q10kCO

About the author

Guillén Torres is a PhD researcher and Lecturer at the Department of Media Studies, University of Amsterdam. His research focuses on how datafication may foster the political action of minoritized communities. Within the Digital Methods initiative, Guillén's work revolves around the role of platforms in mediating access to information.

3   The scale of Facebook's problem depends upon how "fake news" is classified

Richard Rogers[1]

Abstract

Ushering in the contemporary "fake news" crisis, Craig Silverman of *Buzzfeed News* reported that it outperformed mainstream news on Facebook prior to the 2016 U.S. presidential election. Here the report's methods are revisited for 2020. Examining Facebook user engagement of election-related stories, and applying Silverman's classification of fake news, it was found that the problem has worsened. If, however, one were to classify "fake news" in a stricter fashion, as Facebook and others do with the notion of "false news," the scale of the problem shrinks. A smaller scale problem could imply a greater role for fact-checkers, while a larger one could lead to the further politicization of source adjudication, where labeling certain sources as "fake" results in backlash.

Keywords: Fake news, false news, junk news, hyperpartisan, media labeling

Research questions

To what extent is "fake news" (as defined in the 2016 seminal news article) present in the most engaged-with, election-related content on Facebook in the run-up to the 2020 U.S. presidential elections? How does the current

---

1   The first period of the analysis was reported in Rogers, 2020a. The research benefited from research assistance by Paul Bugeja, Maria Lompe, Yumeng Luo, Rimmert Sijtsma, Tatiana Smirnova, Giulio Valentini, Ilian Velasco and Nina Welt.

Rogers. R. (ed.), *The Propagation of Misinformation in Social Media: A Cross-platform Analysis.*
Amsterdam: Amsterdam University Press 2023
DOI: 10.5117/9789463720762_CH03

"fake news" problem compare to that of the 2016 election period, both with the same as well as a stricter definition of "fake news"? Is there more user engagement with hyperpartisan conservative or progressive sources in political spaces on Facebook? How does such engagement imply a politicization of the "fake news" problem?

Essay summary

In all, it was found that the "fake news" problem around the U.S. elections as observed in 2016 has worsened overall on Facebook in 2020. While "fake news" did not outperform mainstream news in any period under study (as it did in August to November of 2016) the proportion of user engagement with "fake news" to mainstream news stories was higher compared to 2016. In the seven full quarters under study in the run up to and aftermath of the 2020 elections (from March 2019 to December 2020) the proportion of engagement of "fake news" to mainstream was on average 1:1.8 compared to 1:2.6 in 2016. It is both an observation concerning the persistence of the problem and an admonition that the measures undertaken to date have not lessened the phenomenon.

If one applies a stricter definition of "fake news" such as only imposter news and conspiracy sites (thereby removing hyperpartisan sites as in Silverman's original definition), mainstream sources outperform "fake" ones by a much greater proportion.

The findings imply that how one defines such information has an impact on the perceived scale of the problem, including the types of approaches to address it. With a smaller-scale problem, fact-checking and labeling become more viable alongside the "big data" custodial approaches employed by social media firms.

Given there are more hyperpartisan conservative sources engaged with than hyperpartisan progressive ones, the research points to how considerations of what constitutes "fake news" may be politicized. Targeting "fake news" presumably would affect hyperpartisan conservative sources to a greater degree than progressive ones. It thereby could invite criticism of "big tech," including claims of censorship on one side of the political spectrum. It also could prompt social media firms to become less open to critical scrutiny by scholars and journalists alike interested in which sources and stories are being degraded or deplatformed.

The findings are made on the basis of Facebook user engagement of the top 200 stories returned for queries for candidates and social issues. Based on existing labeling sites, the stories and by extension the sources are classified along a spectrum from more to less problematic as well as partisan.

Implications

The initial "fake news" crisis (Silverman, 2016; 2017) had to do with fly-by-night, imposter, conspiracy as well as so-called "hyperpartisan" news sources outperforming mainstream news on Facebook in the three months prior to the 2016 U.S. presidential elections. In a sense it was both a critique of Facebook as "hyperpartisan political-media machine" (Herrman, 2016) but also that of the quality of a social media landscape witnessing a precipitous rise in the consumption and sharing of "alternative right" news and cultural commentary (Benkler et al., 2017; Holt et al., 2019).

The events of the first crisis have been overtaken by a second one where politicians as former President Trump in the U.S. and elsewhere employ the same term for certain media organizations in order to undermine their credibility. Against the backdrop of that politicization as well as rhetorical tactic, scholars and platforms alike have demurred on using the term "fake news" and instead offered "junk news," "problematic information," "false news" and others (Vosoughi et al., 2018). Some definitions (as junk news and problematic information) are roomier, while others are stricter in their source classification schemes. Subsumed under the original "fake news" definition are imposter news, conspiracy sources and hyperpartisan, defined as "overly ideological web operations" (Herrman, 2016) or sources that "expressly promotes views" (Otero, 2017). The newer term, "junk news," covers the same types of sources but adds the connotation of attractively packaged junk food that when consumed could be considered unhealthy (Howard, 2020; Venturini, 2019). It also includes two web-native source types. "Clickbait" captures how the manner in which it is packaged or formatted lures one into consumption, and "computational propaganda" refers to dubious news circulation by bot and troll-like means, artificially amplifying its symbolic power. Problematic information is even roomier, as it expands its field of vision beyond news to cultural commentary and satire (Jack, 2017). Stricter definitions such as "false news" would encompass imposter and conspiracy but are less apt to include hyperpartisan news and cultural commentary, discussing those sources as "misleading" rather than as "fake" or "junk" or as not being "news" in the first instance (Kist and Zantingh, 2017).

Rather than an either/or proposition, "fake news" could be understood as a spectrum with problematic information (the roomiest notion) on one end and "false news," the strictest, on the other, with junk news and fake news in the middle (Wardle, 2016; 2017). While beyond the scope, the purview could be widened even further to include more media than stories and sources, such as video and images.

Depending on the definition, the scale of the problem changes as does the range of means to address it (Gillespie, 2020). With "false news," it grows smaller, and fact-checking again could be a profession to which to turn for background research into the story and the source. Fact-checking's effectiveness is occasionally regarded as limited, given the enormity of the task, the large reach of some fake news stories (well before fact-checks have appeared) and the number of fact-checks an organization can complete per day (Annany, 2018). Moreover, the audiences of "fake news" and fact-checked "fake news" also may differ significantly, meaning that corrections rarely reach the original consumers of the offending content (Bounegru et al., 2018). More attention may be paid to the stories that have merited a fact-check or a label, expanding their reach and engagement.

Facebook's content moderation is multi-facetted, relying on human review, user reporting and automated approaches (Roberts, 2016; Gillespie, 2018; Facebook, 2021b). Where their approach to misinformation is concerned, Facebook has striven to work with fact-checking bodies, though some of the fledgling partnerships ended after a year or two (Madrigal, 2019). For the remaining partner organizations, there is a Facebook dashboard, populated with content flagged through crowd-sourcing and automated techniques, where the fact-checkers can choose articles and write their reports, from two to five per day per fact-checker (Annany, 2018). These reports result in content removal or downgrading. When the problem is scaled down, these approaches become more viable as do other qualitative approaches such as labeling, with adjudicators sifting through posts one by one.

Roomier definitions make the problem larger and result in findings such as the most well-known "fake news" story of 2016. "Pope Francis Shocks World, Endorses Donald Trump for President" began as satire and was later circulated on a hyperpartisan, fly-by-night site (Ending the Fed). It garnered higher engagement rates on Facebook than more serious articles in the mainstream news. When such stories are counted as "fake," "junk" or "problematic," and the scale increases, industrial-style "scalable" solutions may be preferred such as automated review and commercial content moderation (rather than journalist fact-checking).

As more content is taken down as a result of roomy source classification schemes, debates about freedom of choice may become more vociferous rather than less. It recalls the junk food debate, and in this regard, Zygmunt

Bauman stressed how we as *homo eligens* or "choosing animals" are wont to resist such restrictions, be it in opting for "hyperprocessed" food or hyperpartisan news and cultural commentary (2013).

Labeling hyperpartisan news as "fake" or "junk," moreover, may lead to greater political backlash. Indeed, as our findings imply, the "fake news" or "junk news" problem is largely a hyperpartisan conservative source problem, whereas the "false news" one is not. As recently witnessed in the Netherlands, the designation of hyperpartisan conservative sources as "junk news" drew the ire of sources so labeled as well as the leader of a conservative political party, who subsequently labeled mainstream news as "junk fake news" (Rogers and Niederer, 2020; Van Den Berg, 2019). Opting for the narrower "false news" classification would imply a depoliticization of the problem.

Finally, it should be remarked that the sources outputting questionable content in 2020 do not appear to be the fly-by-night, imposter news sites in operation in 2016, but rather more "established" conspiracy and hyperpartisan sites. If Facebook, as its policy states (2021), were to degrade the posts in the News Feed from at least the conspiracy sites, thereby affecting their reach and engagement, then the scale of "false news" problem may be reduced. The circulation of hyperpartisan sources would remain, however, making the platform still the site where the competition between mainstream and "problematic information," "junk news" and "fake news" will remain.

Source and story classification tensions remain. Certain sources may have hyperpartisan commentary but run mainstream stories from wire services. Hyperpartisan sources may gradually mainstream. Distinctions between the hyperpartisan and conspiracy may be difficult to disentangle. Conspiracy theories may become more legitimate with time such as the lab origins of the coronavirus.

Findings

This study revisits the initial "fake news" findings made by Craig Silverman of *Buzzfeed News* in 2016, where it was found that in the three months prior to the 2016 U.S. presidential elections "fake news" stories received more interactions on Facebook than mainstream stories (see Figure 3.1). It ushered in the "fake news" crisis with Facebook at its center.

Finding 1: If we employ the same definition of "fake news" as Silverman did during 2016, to date the problem has worsened somewhat. Whereas 1 in 2.6 "fake news" sources (on average per quarter) were most engaged-with in February–November 2016, from March, 2019 to December, 2020 it is now 1

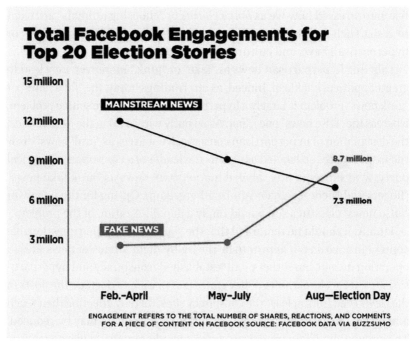

Figure 3.1 "Fake news" outperforms mainstream news in the months prior to the 2016 U.S. presidential elections. Source: Silverman, 2016.

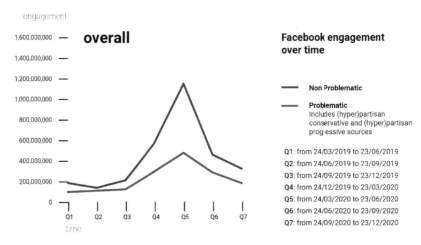

Figure 3.2 Facebook engagement scores of "fake news" (Silverman's roomy definition) versus mainstream news for political candidate and social issue queries overall, March 24, 2019–December 23, 2020. Data source: Buzzsumo.com. Graphic by Carlo De Gaetano and Federica Bardelli.

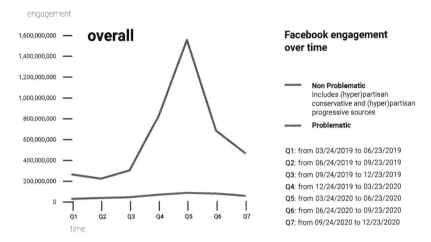

Figure 3.3 Facebook engagement scores of "fake news" (narrow definition) versus mainstream news for political candidate and social issue queries overall, March 24, 2019–December 23, 2020. Data source: Buzzsumo.com. Graphic by Carlo De Gaetano and Federica Bardelli.

in 1.8 (see Figures 3.1 and 3.2). The main finding, in other words, is that the "fake news problem" of 2016 has not been remedied four years later.

Finding 2: If, however, one tightens the definition of "fake news" sites to imposter and conspiracy sites (as the definition of "false news" would have it), thereby removing hyperpartisan sources from the categorization scheme, the proportion of most engaged-with "fake news" to mainstream news in March 2019 to December 2020 lessens to 1 in 12 (see Figure 3.3). After a spike in the run up to the elections, there is a general downward trend in the engagement with such sites.

Note that the 2016 problem also could be thought to diminish if one were to disaggregate Silverman's original source list and remove hyperpartisan stories and sites. An examination of his list per period in question indicates in the first two quarters (February through July 2016) most sources are hyperpartisan and satirical (Silverman, 2016). Only in the period between September and the election do we find imposter sites. A case in point is the Denver Guardian (which is no longer online); as the *Denver Post* wrote, "[t] here is no such thing as the Denver Guardian, despite that Facebook post you saw" (Lubbers, 2016). Imposter sites, however, are in the minority and most engagement is driven by the hyperpartisan and the satirical such as Ending the Fed, Breitbart News and the World News Daily Report. In other words, their removal from the "fake news" classification would put mainstream news back on top.

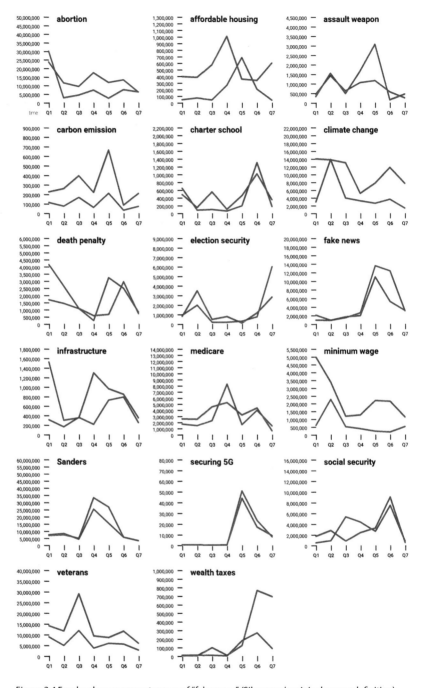

Figure 3.4 Facebook engagement scores of "fake news" (Silverman's original roomy definition) versus mainstream news for political candidate and social issue queries, March 2019–December 2020. Absolute numbers shown for the sake of trend comparison. Data source: Buzzsumo.com. Graphic by Carlo De Gaetano and Federica Bardelli.

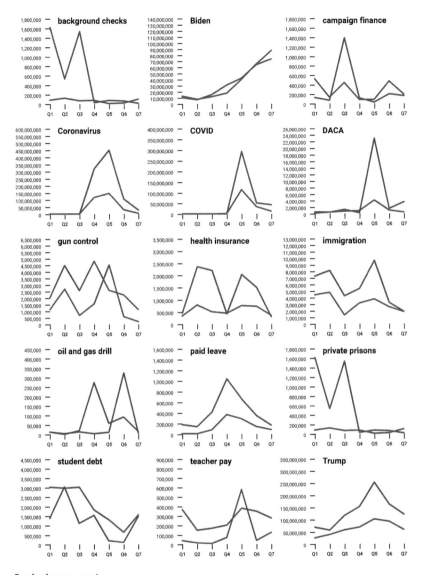

Facebook engagement over time

— Non Problematic

— Problematic
Includes (hyper)partisan
conservative and (hyper)partisan
progressive sources

Q1: from 03/24/2019 to 06/23/2019
Q2: from 06/24/2019 to 09/23/2019
Q3: from 09/24/2019 to 12/23/2019
Q4: from 12/24/2019 to 03/23/2020
Q5: from 03/24/2020 to 06/23/2020
Q6: from 06/24/2020 to 09/23/2020
Q7: from 09/24/2020 to 12/23/2020

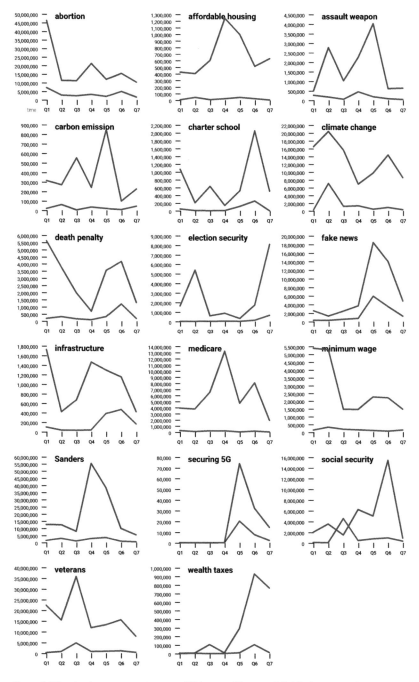

Figure 3.5 Facebook engagement scores of "fake news" (narrow definition) versus mainstream news for political candidate and social issue queries, March 2019–December 2020. Absolute numbers shown for the sake of trend comparison. Data source: Buzzsumo.com. Graphic by Carlo De Gaetano and Federica Bardelli.

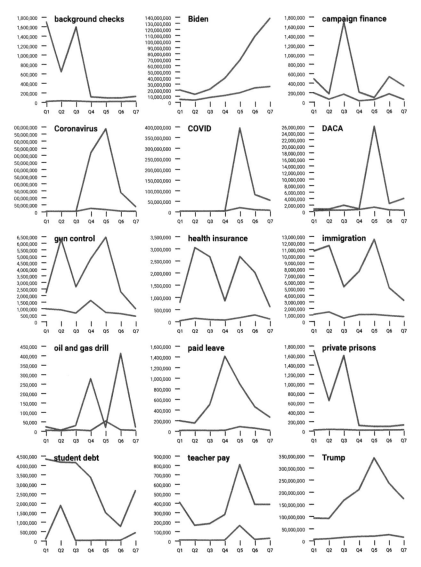

**Facebook engagement
over time**

Non Problematic
Includes (hyper)partisan
conservative and (hyper)partisan
progressive sources

Problematic

Q1: from 03/24/2019 to 06/23/2019
Q2: from 06/24/2019 to 09/23/2019
Q3: from 09/24/2019 to 12/23/2019
Q4: from 12/24/2019 to 03/23/2020
Q5: from 03/24/2020 to 06/23/2020
Q6: from 06/24/2020 to 09/23/2020
Q7: from 09/24/2020 to 12/23/2020

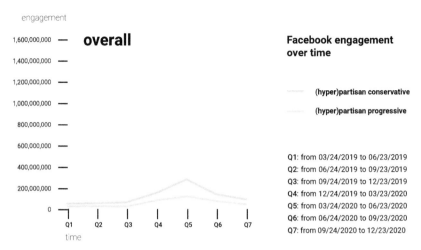

Figure 3.6 Facebook engagement scores of hyperpartisan conservative and hyperpartisan progressive sources for political candidate and social issue queries, overall, March 2019–December 2020. Data source: Buzzsumo.com. Graphic by Carlo De Gaetano and Federica Bardelli.

Finding 3: There are certain issues where more alternative sources provide the coverage that was consumed (see Figure 3.4), but, with the strict definition, in no case did they (consistently) outperform mainstream sources (see Figure 3.5). If we return to the original "fake news" definition (that includes hyperpartisan sites), alternative sources outperform mainstream ones (either overall or in certain weeks) for certain divisive issues such as abortion, death penalty, gun control, social security as well as the issue of fake news itself (see Figure 3.4). There is also one issue (social security) where there is more engagement with "fake news" in the narrow sense than with mainstream news (see Figure 3.5), but overall the mainstream outperforms fake news in a narrow sense across most all issues and periods. With respect to the candidates, Biden has proportionately more "fake news" (and "false news") associated with it than Trump, though Trump has a higher quantity overall. The most engaged-with "fake news" story (PJ Media) relates to Trump and reads "military ballots found in the trash in Pennsylvania all were Trump votes."

Finding 4: There is more engagement with hyperpartisan conservative sources than hyperpartisan progressive ones both overall as well as for the majority of the candidates and issues (see Figures 3.6 and 3.7). The finding suggests that any "fake news" definition that includes hyperpartisan sources will associate the problem more with conservative sources. When adjusting the definition to exclude such sources, "fake news" itself becomes less politicized.

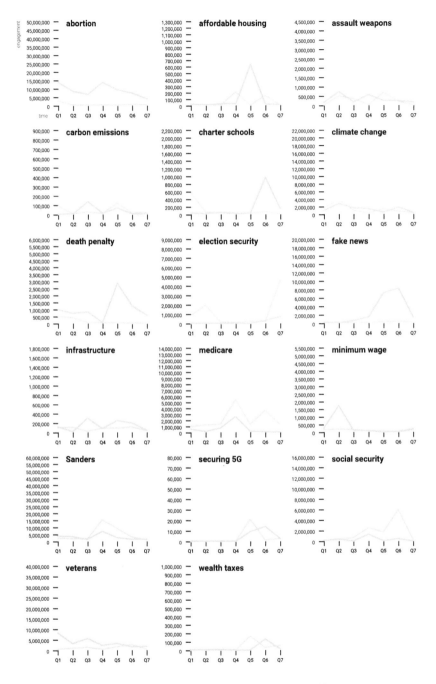

Figure 3.7 Facebook engagement scores of hyperpartisan conservative and hyperpartisan progressive sources for political candidate and social issue queries, March 2019–December 2020. Absolute numbers shown for the sake of trend comparison. Data source: Buzzsumo.com. Graphic by Carlo De Gaetano and Federica Bardelli.

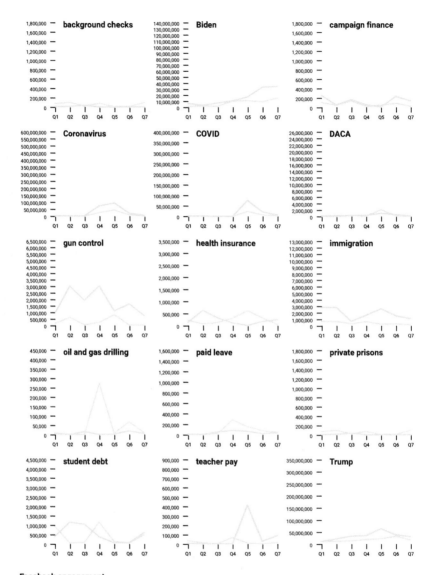

**Facebook engagement
over time**

── (hyper)partisan conservative

── (hyper)partisan progressive

Q1: from 24/03/2019 to 23/06/2019
Q2: from 24/06/2019 to 23/09/2019
Q3: from 24/09/2019 to 23/12/2019
Q4: from 24/12/2019 to 23/03/2020
Q5: from 24/03/2020 to 23/06/2020
Q6: from 24/06/2020 to 23/09/2020
Q7: from 24/09/2020 to 23/12/2020

Methods

This study builds upon the "fake news" report written by Craig Silverman and published in *Buzzfeed News* in 2016. It employs a similar methodology, albeit introducing a "slider" or gradient to indicate the extent of the problem depending on how one classifies sources. The research enquires into the current scale of the problem and compares it to the same timeframe in 2016. It also demonstrates how roomier definitions of "fake news" make the problem appear larger, compared to stricter definitions.

First, a list of candidates and social issues is curated. The candidates chosen are the ones from the major parties, still in the race and campaigning at the time of the study. For social issues, the issue lists at four voting aid sources are first merged, and then filtered for those that appear on multiple lists: Politico, VoteSmart, On the Issues and Gallup (see Table 3.1).

Table 3.1   The list of candidates and issues queried in BuzzSumo.com in March 2020 and January 2021.

Trump	Carbon emissions	Gun control	Private prisons
Biden	Charter schools	Health insurance	Securing 5G
Sanders	Climate change	Immigration	Social security
Abortion	Coronavirus	Infrastructure	Student debt
Affordable housing	DACA	Medicare	Teacher pay
Assault weapons	Death penalty	Minimum wage	Veterans
Background checks	Election security	Oil and gas drilling	Wealth taxes
Campaign financing	Fake news	Paid leave	

Next, we queried Buzzsumo, the marketing research and analysis tool, for each candidate and issue keyword, using the date ranges of March 23, 2019 to March 23, 2020 and March 24, 2020 to January 4, 2021, and the filter "English." (We limited our analysis to the end date, December 23, 2020, thereby covering seven three-month periods.) We also retained non-American sources, in order to ensure that we did not miss highly engaging, problematic sources that are from outside the U.S. Buzzsumo returns a list of web URLs, ranked by interactions, which is the sum of reactions (including likes), shares and comments. The study of engagement (or interactions) concerns a combination of rating (like), reading (comment) and circulating (share). In that sense, it is a rather comprehensive measure. For every candidate and issue, we examined only the top 200 stories returned, which is a limitation. Analyzing Facebook user engagement of "top" content follows Silverman's original method. Silverman's included top 20 sources, whereas "top" content is greater by a factor of 10.

Each of the source names, headlines and any description text are read, and the sources are roughly labeled by concatenating pre-existing source classification schemes (or when in disagreement choosing the majority label). To gain an indication of their genre (non-problematic or problematic news including imposter news, conspiracy site, or clickbait) and (hyper)partisanship, the sources are checked against media bias labeling sites including AllSides (2020), Media Bias/Fact Check (2020), "The Chart" (Otero, 2017) and NewsGuard (2020); news sources' Wikipedia entries are also consulted. We also searched for them online and consulted news and analysis that mention the sources. Additionally, we checked the source lists returned by Buzzsumo against a study of imposter sources called "pink slime sites," or sites that imitate local or national news sites (Bengani, 2019). Throughout the entire period and across all issues in the top 200 most engaged-with stories just one pink slime site was found.

Subsequently, we characterized the stories as problematic or non-problematic, where the former adheres to the strict "false news" definition (imposter or conspiracy sites). These are then graphed overtime using RAW graphs. We also applied the roomier definitions of "fake news," which adds to imposter and conspiracy sites "hyperpartisan" sources. We graphed these values anew. These graphs display the proportion of "fake news" versus non-problematic sources in Facebook for the results of each candidate and social issue query over the election campaigning timeframe and its aftermath, March 2019 to December 2020.

We then compared the 2020 findings with the 2016 results, in two ways. First, we compared the 2020 results with the roomier definition (imposter + conspiracy + hyperpartisan) to the "fake news" findings of 2016 as proportions, finding that in 2019–2020, on average per quarter, there are 1 in 1.8 sources that are "fake" compared to 1 in 2.6 in 2016. Thus, the "original" "fake news problem" has worsened. Second, we examined the source list from February to November 2016 in order to ascertain whether the findings were based on a strict or roomy definition for that timeframe. Early in the 2016 campaign, those sources were largely hyperpartisan or satirical, but the best-performing story by far was from a reputable source that mistakenly published a "fake story," originating from a tweet by Sean Hannity of *Fox News* that the then candidate Trump had used his own private plane to transport "200 stranded marines" (American Military News, 2016). Right before the 2016 election (August to November), the best-performing sources were again hyperpartisan or satirical ones (as Ending the Fed, Breitbart and World News Daily Report), though imposter sites also make an appearance (Denver Guardian). For a sense of how definitions of fake news politicize, we also examined which candidates were associated with hyperpartisan news, noting how Biden is targeted far more often in such sources.

To study the politicization of the "fake news" problem further, we compared the overall engagement on Facebook of hyperpartisan sources, both conservative and progressive, as well as the candidates and issues that had each type most associated with it, finding that conservative, so-called hyperpartisan sources outperformed hyperpartisan progressive ones.

References

AllSides (2020). Media Bias Ratings. https://www.allsides.com/media-bias/media-bias-ratings#ratings.

American Military News (2016, May 23). Article removed—Here's why. *American Military News*, https://americanmilitarynews.com/2016/05/donald-trump-sent-his-own-plane-to-transport-200-stranded-marines/.

Annany, M. (2018, April 4). The partnership press: Lessons for platform-publisher collaborations as Facebook and news outlets team to fight misinformation. *Columbia Journalism Review*. https://www.cjr.org/tow_center_reports/partnership-press-facebook-news-outlets-team-fight-misinformation.php.

Bauman, Z. (2013). *Does the richness of the few benefit us all?* Polity.

Bengani, P. (2019, December 18). Hundreds of "pink slime" local news outlets are distributing algorithmic stories and conservative talking points. Tow Center for Journalism, Columbia University. https://www.cjr.org/tow_center_reports/hundreds-of-pink-slime-local-news-outlets-are-distributing-algorithmic-stories-conservative-talking-points.php.

Benkler, Y., Faris, R., Roberts, H. and Zuckerman, E. (2017, March 3). Study: Breitbart-led right-wing media ecosystem altered broader media agenda. *Columbia Journalism Review*. https://www.cjr.org/analysis/breitbart-media-trump-harvard-study.php.

Bounegru, L., Gray, J., Venturini, T. and Mauri, M. (2018). *A field guide to "fake news" and other information disorders*. Public Data Lab.

Facebook (2021b, May 25). False news, Facebook Transparency Center. https://transparency.fb.com/policies/community-standards/false-news/.

Herrman, J. (2016, August 24). Inside Facebook's (totally insane, unintentionally gigantic, hyperpartisan) political-media machine. *New York Times*. https://www.nytimes.com/2016/08/28/magazine/inside-facebooks-totally-insane-unintentionally-gigantic-hyperpartisan-political-media-machine.html.

Holt, K., Figenschou, T.U. and Frischlich, L. (2019). Key dimensions of alternative news media. *Digital Journalism*, 7(7), pp. 860–869. https://doi.org/10.1080/2167 0811.2019.1625715

Gillespie, T. (2018). *Custodians of the internet: Platforms, content moderation, and the hidden decisions that shape social media.* Yale University Press.

Gillespie, T. (2020). Content moderation, AI, and the question of scale. *Big Data & Society*, July–December: 1–5, https://doi.org/10.1177/2053951720943234.

Howard, P. (2020). *Lie machines.* Yale University Press.

Jack, C. (2017) Lexicon of lies: Terms for problematic information. Data & Society Research Institute. https://datasociety.net/library/lexicon-of-lies/.

Kist, R. and Zantingh, P. (2017, March 6). Geen grote rol nepnieuws in aanloop naar verkiezingen. *NRC Handelsblad*. https://www.nrc.nl/nieuws/2017/03/06/fake-news-nee-zo-erg-is-het-hier-niet-7144615-a1549050.

Lubbers, E. (2016, November 5). There is no such thing as the Denver Guardian, despite that Facebook post you saw. *The Denver Post*. https://www.denverpost.com/2016/11/05/there-is-no-such-thing-as-the-denver-guardian/.

Media Bias/Fact Check (2020). Filtered search. https://mediabiasfactcheck.com.

NewsGuard (2020). NewsGuard Nutrition Label. https://www.newsguardtech.com.

Otero, V. (2017). The chart, version 3.1, ad fontes media. https://www.adfontesmedia.com/the-chart-version-3-0-what-exactly-are-we-reading/.

Roberts, S.T. (2016). Commercial content moderation: Digital laborers' dirty work. In S.U. Noble and B.M. Tynes (Eds.), *The intersectional internet: Race, sex, class and culture online* (pp. 147–160). Peter Lang.

Rogers, R. and Niederer, S. (Eds.) (2020). *The politics of social media manipulation.* Amsterdam University Press.

Silverman, C. (2016, November 16). This analysis shows how viral fake election news stories outperformed real news on Facebook, *Buzzfeed News*. https://www.buzzfeednews.com/article/craigsilverman/viral-fake-election-news-outperformed-real-news-on-facebook.

Wardle, C. (2016, November 18). 6 types of misinformation circulated this election season. *Columbia Journalism Review*. https://www.cjr.org/tow_center/6_types_election_fake_news.php.

Wardle, C. (2017, February 16). Fake news. It's complicated. First Draft. https://firstdraftnews.org/latest/fake-news-complicated/.

Van Den Berg, E. (2019, July 30). Opnieuw misser bij Forum voor Democratie: Persoonlijke advertentie Thierry Baudet offline gehaald. NPO3. https://www.npo3.nl/brandpuntplus/opnieuw-misser-bij-forum-voor-democratie-persoonlijke-advertentie-thierry-baudet-offline-gehaald.

Venturini, T. (2019) From fake to junk news: The data politics of online virality. In D. Bigo, E. Isin, and E. Ruppert (Eds.) *Data politics: Worlds, subjects, rights* (pp. 123–144). Routledge.

Vosoughi, S., Roy, D., and Aral, S. (2018). The spread of true and false news online. *Science*, *359*(6380), pp. 1146–1151. https://doi.org/10.1126/science.aap9559.

Data availability

https://doi.org/10.7910/DVN/VFMJUH

About the author

Richard Rogers, PhD, is Professor of New Media & Digital Culture, Media Studies, University of Amsterdam, and Director of the Digital Methods Initiative. He is author of *Information Politics on the Web* and *Digital Methods* (both MIT Press) and *Doing Digital Methods* (SAGE).

4   When misinformation migrates

Cross-platform posting, YouTube and the deep vernacular web

Anthony Glyn Burton[1]

Abstract
This chapter investigates the political information ecologies of the "deep vernacular web" by studying the cross-posting of links on 4chan's "politically incorrect" board and a host of political subreddits. It finds that Reddit's banning of political subreddits in June 2020 proved effective in culling the spread of misinformation. 4chan users turned from sharing propagandistic content towards conspiratorial links as the 2020 U.S. election approached. This turn towards conspiracy parallels the decline in popularity of alt-right punditry on both platforms, reflected in the shift in presence over time of these types of videos. The chapter offers an example of how URLs and YouTube links can be used as a cross-platform digital method in studying the spread of misinformation.

Keywords: 4chan, Reddit, misinformation, digital methods, YouTube

Research questions

To what extent do U.S.-based political boards and forums on 4chan and Reddit share misinformation and "junk" content? Are algorithmically generated imposter news websites among the misinformation that circulates? How can we quantify and qualify the degree to which "alternative influence

1   Parts of this chapter are drawn from Burton and Koehorst, 2020. The research team included Dmitri Koehorst and Martijn van Schjip, who aided in the first round of research, and Yentel Boot, Frederikke Christiansen, David Dijkhuis, Morris Nieuwenhuis, and Alejandra O'Connor, who aided in the second round.

Rogers. R. (ed.), *The Propagation of Misinformation in Social Media: A Cross-platform Analysis.* Amsterdam: Amsterdam University Press 2023
DOI: 10.5117/9789463720762_CH04

networks" proliferate on these sites? How might we characterize the shift in the information ecologies of these spaces around the time of the 2020 U.S. election?

Essay summary

This chapter takes up these questions through a quantitative analysis of the news links shared on the spaces of the subcultural political web. It details the results of two separate studies. The first dataset covers the beginning of the 2020 presidential primaries, while the second period the lead-up and follow-through of the November 3, 2020 election. We employed a variety of methods to tackle these questions, of which the "haystack-to-needle" deductive method pioneered by Hagen and Jokubauskaite (2019) produced the best results in investigating the texture of informational websites shared.

Constructing a coding schema based on Benkler et al.'s work studying the 2016 U.S. election, we first investigated the presence of "junk" news on each platform, which Howard et al. define as content "extremist, sensationalist, conspiratorial, masked commentary, [or] fake" that presents itself as news (Howard et al. 2017; see also Gray et al., 2019). The presence of junk news on each platform remained relatively stable, comprising approximately a third of sources on 4chan and a fifth on Reddit.

We then investigated those sources coded as news proper and as well as for partisanship using a variety of expert sources. We find that while the first collection period was characterized by a plurality of websites coded as neutral news, the period leading up to and through the election marks a shift towards partisanship in the news ecologies of both spaces.

Finding YouTube as an outsized source in both spaces—in both time-frames making up a higher share of links on 4chan than all other sites combined, and a stark presence on Reddit—we focus further on the types of videos that characterize each platform's YouTube shares. While the network of right-wing pundits that make up what Lewis (2018) dubs the "alternative influence network" constituted a strong presence in the first dataset, their popularity in the lead-up to the election dramatically wanes—replaced by video clips that purport to illustrate the very theories that the AIN traffics in, and illustrating a potential abandonment of the mediated, parasocial relationships that make up the AIN's appeal (Lewis, 2020). Methodologically speaking, this chapter's cross-platform methods—using hyperlinks as metaphors for interest as opposed to tracking infrastructural syntaxes specific to particular platforms—offers a further potential avenue for study in the face of deplatforming and the migration of user audiences across platforms (Rogers, 2020b).

Implications

The accelerated informational exchange and ease of publication afforded by social media took on a dystopic turn during the 2016 U.S. election, where coordinated campaigns to manipulate information ecologies on mainstream social media platforms like Twitter sounded an epistemic alarm and added "misinformation" to the cultural lexicon (Shao et al., 2018). But as platforms strengthen their harmful content policies in response to criticism for harboring misinformation and hate speech, especially after the election (Einwiller and Kim, 2020; Donovan and boyd, 2018), we began to see alternative spaces such as the relatively unmoderated and historically uncensored subcultural political web found on spaces like Reddit and 4chan as primary hubs for the spread of misinformation (Coppins, 2020). The lack of oversight in these spaces marks a continuation of what Starbird et al. refer to as the "echo-systems" that characterized the spread of misinformation in 2016, wherein particular news sources are amplified within a discursive space and iteratively gain volume and attention (2018). And while Reddit banned a number of subreddits in June 2020 for violating their hate speech policy—including the notorious alt-right subreddit "r/The_Donald" (included in our dataset)—the pseudonymous nature, sheer scale, and ideological underpinnings of these platforms set up a "propaganda pipeline" where misinformation and its correlates gain vivacity (Benkler et al., 2019). These subcultural political platforms make up what Tuters calls the "deep vernacular web" (2019), characterized by pseudonymous participation and its antecedent trolling, playfulness, and dreams of unfettered freedom of speech (Massanari, 2017; Coleman, 2012; Buyukozturk et al., 2018), and are thus important players in contemporary news ecologies. But to characterize every user of these spaces as a part of this propaganda pipeline would be too general. What does news circulation on these spaces look like? How are common narratives and shared realities drawn in these spaces? And what might be different about their conceptions of information, political punditry, and mediated verification?

Findings: News ecologies, compared

Increasing junk news as the election drew near

We observed that "junk news" aesthetically or through the adoption of techniques masquerading as news websites either pushed conspiracy theories or presented content with the aims of sensationalizing or propagandizing. On 4chan, the presence of junk news remained relatively stable across our datasets, with 32% of links posted falling under the category in the first time period and 31% of websites in the second time period. On the other hand, the stark shift in the presence of junk news on Reddit between our first and second datasets points to the fact that Reddit's banning of starkly political subreddits may have played a role in the information ecologies of the site: while 17% of links shared fell under the category of junk news in our first dataset, it fell to about 4% in the second dataset, with propaganda making up little over 1% of links, sensationalist media counting 3%, and conspiracy a paltry 0.5%.

The types of junk news that appear on each website provide us with further insight on changes that occurred as the election approached, especially on 4chan. While propaganda was in relative abundance in the initial data collection period—with 20.2% of total links falling under the category, compared to 10.7% as sensationalist and 1.2% as conspiratorial—the lead-up to the election saw propaganda junk news fall by almost half, to 10.4% of total news links posted. Sensationalist news decreased slightly to 6.9%. Most notably, 14.4% of links in our second dataset were categorized as conspiratorial. This is an increase by a factor of 14. And while it is still outranked by the first dataset's number of propagandistic links, the increase in conspiracy as the election approached signals a dramatic shift.

Increasing partisanship as the election drew near

Compared to junk news, websites which appeared to follow journalistic standards made up the majority of links in both datasets. The changes over time, however, are notable: while both Reddit and 4chan hovered around 60% of all links being to news websites in the first data collection period, news links on 4chan slightly lowered to 58% on the second run while Reddit's number increased by almost a third to 83%. But what appears on the surface as a relatively stable and socially endorsed informational ecology belies the partisan shift that occurred as the election approached.

In the first dataset, Reddit's news sources contained a plurality of neutral sources—48% of all websites, and 57.8% of all websites coded as "news." Left-leaning sources made up 24.8% of all links, while right-leaning sources made up 9.9% of news links. The second dataset saw a marked shift in the political valence of hostnames, however. In this period, left-leaning websites made up a plurality of the links, with 42.0% of links posted being categorized as such. Much of this gain was at the loss of neutral links, which numbered 21.1% of all total news links; meanwhile, the number of right-leaning links decreased to 3.9% of all news links.

The shift towards partisanship (according to our coding) was starker on 4chan. In the first dataset, news websites categorized as neutral made up 46.4% of the total information websites posted, while right-leaning websites made up 12.3% of links and left-leaning websites just 4.1%. In the run-up to the election, however, the amount of neutral websites that appeared decreased by more than half, comprising just 17.5% of total news-coded links. This decrease was counterbalanced by a tripling of both left- and right-leaning links. Left-leaning links appeared 15.9% of the time in the second dataset, while right-leaning links made up over a third of all news links, appearing 35.0% of the time.

Video ecologies: Categories versus our own coding

On both 4chan's /pol/ and in the political subreddits, video plays an important part in collective information habits. In both datasets, links to YouTube on 4chan were higher than all other links combined; on Reddit, YouTube was the top-linked website. In the first run-through of the dataset, we focused on studying the videos posted by using YouTube's own categories to characterize videos. "News & Politics" made up the majority of links shared on both websites, with "People & Blogs" being the second highest. "News & Politics" contains political content, news clips, broadcasts, and other related content, while the purview of "People & Blogs" is slightly larger, containing talk shows, interviews, video casts of podcast recordings, and vlogs. Despite these core similarities, "Education" and "Nonprofits and Activism" made up the third- and fourth-highest categories in the Reddit data, while "Entertainment" and "Music" made up the third- and fourth-largest categories on 4chan. Given the lack of granularity of these categories we performed our own coding for the second dataset, applied to YouTube links on both 4chan and Reddit, detailed in Table 4.1.

Table 4.1   Coding scheme of YouTube videos.

Video type	Definition
Clip	Short, standalone clip without context
Shitposting	Deliberately low-quality content that provokes attention and disrupts discursive exchange Colley and Moore 2020, 22)
Discussion	Conversation or debate surrounding a particular issue
Press Conference	Videos of partial or full press conferences held by officials
Interview	Interviews between individuals
Reportage	Reporting of an event by press or individuals
Livestream	The live filming and transmission of an event
Compilation	An edited collection of videos, clips, reporting, etc.
Campaign Video	Videos created by political consultants or staff with a direct promotional purpose
Meme	Videos of a typically humorous nature with viral qualities
Audiobook	A video containing a narrativized recording of a book
Other	Any content that does not fit in the above categories

On 4chan a significant number of videos shared were categorized as shitposting, followed by discussion and clip (see Table 4.2). On Reddit, the top categories differed, with audiobooks, discussions, and interviews making up the top three. There was likewise a much higher level of homogeneity among videos shared on Reddit: only five of the twelve categories appeared on Reddit, while 4chan's shared videos ran across the different types.

Table 4.2   YouTube video types per platform (Reddit and 4chan).

Video type	Reddit appearances	4chan appearances
Clip	17.04%	30.81%
Shitposting	0%	18.23%
Discussion	22.69%	12.88%
Press Conference	0%	5.93%
Interview	26.2%	2.77%
Reportage	24%	8.36%
Livestream	0%	2.21%
Compilation	0%	10.02%
Campaign Video	0%	5.37%
Meme	0%	2.12%
Audiobook	10.07%	0%
Other	0%	1.31%

The decline of the alternative influence network

While these categories were not used in the first round of data collection, qualitative observation of the data indicates that the type of videos shared shifted strongly over two datasets: the direct viewer address of alt-right political punditry gave way to a documentarian form of video clip, usually taken out of its overall context, designed to act as "unmediated" footage of depicted events. At the beginning of the election period, videos from a group of alt-right pundits that Rebecca Lewis calls the "alternative influence network" constituted these spaces' video culture. The AIN is a group of loosely associated pundits that form a sort of "network," in Lewis's terminology, by appearing on each other's YouTube channels and repeating talking points brought up by websites such as Breitbart and the Daily Caller. The cast of characters on this network differentiate themselves by peddling their own particular brands of misinformative and conspiratorial content that ideologically speaking ranges from the Trumpian Republican party line to neo-Nazism. AIN member Richard Spencer regularly propagandizes for a white ethnostate (Kaplan, 2017); Paul Joseph Watson of Prison Planet pushes the conspiracy that 9/11 was a covert government operation (Hines, 2018); Jordan Peterson shot to fame by claiming a Canadian government bill introducing gender identity as grounds for discrimination was an example of creeping "post-modern radical leftism" (Peterson, 2016). The AIN could be described as reactionary politics pivoting to video: by explicitly positioning themselves as alternatives to legacy and mainstream news outlets, members can adopt the techniques of social media influencers to "build audiences and 'sell' them on far-right ideology" (Lewis, 2018, p. 4).

In the earlier dataset, these links made up 596 of the total YouTube links shared on 4chan, and 3989 of the links shared on Reddit. The second dataset paints a different picture of the video cultures of the deep vernacular web: the AIN made an appearance on 4chan just 337 times, for a 42.5% reduction, while Reddit users shared videos from the AIN just 458 times, a reduction of 88.6%. The Reddit numbers are likewise boosted by 378 shares of a video by Mike Cernovich titled "Un/Convention: Exposing Fake News at the RNC and DNC" (2016). The second-most popular AIN members—Ben Shapiro's "Daily Wire," Rick Rubin's "Rubin Report," and Tim Pool—were only shared 15 times apiece.

One possible explanation is that a combination of deplatforming and subreddit banning could explain their decline, but it does not bear out. The most popular AIN figures on 4chan and Reddit in the earlier dataset, Joe Rogan and Ben Shapiro ("PowerfulJRE" and "The Daily Wire," in channel-name terms), remain on YouTube, as do 4chan's two favorites, Sargon of Akkad and Tarl Warwick ("The Thinkery" and "Styxhexenhammer666," respectively). And while Reddit banned a significant number of subreddits between the first and second data collection periods, as detailed above, this would have no bearing on 4chan's sharing numbers, which show a decline in viewing by nearly half.

Alternative or mainstream influence network?

From the purview of the subcultural spaces under study, the AIN's designation as alternative could be revisited. Put differently, they could have mainstreamed or normified, in the sense that all the figures above as well as many others in the AIN still enjoy robust followings and high YouTube subscriber counts outside of the subcultural spaces discussed here. Yet the video consumption tastes of their original fans seem to have shifted. Instead of pointing to AIN pundit commentaries on political clips, they point increasingly to clips discussed by lesser-known YouTube accounts. Three of the top five shared YouTube videos on 4chan in the second dataset fall under this category, and all are documentary-style recordings recontextualized to articulate a particular political or empirical theory by non-AINs. One "Amy Adams" has two of the top shared videos. The first is a 35-second undated clip of Joe Biden, posted in 2016, titled "SHOCKING: Joe Biden discusses the left's globalist agenda" (Adams 2016). The other is "KRAKEN UNLEASHED: The press conference they don't want you to see..." (2020). Another is a 70-second clip from 2017 titled "Senator Schumer says God made him a guardian of Israel," posted by the user "If Americans Knew," who describe themselves on their biography page as "an independent research and information dissemination institute, with particular focus on the Israeli-Palestinian conflict, U.S. foreign policy regarding the Middle East, and media coverage of this issue. Specifically, the organization's objective is to provide information that is to a large degree missing from American press coverage of this critical region" (2017).

Migrating misinformation

Two observations may be made from a comparison of these two periods. When it comes to "cleaning up" the junk news strewn about on a platform, eliminating spaces—not necessarily users, which would be considered deplatforming and is another discussion (see, e.g., Rogers, 2020; de Keulenaar and Burton, 2021; Urman and Katz, 2020)—may lead to precipitous reductions. Reddit's banning of politically charged subreddits, especially the notorious r/the_Donald, coincided with a steep decline in dubious content on Reddit. The amounts also dwarf those in comparison with 4chan. If we think of the changes in 4chan data as a rough way to normalize the Reddit changes, the fact that only 4% of links were categorized as junk news at all (let alone a particular type of junk news) while the amount of junk news on 4chan remained relatively stable lends credence to arguments concerning the effectiveness of such actions.

As was found in a previous study of subreddit closures, users of r/the_Donald are not known to have migrated en masse to any other particular subreddit but rather moving to the group of independent ".win" platforms (Goforth, 2021). While the ".win" platforms were outside the scope of this study, it's also possible that some of the purged users from Reddit made their way to 4chan/pol/ after June 2020. It could explain the rise of conspiratorial content on 4chan in the run-up to the election: not necessarily a shift in existing user sentiment, but a migration of users themselves. It is worthy of further investigation given how that subreddit and /pol/ have been credited with an outsize influence on the spread of political misinformation (Blackburn, 2018; Zanettou et al., 2017).

The second notable observation in the dataset is the decline in popularity of the alternative influence network in these spaces, paralleled on 4chan by the rise in conspiratorial "found footage," documentary-style clips. Out of the videos shared over 100 times on 4chan in the run-up to the election, these clips made up 30.81% of all total videos—almost double the runner-up, "shitposting," at 18.23%. While these clips do not carry the explicitly political explanations or expressions that characterize the AIN, they instead act to support pre-existing conspiratorial narratives on the far right. Adopting the generic affordances of documentary footage, they play into narratives of election irregularities, COVID-19 hoax theories, and Hunter Biden's alleged ties to Ukraine. Thus, the stark rise in conspiratorial links on 4chan is paralleled by the rise in popularity of these fodder-style videos, which is likewise paralleled by Reddit's closing of r/the_Donald and other politically unsavory subreddits. Investigating this further would require a closer lens on the months surrounding the subreddit's banning as well as innovations in method to determine an appropriate proxy for user migration, considering Reddit's pseudonymity and 4chan's anonymity.

What's clear is that the instability of contemporary platform ecologies requires a robust framework for studying them across particular spaces and that the open nature of hyperlinks, despite being one of the web's oldest infrastructural elements, provides a way to track these spatial conflations.

It's also clear that in order for the misinformation epidemic to stay under the grasp of those tracking it, further research is needed on both the ecologies that spring up on migratory platforms as well as the role these shifts play in the evolution of verification, epistemologies, and political narratives.

Method: Finding links in a web stack

This project consisted of two periods of data collection: from the beginning of the 2020 U.S. presidential campaign to its middle, and then the end of the campaign and two months of its aftermath. We took Tulsi Gabbard's campaign announcement for the Democratic Party nomination on January 11, 2019 as marking the beginning of the campaign period. This research window ran until March 25, 2020, the day we began our data collection. The second round of research, conducted from January 7–10, 2021, picked up where the first research window left off, up to December 31, 2020.

Methodologically, we oriented our data collection around the political spaces of the respective platforms. On 4chan, we drew our data from the /pol/ board. Titled "politically incorrect," /pol/ is the forum's largest board and contains a few unique infrastructural syntaxes that allowed us to narrow our research. User posts are tagged with a small flag, which is automatically chosen based on the geographic location of the user's IP address. We thus queried for user posts tagged with a U.S. flag in our given time periods. The flag is not a perfect proxy for location, because users can manually select custom flags such as "Communist" and "European" alongside explicitly offensive and anachronistic flags like the Rhodesian flag (for context, during our first data collection period there were 4,173,476 posts with custom flags on the entirety of the board, and 25,872,606 posts with U.S. flags). Users cannot change their flag to another geographic location, however, so while our collection did not incorporate users with custom flags, those U.S. flags we did capture can reliably be said to originate in the U.S.

For Reddit, we relied on the Reddit bot named "userleansbot," in order to collect political subreddits. Userleansbot is designed to provide "information and transparency to the users engaged in political communities across reddit" (userleansbot, 2020). Userleansbot's primary purpose is to provide the political leaning of Reddit users on request. By replying to a user's post and tagging the bot, userleansbot analyzes the posting history of the initial poster and quantify the frequency of their participation on various subreddits in order to provide an estimation of their political leanings. The list from which userleansbot sources its information is crowd-sourced from various Reddit users through personal threads as well as direct suggestions via Reddit's direct messaging feature. The bot is popular on Reddit: users have awarded it 50,254 karma points, a (high) score that refers to Reddit's infrastructural points system that allows users to endorse the activity of other users (userleansbot, 2020). In order to build our list for analysis, we took the list of subreddits that userleansbot relies on to code partisanship and then selected those subreddits that dealt with U.S. national politics.

In the first round of data collection, we began our research by employing the "needle-to-haystack" method (Hagen and Jokubauskaite, 2018). This method entails inductive investigation, looking for a "needle" of particularly defined URLs within the "haystack" of collected data. We employed the 4chan Capture and Analysis Toolkit, or 4CAT (Peeters and Hagen, 2018), to collect all posts in our time range from 4chan/pol/ with U.S. flags, and from our collected political subreddits. Given that our initial research questions revolved around the presence of "pink slime" websites outlined in Bengani (2019), we used a list of these websites as our needle and our collected data as the haystack. There were no pink slime websites found in either dataset. We then turned to the "haystack-to-needle" method, taking a deductive approach to investigate the news ecologies of each space. In our first collection period, we wrote a python script to filter for a regular expression that matched URLs to construct this dataset. In the second collection period, we used 4CAT's functionality to extract hostnames from our datasets (which uses a similar regular expression strategy on its backend).

Hostnames were then manually coded according to the coding schema adapted from Benkler et al.'s study of the media ecologies of the 2016 U.S. election (Table 4.1), using a combination of the qualitative study of each website's front page alongside information from Media Bias/Fact Check (2020) (when the political valence was still unclear after consulting Media Bias/Fact Check, both NewsGuard and AllSides.com were used). Media Bias/Fact Check codes websites according to their political partisanship into 9 categories, using a qualitative methodology to rank sources on 4 metrics: Biased Wording/Headlines, Factual/Sourcing, Story Choices, and Political Affiliation. While we drew basic readings from Media Bias/Fact Check, we used it as a guide for our first reading of the websites as opposed to adapting its coding schema directly because of its breadth. We coded news websites as those that adhered to journalistic standards, while websites that made no attempt or posture towards the appearance of presenting news were coded as "non-news." The remainder, which we classified as "junk news," was further split into conspiracy (circulating conspiratorial narratives), propaganda (misrepresenting facts for political aims), and sensational (websites aiming to emphasize salacious perspectives or "clickbait"-style content). These coding definitions are found in Table 4.3.

Table 4.3   Coding schema for hostnames. Adapted from Benkler et al., 2019.

Code	Definition
News	Websites that adhere to a framework of "professional journalistic norms," including the imposition of "higher reputational costs on sites and authors who propagate rumor" and the focus on "relatively rapid fact checking, criticism of false claims, and rapid dissemination of and coalescence around corrected narratives" (2018, p. 74).
Conspiracy	Sites whose primary narrative or ideological focus is "alternative," "conspiratorial," or otherwise outside of mainstream established truths as articulated by outlets who fall under the "news" category.
Propaganda	Content focused on "manipulating and misleading people intentionally to achieve political ends" (2018, p. 24).
Sensationalist	Clickbait or disinformation focused on "partisan-confirming news emphasized over truth." As distinct from propaganda, sensationalist content is organized based on the acquisition of attention (and, in turn due to the infrastructure of digital news, profit) as opposed to intentional political manipulation (2018, p. 274).
Campaign	Any website directly related to or directly promoting the political campaign of a presidential candidate or public servant
Non-news	Any website that does not fall into the above categories (examples include Wikipedia, YouTube, recipe websites, etc.).

News was further divided based on a rough indication of political and ideological biases, based on an expert list informed by such media and news bias sources as Allsides.com, Media Bias/Fact Check and NewsGuard (see Table 4.4).

Table 4.4   Political valence coding scheme with examples.

Political valence	Examples
Neutral	*NBC; Monthly Review*
Liberal	*The Guardian; The Nation*
Conservative	*Fox News; Wall Street Journal*

Adapted from Media Bias/Fact Check, AllSides, and NewsGuard.

In the first observational period of this research, we selected our news sites to code based on whether they appeared over 2,000 times on Reddit and 400 times on 4chan. From this, our coding dataset contained 204 websites from Reddit and 182 from 4chan. We used Bernhard Reider's YouTube Data Tools (2015) to collect video metadata, including category, view count, date published, and title. Since the YouTube Data Tools use the YouTube API, which occasionally returns malformed data, we scripted a separate call in Python to the YouTube API that individually verified each video returned and whether it was deleted since its appearance in the links dataset.

Both our tooling and sampling criteria were changed for the second observational period. Between our observational periods, Reddit banned four subreddits that together constituted a large portion of data in our first study: r/ChapoTrapHouse, r/The_Donald, r/RightwingLGBT, and r/TheNewRight (Ingram and Collins, 2020). Our second observational period spanned the period of 9 months, in contrast to the 15 months observed between January 2019 and March 2020. Because of this smaller window, we reduced the cut-off we used for coding hostname links on Reddit from 2,000 to 100, which resulted in 220 hostnames from Reddit being coded. On 4chan, likewise, we reduced the cutoff for coding websites from 400 mentions to 200, which yielded 219 results. Regressions and limitations introduced into YouTube's API between the first observational period and the second led us to writing a custom script using youtube-dl (ytdl-org, 2021), in order to capture video metadata. Instead of using YouTube's API, youtube-dl programmatically scrapes the information from the video by simulating the loading of what a casual user would see on a video page. While this took longer to run than using the YouTube Data Tools, our requests were not malformed or subject to the unknowns of YouTube's API interface.

References

Adams, A. (2016, August 25). SHOCKING: Joe Biden discusses the left's globalist agenda. https://www.youtube.com/watch?v=KaCBYrVsic4. Accessed April 21, 2021.

Adams, A. (2020, November 20). KRAKEN UNLEASHED: The press conference they don't want you to see... https://www.youtube.com/watch?v=_u34jhCKT2U. Accessed April 21, 2021.

AllSides (2020). Media Bias Ratings. https://www.allsides.com/media-bias/media-bias-ratings#ratings.

Benkler, Y., Faris, R., and Roberts, H. (2018). *Network propaganda: Manipulation, disinformation, and radicalization in American politics.* Oxford University Press.

Blackburn, J. (2018, February 16). *How 4chan and The_Donald influence the fake news ecosystem.* FIC Observatory. https://observatoire-fic.com/en/

how-4chan-and-the_donald-influence-the-fake-news-ecosystem-by-jeremy-blackburn-university-of-alabama-at-birmingham/. Accessed April 21, 2021.

Buyukozturk, B., Gaulden, S. and Dowd-Arrow, B. (2018). Contestation on Reddit, Gamergate, and movement barriers. *Social Movement Studies*, 17(5), pp. 592–609. https://doi.org/10.1080/14742837.2018.1483227

Cernovich, M. (2016, September 14). Un/Convention: Exposing fake news at the RNC and DNC. YouTube video. https://www.youtube.com/watch?v=cNwgKR88UD0.

Coleman, E.G. (2014). *Hacker, hoaxer, whistleblower, spy: The many faces of Anonymous*. Verso.

Colley, T. and Moore, M. (2020). The challenges of studying 4chan and the Alt-Right: "Come on in the water's fine." *New Media & Society*, 1461444820948803. https://doi.org/10.1177/1461444820948803.

Coppins, M. (2020, March). The billion-dollar disinformation campaign to reelect the president. *The Atlantic*. https://www.theatlantic.com/magazine/archive/2020/03/the-2020-disinformation-war/605530/.

Donovan, J. and boyd, d. (2018, June 1). The case for quarantining extremist ideas. *The Guardian*. http://www.theguardian.com/commentisfree/2018/jun/01/extremist-ideas-media-coverage-kkk.

Einwiller, S.A. and Kim, S. (2020). How online content providers moderate user-generated content to prevent harmful online communication: An analysis of policies and their implementation. *Policy & Internet*, 12(2), pp. 184–206. https://doi.org/10.1002/poi3.239.

Goforth, C. (2021, January 21). Notorious pro-Trump forum rebrands as "patriots" after post-Capitol riot infighting. *The Daily Dot*. https://www.dailydot.com/debug/pro-trump-site-renamed-internal-conflict/.

Gray, J., Bounegru, L., and Venturini, T. (2020). "Fake news" as infrastructural uncanny. *New Media & Society*, 22(2), pp. 317–341. https://doi.org/10.1177/1461444819856912.

Hagen, S., Burton, A., Wilson, J., and Tuters, M. (2019, September 8). Infinity's abyss: An overview of 8chan. *OILab*. https://oilab.eu/infinitys-abyss-an-overview-of-8chan/.

Hagen, S. and Jokubauskaite, E. (2019). Dutch junk news on 4chan and Reddit /pol/. In R. Rogers and S. Niederer (Eds.), *The politics of social media manipulation* (pp. 115–151). Dutch Ministry of the Interior and Kingdom Relations.

Hines, N. (2018, April 22). Alex Jones' protegé, Paul Joseph Watson, is about to steal his crackpot crown. *The Daily Beast*. https://www.thedailybeast.com/alex-jones-protege-paul-joseph-watson-is-about-to-steal-his-crackpot-crown.

Howard, P. N., Bolsover, G., Kollyani, B., Bradshaw, S., and Neudert, L.-M. (2017). Junk news and bots during the U.S. election: What were Michigan voters sharing over Twitter? Data Memo 2017.1, Project on Computational Propaganda, Oxford Internet Institute. http://blogs.oii.ox.ac.uk/politicalbots/wp- content/uploads/sites/89/2017/03/What-Were-Michigan-Voters-Sharing-Over-Twitter-v2.pdf.

If Americans Knew. (2017, February 3). Senator Schumer says God made him a guardian of Israel. YouTube video. https://web.archive.org/web/20210417224317/https://www.youtube.com/c/IfAmericansKnew-Video/about. Accessed August 2, 2020.

Ingram, D. and Collins, B. (2020, June 29). Reddit bans hundreds of subreddits for hate speech including Trump community. *NBC News*. https://www.nbcnews.com/tech/tech-news/reddit-bans-hundreds-subreddits-hate-speech-including-trump-community-n1232408.

Kaplan Sommer, A. (2017, October 19). White nationalist Richard Spencer gives Israel as example of ethno-state he wants in U.S. *Haaretz*. https://www.haaretz.com/us-news/richard-spencer-gives-israel-as-example-of-ethno-state-he-wants-in-u-s-1.5459154.

Lewis, R. (2018). Alternative influence: Broadcasting the reactionary right on YouTube. Data & Society Research Institute. https://datasociety.net/library/alternative-influence/.

Lewis, R. (2020). "This is what the news won't show you": YouTube creators and the reactionary politics of micro-celebrity. *Television & New Media*, *21*(2), pp. 201–217. https://doi.org/10.1177/1527476419879919.

Massanari, A. (2017). #Gamergate and the fappening: How Reddit's algorithm, governance, and culture support toxic technocultures. *New Media & Society*, *19*(3), pp. 329–346. https://doi.org/10.1177/1461444815608807.

Media Bias/Fact Check (2020). Filtered search. https://mediabiasfactcheck.com.

NewsGuard (2020). NewsGuard Nutrition Label. https://www.newsguardtech.com.

Peeters, S. (2020, May 15). Normiefication of extreme speech and the widening of the Overton window. Open Intelligence Lab. https://oilab.eu/normiefication-of-extreme-speech-and-the-widening-of-the-overton-window/.

Peeters, S. and Hagen, S. (2018). 4CAT: 4chan Capture and Analysis Toolkit [software]. https://4cat.oilab.eu.

Peterson, J. (2016, November 8). Jordan Peterson: The right to be politically incorrect. National Post. https://nationalpost.com/opinion/jordan-peterson-the-right-to-be-politically-incorrect.

Phillips, W. (2018). The oxygen of amplification. Data & Society Research Institute. https://datasociety.net/output/oxygen-of- amplification/.

Reider, B. (2015). YouTube Data Tools [software]. https://tools.digitalmethods.net/netvizz/youtube/index.php.

Rogers, R. (2020b). Deplatforming: Following extreme internet celebrities to Telegram and alternative social media. *European Journal of Communication*, *35*(3). https://doi.org/10.1177/0267323120922066.

Shao, C., Ciampaglia, G. L., Varol, O., Yang, K.-C., Flammini, A., and Menczer, F. (2018). The spread of low-credibility content by social bots. *Nature Communications*, *9*(1), p. 4787. https://doi.org/10.1038/s41467-018-06930-7.

Tuters, M. (2019). LARPing & liberal tears: Irony, idiocy & belief in the deep ver-
    nacular web. In M. Fielitz and N. Thurston (Eds.) *Post-digital cultures of the far
    right: Online actions and offline consequences in Europe and the U.S.* (pp. 37–48).
    Transcript.

Urman, A. and Katz, S. (2020). What they do in the shadows: Examining the far-right
    networks on Telegram. *Information, Communication & Society*, pp. 1–20. https://
    doi.org/10.1080/1369118X.2020.1803946.

userleansbot. (n.d.). List of political subreddits used by userleansbot. Reddit.
    https://www.reddit.com/user/userleansbot/comments/cfzho2/list_of_politi-
    cal_subreddits_used_by_userleansbot/.

ytdl-org. (2021, February 1). *Youtube-dl*. Youtube-Dl: Download Videos from YouTube
    (and More Sites). http://ytdl-org.github.io/youtube-dl/.

Zannettou, S., Caulfield, T., De Cristofaro, E., Kourtelris, N., Leontiadis, I., Sirivianos,
    M., Stringhini, G., and Blackburn, J. (2017). The web centipede: Understanding
    how web communities influence each other through the lens of mainstream
    and alternative news sources. *Proceedings of the 2017 Internet Measurement
    Conference IMC'17* (pp. 405–417). ACM. https://doi.org/10.1145/3131365.3131390.

About the author

Anthony Glyn Burton is SSHRC Joseph Armand Bombardier Doctoral
Scholar in the Department of Communication, Simon Fraser University
and holds a SFU-Mellon Critical Data Studies fellowship at the Digital
Democracies Institute. His dissertation work investigates the relationship
between optimization and fascism.

5 Fringe players on political Twitter

Source-sharing dynamics, partisanship and problematic actors

Maarten Groen and Marloes Geboers

Abstract

Focusing on the (early) run-up to and aftermath of the 2020 U.S. presidential elections, this study examines the extent of problematic information in the most engaged-with content and with the most active users in "political Twitter." It was found that mainstream sources are shared more often than problematic ones, but their percentage was much higher prior to the Capitol riots of January 2021. Significantly, (hyper) partisan sources are close to half of all sources shared, implying a robust presence. By March 2021, though, both the share of problematic and of (hyper)partisan sources decreased significantly, suggesting the impact of Twitter's deplatforming actions. Additionally, active, problematic users (fake profiles, etc.) were found across the political spectrum, albeit more abundantly on the conservative side.

Keywords: hyperpartisanship, misinformation, U.S. elections, deplatforming, Capitol riots, digital methods

Research questions

To what extent are problematic sources present in the most engaged-with content in political and social issue spaces on Twitter in the run-up to and aftermath of the 2020 U.S. elections? Has Twitter's deplatforming affected the quality of sources shared? Are there problematic users among the most active, and are they typically of a particular political leaning?

Rogers. R. (ed.), *The Propagation of Misinformation in Social Media: A Cross-platform Analysis.*
Amsterdam: Amsterdam University Press 2023
DOI: 10.5117/9789463720762_CH05

Essay summary

To probe the extent to which problematic sources are present on political Twitter, the study queries political keywords and investigates the most shared news sources and their credibility as well as the most active users, their authenticity and partisanship. Problematic sources refer to Jack's characterization as containing information that is "inaccurate, misleading, inappropriately attributed, or altogether fabricated" (2017, p. 1). Most engaged-with content on Twitter refers to the most retweeted tweets and/ or most frequently shared sources within the given time periods. Most active users or accounts are those with the highest tweeting activity, and problematic ones are fake accounts, bots or locked/suspended users. Political and issue spaces on Twitter (or "political Twitter") refer to the result sets from keyword and hashtags queries for presidential candidates, political parties and social issues.

In March 2020 the amount of problematic news sources shared on Twitter was 16% of all shared news sources. By December 2020 the share of problematic news sources almost had doubled to 30%. In March 2021 we found a sharp decline in those shared, at just over 10%. While it may have to do with the decline in source sharing during that time frame, it also could reflect the significant purge of user accounts by Twitter in the days after the Capitol riots of January 6. The purge likely affected users who were involved in sharing problematic sources.

In the first two time spans under study (March 2020 and December 2020/ January 2021), close to half of the non-problematic sources circulating the news were classified as (hyper)partisan,[1] suggesting that Twitter, like Facebook before it, is a platform where such sources perform well (Silverman, 2016). In March 2021, the third timeframe, we saw a drop to 34% in that category. The first two periods set themselves apart from the third in that they witnessed the dominance of conservative (hyper)partisan sources which were no longer as strongly in evidence in the third period of time (after the deplatforming).

In terms of the users, in 2016 it was mostly pro-Republican fake and bot accounts that shared problematic information on Twitter (Bovet and Makse, 2019). We noticed, however, that there are also pro-Democrat fake and bot

---

1   (Hyper)partisan is used with the parentheses not only to indicate an amalgamation of the hyperpartisan and partisan source types, but also to signal the difficulty in consistently disentangling them. Below we use (hyper)partisan when discussing sources that were labeled as such in the study.

accounts actively circulating such information. In addition, instead of using their own hashtags, both Democrat and Republican supporters tend to use each other's hashtags to draw attention from their opposition.

Implications

Ever since its tagline changed from *What are you doing?* to *What's happening?* (2009) Twitter has become regarded less as an ambient friend-following medium than as a "reporting machine" at least in the Western social media realm (Rogers, 2014; Tate, 2009). In the past decade, Twitter also has been regarded as a space for doing politics, exemplified by Donald Trump's usage of the platform as a political tool in his campaigning for the presidency in 2015–2016 and later by its integration into his administration. Trump's tweeting changed the nature of the presidency and allowed him to leverage a relatively novel form of media power (Enli, 2017), at least up until the banning of his account on January 8, 2021, as a response to the Capitol building riots and violence two days before, given the role that Trump played in fueling and "glorifying" them.

Given the dominant presence of Trump on Twitter, but also of other candidates and their supporters and observers, it arguably became the key social media platform where the politics of the 2020 U.S. presidential elections played out. Trump's "populist anger" (Wahl-Jorgensen, 2019, p. 117) was not only on display on Twitter but connected to a hybrid media system in which mainstream media co-mingle with "fringe" players (Chadwick, 2017; Wahl-Jorgensen, 2019). It is the extent of this co-mingling that one is able to study on Twitter.

In this regard, it is important to note how social media posting not only "folds into" (Niederer, 2019, pp. 119–120) the content of mainstream media (within which we distinguish more or less partisan sources) but also impacts their "affective styles" (Wahl-Jorgensen, 2019, p. 116). A broad set of transformations have accompanied these new media, enabling a media regime to emerge in which there is a "normalization of a new set of 'emotion rules' that allow a president to consistently make statements that are verifiably false, be called out on these falsehoods and pay no political price for them" (Delli Carpini, 2018, pp. 18–20).

Twitter is a space that is vulnerable to problematic information and the presence of potentially problematic users such as fake accounts and bots (Boyd et al., 2018). We identified such problematic activity during the periods under study, each of which with distinctive user activity. The initial time span is the period around "Super Tuesday" on March 3, 2020, when the greatest number of states hold their primaries or caucuses. We then repeated our analyses in the final days of 2020 from late December up until January 4, 2021, which covers the post-election time span and the significant U.S. Senate run-off elections in Georgia on January 5 which would result in a Senate majority for the Democrats. In retrospect, these days were also close to the Capitol riots of January 6 that were spurred by ongoing speculations about election fraud. This time frame represents a Twitter discourse centering on speculations concerning the balance of power after the Senate run-offs as well as allegations of election fraud and subsequent calls for protesting the "vote steal." The final time span under study covers March 10 to 22, 2021 and can be characterized as not only post-election but also post-purge after Twitter deplatformed over 70,000 accounts (many linked to QAnon conspiracies) between January 9 and 12, in response to the aforementioned riots (Conger, 2021).

Overall, our findings show that mainstream sources outperform (or are shared more often than) problematic sources on political Twitter. Though the circulation of problematic sources was higher just after the election, they never outperformed mainstream sources as was the case on Facebook in the run-up to the 2016 elections (Silverman, 2016). We do see a significant drop in March 2021 in the circulation of problematic sources after the Twitter purge.

In both March 2020 and December 2020/January 2021 nearly half of the sources shared were coming from sources that we sub-categorized as (hyper) partisan progressive or (hyper)partisan conservative. We also witnessed a noticeable uptick in problematic sources shared in the aftermath of the elections which spans the weeks in which the Twitter discourse was dominated by allegations of electoral fraud. While (hyper)partisan sources do not share conspiracy or pseudo-science and are not problematic in that sense, the findings point to a particular kind of hybrid media landscape. It provides plenty of space for (hyper)partisanship and problematic information to co-mingle with mainstream sources. Put differently, mainstream news is increasingly confronted with more partisan players in the field, at least on Twitter in the run-up to and aftermath of the U.S. elections.

Though beyond the scope of this study, our findings imply that more problematic information is engaged with on social media than in other online media spaces such as the web, where the top-ranked media properties (by traffic) are rather mainstream and include NBC, CBS, Disney and Turner (ComScore, 2019), though a separate measure should be taken of the "political web." This disparity between Twitter and the web aligns with what Barnidge and Peacock (2019) point out concerning the reliance on social media for the dissemination of hyperpartisan (and problematic) sources.

In the run-up to the presidential elections in 2016, multiple studies indicated that suspect accounts were mostly spreading problematic, pro-Republican information on Twitter (Bovet and Makse, 2019). During the campaigning and in the (immediate) aftermath of the 2020 elections, however, we also identified problematic, pro-Democrat accounts actively spreading problematic information across Twitter, though they do not outnumber those on the other side of the political spectrum. That is, compared to the findings of previous studies concerning the type of problematic accounts, to date there are indications of a shift from mainly conservative to a mix of conservative as well as progressive problematic accounts. Additionally, among the datasets of most active users we found more problematic accounts than authentic ones, implying that highly active accounts during election campaigning deserve scrutiny.

With respect to the most engaged-with tweets, the vast majority is posted by influential users, and they do not circulate many problematic sources. The finding indicates that most retweeted content (rather than most tweeted content only) is a quality indicator, at least in this brief study. The role of follower counts is thus important as there is a direct relationship between follower and retweet counts. If problematic users would attain influential masses of followers, such analyses might look different.

In light of the societal consequences of disseminating problematic or hyperpartisan sources, it is important to stipulate that the link between sharing and the actual visibility of such sources is not clear cut, given how visibility is algorithmically determined. We can assume a higher probability of exposure, however, when tweets are retweeted (Kwak et al., 2010). Meier et al. (2014) found that retweeting and liking could be regarded as audience engagement in a conversation and attention to the messages, which facilitates information transmission.

Situating the findings: Diversification and polarization on Twitter

We situate our findings around the sharing of problematic and non-problematic sources in the affordances of a platform that, to a certain extent, democratized news sharing in the sense of opening the gates for non-mainstream sources to circulate and be amplified. In order for sources to be successful on Twitter, we need to understand both how people are exposed to news sources and what makes (news) content prone to amplification in that realm. The rise of social platforms has posed challenges to theorizing selective exposure to news. Barnidge and Peacock (2019) distinguish two ways in which social media have restructured selective exposure to news. Both ways provide a means to assess the implications of our findings that social media diversify social connections and facilitate the rise of hyperpartisan news.

The diversification aligns with Bruns's reflections (2019) on the existence of filter bubbles and echo chambers (Pariser, 2011; Sunstein, 2001). Such structures of isolated communities are based on a belief that social media inevitably promote echo chambers and filter bubbles as they personalize content to the extent that individuals consume news in isolated ways. Empirical research into the existence of such structures have not found evidence to support this belief (O'Hara and Stevens, 2015; Barnidge, 2017). Bruns (2019) modified these concepts through introducing degrees of "bubbleness" or "chamberness": scholars can quantify the extent to which people connect or communicate *within* and beyond ideological groups. This modification does justice to the fact that by far most people use multiple sources for their news consumption (Dubois and Blank, 2018) and that people befriend others not just on the basis of their political leanings. Bruns (2019) backs the latter argument by stating how people are not primarily on social media (or at least on Facebook) to talk politics. We would like to note that Twitter's use culture is more geared toward talking politics than is Facebook's, for example, which might lead to different ways of curating one's social network.

Though Twitter users may have diverse social networks and the information that people are exposed to is varied, the findings from our study underscore how sharing sources seems to largely follow one's own political leaning: in the datasets where Republican leaning users were most active, the (hyper)partisan sources were mainly conservative in kind and vice versa. Note, too, how the Republicans are overrepresented in the data demarcated by keywords pertaining to the Democrats, which is related to how Twitter users are calling out or attacking their opponents in their tweets.

Within all datasets we found a pattern whereby users employ the opposition's keywords and hashtags, in order to target each other. It occurs in political spaces organized around both political parties and candidates. Within these supporter spaces, there appear to be more sources shared that attack the opponent rather than support the candidate. (See also Starbird (2017) as well as Groshek and Koc-Michalska (2017) for investigations into strategies of attack and trolling of mainstream media, especially apparent on Twitter.) Our findings thus reiterate how the relentless targeting of people through hyperpartisan viewpoints continues and is a phenomenon practiced on both sides of the political spectrum. One methodological implication is that one cannot neatly demarcate a supporter space through hashtag and/ or keyword queries only.

Barnidge and Peacock (2019) point out that alongside the diversification of information described above, social media also allow hyperpartisan voices to reach a wider audience that is now able to share messages independently of mainstream media. Hyperpartisan news could be described as having a slanted political agenda and making scant effort to balance opposing views. It could be said to push anti-system messages that are critical of mainstream media and established politicians, relying on dubious information or misinformation to do so. It also depends heavily on social media for its dissemination (Barnidge and Peacock, 2019).

Through challenging mainstream narratives, hyperpartisan media also overlap with notions of alternative media. Strengthening Bruns's argument about the absence of isolated bubbles, Peacock et al.'s empirical investigation (2019) found that strong partisans on social media are exposed to both left- as well as right-leaning news. In order to proffer an "alternative perspective" to mainstream news, hyperpartisan media and users have to monitor mainstream sources to know how these outlets talk about issues. They attach commentary to the narratives of mainstream media. As O'Hara and Stevens point out: "engaging with the enemy does not necessarily make a group less partisan" (2015, p. 418). Bruns (2019) expands on this point and situates exposure to diversified information as intensifying polarization through in-group identification and providing an outside "other" that serves as an embodiment of the political enemy. We might not live in isolated bubbles; rather, it is the diversification of information on platforms that seems to spur polarization because of an increased exposure to opposing views. This observation would involve a much-needed research focus into *how* people perceive and recontextualize news on social media to fit it into their existing beliefs.

Expanding on Bruns' argument about "porous" filter bubbles and echo chambers, we found that many tweets were formatted to call out or attack opponents, e.g., from the dataset that queried GOP: "If we 'move on', the GOP will refuse to concede future elections, then judge-shop until they steal one. There must be a price paid for sedition or we will lose our democracy. This is critically important work in the next couple of years" (Alter, 2021). This strategy of attacking opponents was apparent in the fact that the tweet data collected through (for example) words that relate to Democrats contained largely Republican-leaning users who were calling out or attacking Democrats and vice versa. Note for example that in the March 2020 Republican-oriented dataset, a tweet from a Democrat reads: "Real quick: How are Republicans like Donald ok with 2% of people dying from coronavirus as if 2% is not a very high number. But when you discuss a 2-cent wealth tax on people making over 50 million they freak out like it's the worst thing that could ever happen to them" (Salenger, 2020).

Mainstream media attempts to contextualize and balance the narratives injected by hyperpartisan sources. When terms like "junk news" and "conspiracy theory" are invoked, they seem to trigger political backlash (Rogers, 2020a) and increase distrust in mainstream media. This dynamic can only be further understood if affective and intuitive tactics of people who are consuming and sharing news on social media are taken into account. As Swart and Broersma (2021) found in their analyses of young people's assessments of the trustworthiness of news, it is prior knowledge, lived experiences, and endorsements of sources by people within their own social networks that guide how people assess sources, which in turn plays a vital role in the choice to share particular sources over others.

When it comes to sharing news, the existing literature also steers attention toward the emotive underpinnings of hyperpartisan news and its effects when disseminated in the realm of social media. Twitter's business model is based on an attention economy, which places emotion at the forefront of journalistic practices. While emotion and information are not mutually exclusive, hyperpartisan media tend to exploit anger and a culture of outrage (Barnidge and Peacock, 2019; Berry and Sobieraj, 2014). Berry and Sobieraj (2014) move away from conventional wisdom that the rise of outrage media is the result of increased political polarization and argue for considering the economic underpinnings of what they dub an "outrage industry." They situate this industry in the context of structural changes to the media landscape that have fostered its exponential growth.

Twitter as part of this new media landscape is market-driven and dependent on the stickiness of content circulating on its platform. What makes users stick around (and share)? In the context of problematic and hyperpartisan news media, Berger and Milkman's study into viral news content (2012) is instructive for it examines what animates users to share content by assessing the emotive components of more and less shared content. They found that the virality of the content depends on evoking high-arousal positive (awe) or high-arousal negative (anger or anxiety) emotions. Content that evokes low-arousal, or deactivating, emotions (e.g., sadness) is less viral.[2] Thus outrage is seen as viral, which sheds light on the rise of hyperpartisan news on Twitter, as this kind of news is "meant to cause outrage, cue partisan emotions, and get clicks (i.e., make money). Hyperpartisan news ... provides low-quality news with the goal of making money from people's—in many cases misguided—anger and outrage" (Barnidge and Peacock, 2019, p. 6). Note, however, that a binary opposition between quality journalism that is "informing" and less emotive and a sensationalized form that is merely emotive is false, as Wahl-Jorgensen (2019) also stipulates, in reference to Boltanski (1999). The creation of empathy is a prerequisite for political action. We want to stipulate that our distinction between problematic and non-problematic sources is not based on considerations regarding a distinction between factual and emotive news sources; rather, we point to the role of exploiting outrage through a socio-technical synergy between (hyper)partisan news outlets and a market-driven platform.

Notwithstanding the fact that all journalistic items hold some emotion, the affordances of Twitter facilitate a discursive climate which is more extreme, divisive and polarized than most mainstream news spaces (Shepherd et al., 2015). Trump but also hyperpartisan (and problematic) news outlets have benefitted from this affective shift by crafting messages in such a way that they spill over to mainstream media (Karpf, 2017) that in turn, and perhaps unwantedly, amplify fringe players on the platform. So, although the majority of shared sources is still comprised of mainstream news organizations, problematic and hyperpartisan sources are pushing for more space and might have spillover effects in the form of steering mainstream content and affective styles of communication on the platform.

Though investigating such spillover effects into content and style of legacy media is beyond the scope of our analyses, we did find that in political issue spaces such as that of DACA, mainstream media either followed uptakes in problematic source-sharing (see third time span, Figure 5.4) or seemed to veer upwards after such flares in problematic source-sharing (second time span, Figure 5.4), suggesting that problematic sources can be at the forefront of constructing a particular narrative about an issue at hand that is then taken up by mainstream sources. The latter dynamic can be the result of an algorithmically maintained power disparity between mainstream and fringe sources due to the intensification of majority (already popular)

---

2   These results hold even when the authors controlled for how surprising, interesting, or practically useful content is (all of which are positively linked to virality), as well as external drivers of attention, e.g., how prominently content was featured.

voices, a dynamic also hypothesized by among others Bruns (2019) as well as Bozdag and Van den Hoven (2015). This observation opens a relevant future direction for misinformation research which is more sensitive to detecting the adoption, or the "folding in," of fringe and at times problematic sources in the coverage and affective styles of mainstream media.

Findings

Finding 1: On Twitter the number of mainstream sources attached to political tweets or retweets is greater than problematic sources, however much the high share of (hyper)partisan sources within mainstream sources points to a rather polarized platform. After the Twitter purge of problematic accounts in January 2021, the share of (hyper)partisan sources within mainstream sources decreased significantly.

In the data collected during all three time frames (March 2–22, 2020, December 24, 2020–January 4, 2021 and March 10–21, 2021) around a million links to media articles were shared. Of these, overall, mainstream news sources outperformed problematic sources on Twitter. In March 2020, the share of problematic news sources shared on Twitter was 16% of all shared news sources. In December, the share of problematic news sources almost doubled to 30%. In March 2021, the share of problematic sources dropped significantly to 11%. The source classifications are based on source labeling platforms and contain two main categories indicating whether a source is mainstream or problematic and sub-labels for mainstream sources indicating (hyper)partisanship conservative or (hyper)partisanship progressive. The percentage of mainstream sources shared from sources subcategorized as (hyper)partisan decreased slightly from 48% in March 2020 to 43% in December and further dropped to 33% in March 2021. This drop mostly owes to conservative (hyper)partisan sources being less circulated. Overall, mainstream sources are shared more often than problematic news websites, though closely after the election, there was a significant rise in the share of problematic sources which decreased again in March 2021.

Finding 2: Conservative sources are shared more often when discussing Democrat keywords, and in most cases progressive sources are shared more often when discussing Republican ones. In Twitter we queried for specific keywords and hashtags (see Table 5.1) that represent each party and political candidate and found that in both March periods of 2020 and 2021 conservative sources were shared more than progressive ones when discussing Democrat keywords, and vice versa (Figures 5.2 and 5.3). Only in the December/January

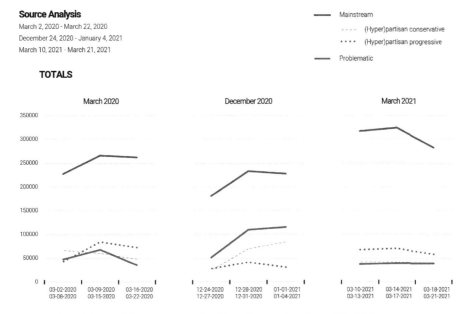

Figure 5.1 Cumulative total of mainstream and problematic hosts shared on political Twitter over three time spans: March 2–22, 2020, December 24, 2020–January 4, 2021 and March 10–21, 2021. Line graphs by Carlo De Gaetano and Federica Bardelli.

period the share of progressive sources in the Republican dataset was lower than that of conservative sources. We also found that in both March periods there were fewer problematic sources shared when discussing Republican keywords than Democrat ones. In December the proportion of problematic sources was much higher which is a trend we see across all datasets. The (hyper)partisan conservative sources in December are shared more often across both Republican and Democrat political spaces.

This finding is in contrast with the results in the other two periods that indicate a crossover of information where (hyper)partisan conservative sources were shared in the Democrat issue space and (hyper)partisan progressive sources were shared in the Republican. The change in December indicates that in the aftermath of the elections, Democrats continue to attack Donald Trump and the Republican party while some problematic and conservative (hyper)partisan sources seem to make a shift and even attack Republicans in the December/January time period when the alleged election fraud was a major topic. One example of this shift is an article[3]

3   https://www.thegatewaypundit.com/2020/12/raffensperger-gets-caught-georgia-ballots-printed-differently-gop-counties-vs-dem-counties-election-rigged/

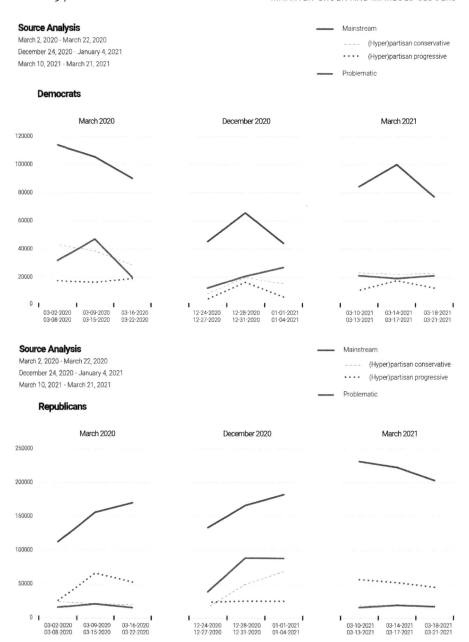

Figures 5.2 and 5.3 Cumulative total of mainstream and problematic hosts shared on political Twitter when querying Republican or Democrat terms for three time spans: March 2–22, 2020, December 24, 2020–January 4, 2021 and March 10–21, 2021. Line graphs by Carlo De Gaetano and Federica Bardelli.

by the Gateway Pundit which made up 25% (23,000 shares) of the total of problematic content shared in that 4-day period, attacking a Republican in Georgia (who had not followed Trump's wishes). In terms of hashtag use, users who support the Democrats would use Republican keywords or hashtags such as #gop and #republicans to tweet against or at them. The same holds for the Republican supporters using the Democrat terms.

Finding 3: Mainstream sources are shared more often than problematic sources concerning social issues related to health care and climate change but not DACA (Deferred Action for Childhood Arrivals) where problematic sources outperformed mainstream sources in certain periods during March and December 2020 as well as in March 2021. In the third time span DACA has fewer partisan sources than in the first two time spans. That is, of those under study, the one issue where problematic sources are shared more often than mainstream sources (only during the first week of March and December 2020) is DACA (Figure 5.4), though the high engagement is largely attributed to a few articles. In the second and third weeks of March 2020, the number of problematic sources in the DACA issue space significantly decreased. Indeed, across the three social issues, with the exception of DACA, few problematic sources were shared.

We note a similar pattern of shared problematic sources across the issues when comparing all time frames. In general, all issue spaces show less engagement in the time periods after the election. For example, there was almost no activity in the Medicare issue space in March 2021, indicating its election relevance rather than a broader societal concern. Note that the sample sizes in these issue spaces are small, so one article can quickly spike engagement.

Finding 4: There were more problematic accounts (fake accounts, bots or locked/suspended) than real accounts on Twitter among selected keyword and hashtag datasets (Democrat, Republican, Trump) except for Biden's dataset in the first time frame. The latter data did contain problematic accounts in the second time span, covering the immediate aftermath of the elections.

We now move to the top 20 users with the highest number of tweets and retweets during two, three-day time frames in March (one during and one after "Super Tuesday," March 3, 2020) and a third time frame (January 1–4, 2021). In the Republican and Democrat keyword and hashtag datasets we noticed that, in total, there were more problematic accounts than real accounts (Figure 5.7) for these time frames. For the Democrat dataset we found only four real accounts in March and one account that clearly labeled itself as a bot that retweets all tweets by Trump. The rest was a combination

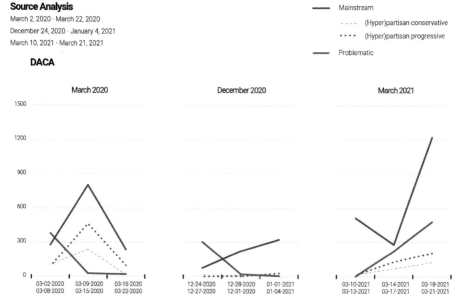

Figure 5.4 Cumulative total of mainstream and problematic hosts shared on political Twitter concerning DACA, during the time spans: March 2–22, 2020, December 24, 2020–January 4, 2021 and March 10–21, 2021. Line graphs by Carlo De Gaetano and Federica Bardelli.

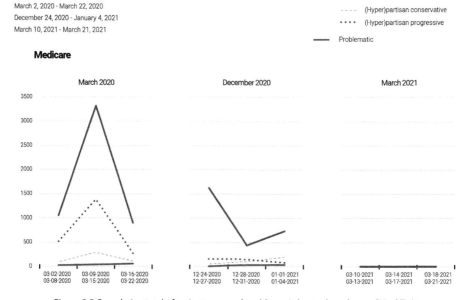

Figure 5.5 Cumulative total of mainstream and problematic hosts shared on political Twitter concerning Medicare, during the time spans: March 2–22, 2020, December 24, 2020–January 4, 2021 and March 10–21, 2021. Line graphs by Carlo De Gaetano and Federica Bardelli.

Source Analysis

March 2, 2020 - March 22, 2020
December 24, 2020 - January 4, 2021
March 10, 2021 - March 21, 2021

——— Mainstream
- - - - (Hyper)partisan conservative
• • • • (Hyper)partisan progressive
——— Problematic

Green New Deal

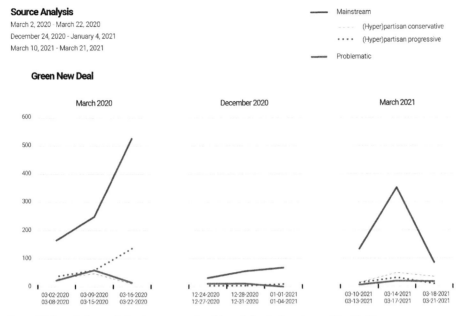

Figure 5.6 Cumulative total of mainstream and problematic hosts shared on political Twitter concerning Green New Deal, during the time spans: March 2–22, 2020, December 24, 2020–January 4, 2021 and March 10–21, 2021. Line graphs by Carlo De Gaetano and Federica Bardelli.

of fake accounts and locked/suspended accounts that had been banned by Twitter. In the Democrat keyword and hashtag dataset, most accounts, whether real or fake, were mostly pro-Republican, indicating again how users are employing the opposing political party's terms. The same applies to the Republican keyword and hashtag dataset, where most users are pro-Democrat as opposed to Republican, though a smaller proportion is fake. Interestingly, in January 2021, the share of fake and bot accounts shifts between these two issue spaces. The number of fake accounts in the Republican hashtag space is now larger than the Democratic space. In our datasets in total, problematic accounts in January make up about 60% of all accounts which is roughly the same as in March.

In 2016 it was found that suspect accounts were mostly Pro-Republican, and these were responsible for spreading most of the problematic information (Bovet and Maske, 2019). In March we found that there was already a rise in problematic accounts associated with pro-Democrats. In January, we found that there are more problematic pro-Democrat accounts compared to March. Thus, it can be argued that Democrats are employing problematic accounts within Republican political spaces to attack the Republican party.

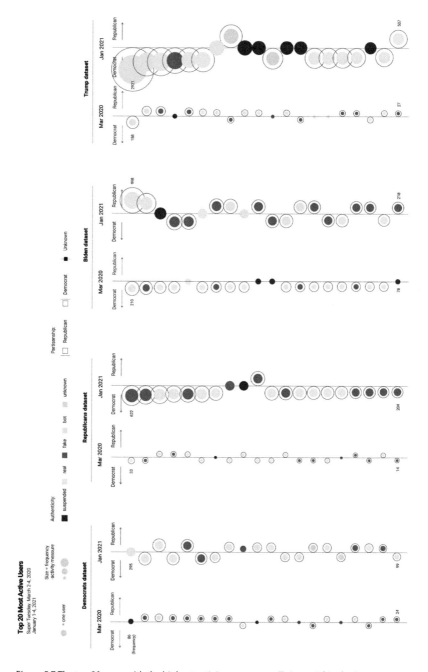

Figure 5.7 The top 20 users with the highest activity measure on Twitter within the Democrat, Republican, Biden and Trump hashtag/keyword datasets, collected March 2–4, 2020 and January 1–4, 2021. Bubble diagrams by Carlo De Gaetano and Federica Bardelli.

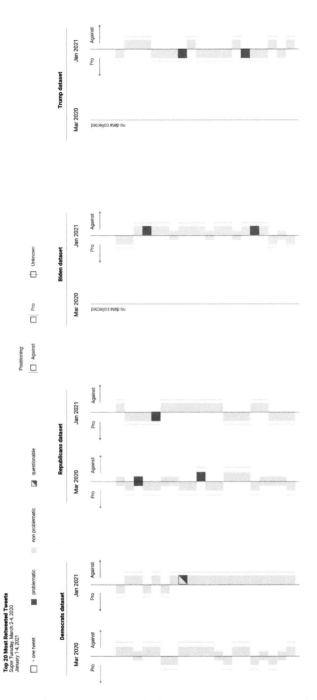

Figure 5.8 The top 20 users with the highest activity measure on Twitter within the Democrat and Republican hashtags/keywords datasets, collected during the time spans: March 2–4, 2020 and January 1–4, 2021. Diagrams by Carlo De Gaetano and Federica Bardelli.

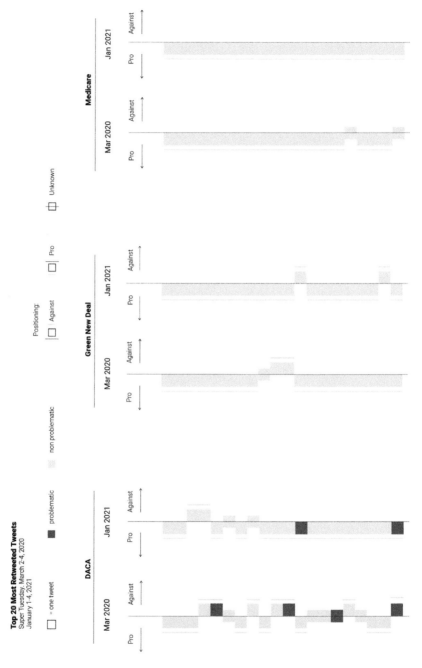

Figure 5.9 The top 20 users with the highest activity measure on Twitter within the hashtag/keyword datasets for the three political issues, collected during the time spans: March 2–4, 2020 and January 1–4, 2021. Diagrams by Carlo De Gaetano and Federica Bardelli.

For the candidates' datasets (Biden and Trump) the same process was followed, but we filtered the top 20 users (by tweeting activity) that @mention each candidate (Figure 5.7). Interestingly, a similar shift can be seen in the Democrat and Republican datasets when comparing the two time frames. In March, the Biden dataset had the highest number of real accounts, with a few fake and locked/suspended accounts. The majority of users that @ mention Biden is not problematic, and they are supporters of his political campaign. The opposite holds for users mentioning Trump where results are equally distributed between bots, fake, and real accounts. In terms of partisanship, the majority is pro-Republican, which indicates that in contrast to the political party spaces, the most active users are supportive. In January, however, the most active users are those who are attacking either candidate. There are more pro-Democrat bots attacking Trump and more real pro-Republican accounts attacking Biden. Overall, the debate seems (even) more polarized in January compared to March.

Finding 5: The most retweeted tweets among all datasets in both March 2020 and December–January 2021 were made mostly by influential accounts like the presidential candidates, members of Congress, organizations, and journalists and largely do not contain any problematic sources. Few problematic sources were found among the top 20 most retweeted tweets in the Democrat and Republican keyword and hashtag datasets in the two time frames (Figure 5.8). For example, the two tweets flagged as problematic in the Republican space in March are linked to the website run by Dan Bongino, a conservative talk show host. A large majority of the retweets are by less controversial, influential people, including presidential candidates, members of Congress and journalists. The results are largely similar for the January 2021 dataset, where one highly resonating retweet opposing Democrats was labeled as questionable. It relates to a news item around electoral fraud from the OAN (One America News), which is a problematic source as per our classification based on Media Bias/Fact Check (see also methods section). Another resonating retweet referred to Breitbart News covering calls for investigating electoral fraud.

Methods

Before initiating our Twitter data collection, we curated a list of queries for political candidates, political parties and social issues, incorporating politician-specific, party-specific and issue-specific keywords and hashtags (Table 5.1). Three social issues (likely to animate both sides of the political spectrum) were selected from a longer issue list made by triangulating issue lists on voter aid sites: Politico, VoteSmart, On the Issues and Gallup. These keywords and hashtags were captured using DMI-TCAT (Borra and Rieder, 2014) from the 2nd until the 23rd of March 2020 and from December 24, 2020 until January 4, 2021. 4CAT[4] was used in the period from March 10 to 22, 2021, when problematic users were not analyzed. In these time spans, close to 3 million tweets were captured that contain a link to a news article. These tweet sets we term "political Twitter."

Table 5.1   Curated list of political keywords and hashtags queried in Twitter.

Topic	Query
Democrat	#democrats, 2020Democrats, BackTheBlueWave, CountryOverParty, DemocraticParty, Democrats2020, Dems, NotMeUs, TowardsADemo-craticPartyICanTrust, VoteBlue, VoteBlueNoMatterWho, VoteBlue-NoMatterWho2020, VoteBlueToSaveAmerica, WelcomeToNotMeUs, democrats, thedemocrats
Republican	#gop, gop, republicans, #republicans, VoteRed, VoteRed2020, VoteRedToSaveAmerica, VoteRedToSaveAmerica2020
Biden	#biden, #joebiden, "joe biden," Biden2020, BidenBounceBack, BidenForPresident, BidenHarris, BidenHarris2020, BidenBeatsTrump, JoeBiden2020, JoeMentum, Mojoe, QuidProJoe, RidinWithBiden, TeamBiden, TeamJoe, WeKnowJoe, biden, joebiden
Trump	#trump, "donald trump," BlackVoicesForTrump, CubansForTrump, DonaldTrumpjr, KAG, KAG2020, KAG2020LandslideVictory, KeepAmeri-caGreat, MAGA, MAGA2020, MAGA2020Landslide, PresidentTrump, PresidentTrump2020, ReElectPresidentTrump2020, TWGRP, Trump2020, Trump2020Landslide, Trump2020LandslideVictory, trump
DACA	Daca
Green New Deal	Greennewdeal
Medicare	medicareforall, medicare4all

The three types of data we collected were most shared links, the top users (in terms of the number of tweets made), and the most retweeted tweets. To study the most shared links, an expert list of sources was created. Each source was labeled into two main categories, mainstream or problematic. Mainstream sources could be sub-categorized as (hyper)partisan conserva-tive, (hyper)partisan progressive or neither. The expert list was created using existing labeling sites such as Allsides.com, Media Bias/Fact Check, "the Chart," and NewsGuard. We consider the categorization as rough. By calculating the total number of times problematic sources were shared

4   https://github.com/digitalmethodsinitiative/4cat

during our duration of study and comparing it with the mainstream sources we were able to show the magnitude of the matter at hand. Are problematic sources present and shared by the users on Twitter who make use of specific political hashtags and keywords? We limited the scope of the top users and hashtags under study to three days in the first two time frames, starting from the 2nd of March 2020 and from the 1st of January 2021. The reason for choosing the specific March period was that it encompassed "Super Tuesday," a day when the largest number of U.S. states hold primary elections, and it would be a reasonable assumption that the Twitter engagement on this day, the day prior, and the day after would be higher than the other days in our date range. The January time frame was just before the deciding Georgia run-off elections for the U.S. Senate on January 5, which would give the Democrats a slim majority and in hindsight, with that time frame, we also captured the days before the Capitol riots of January 6, 2021.

With the dataset of most active users, we investigated the extent to which problematic users/accounts (fake profiles, bots, or locked/suspended users) were present. We examined the top 20 users with the greatest number of tweets on political Twitter. These users were then coded or categorized on two scales: "authenticity" and "partisanship." For the authenticity label, the top 20 users were classified into four types based on their Twitter profiles, where the idea is to gain a sense of the genuineness and legitimacy of the top users: real, fake, bot, and locked/suspended. The categories are adopted from the audience intelligence website, SparkToro, which ranks Twitter users based on their attributes (Fishkin, 2018). For bots, the website categorizes accounts by determining whether they have Twitter's default profile image, if an account has an unusual ratio of followers/following, or posts an abnormal number of tweets per day, among other signals. Fake/real profiles, too, are judged according to (usual/unusual) tweeting habits and behavior. The second categorization is "partisanship," where all the top users' political leanings were labeled independently by two authors by looking at their Twitter profiles and classifying them into one of three categories: Democrat-leaning, Republican-leaning, or unknown. Any disagreements between the authors resulted in labeling the one in question as unknown.

With regards to the most retweeted tweets, the top 20 tweets were extracted from the political spaces, and from the three issue-specific hashtags, DACA, Green New Deal, and Medicare. The most retweeted or the most popular tweets were further categorized into two categories of partisanship and the categories problematic or non-problematic information provider. Similar to the problematic users' segment, the partisanship of the tweets was manually labeled by looking at the language of the tweet and further details about the person who tweeted. To decide if a tweet contains problematic information, we checked whether any news sources linked in the tweets were classified as such in the labeled source list.

References

Alter, J. [jonathanalter]. (2021, January 1). "If we 'move on', the GOP will refuse to concede future elections, then judge-shop until they steal one. There must be a price paid for sedition or we will lose our democracy. This is critically important work in the next couple of years" [tweet]. https://twitter.com/jonathanalter/status/1345074521561292800.

Barnidge, M. and Peacock, C. (2019). A third wave of selective exposure research? The challenges posed by hyperpartisan news on social media. *Media and Communication, 7*(3), pp. 4–7. https://doi.org/10.17645/mac.v7i3.2257.

Barnidge, M. (2017). Exposure to political disagreement in social media versus face-to-face and anonymous online settings. *Political Communication, 34*(2), 302–321. https://doi.org/10.1080/10584609.2016.1235639.

Berger, J. and Milkman, K. L. (2012). What makes online content viral? *Journal of Marketing Research, 49*(2), 192–205. https://doi.org/10.1509/jmr.10.0353.

Berry, J. and Sobieraj, S. (2014). *The outrage industry.* Oxford University Press.

Boltanski, L. (1999). *Distant suffering: Morality, media and politics.* Cambridge University Press.

Borra, E. and Rieder, B. (2014). Programmed method: Developing a toolset for capturing and analyzing tweets. *Journal of Information Management* 66(3), pp. 262–278. https://doi.org/10.1108/AJIM-09-2013-0094.

Bovet, A. and Makse, H.A. (2019). Influence of fake news in Twitter during the 2016 U.S. presidential election. *Nature Communications, 10*(1), p. 7. https://doi.org/10.1038/s41467-018-07761-2.

Boyd, R. L., Spangher, A., Fourney, A., Nushi, B., Ranade, G., Pennebaker, J., and Horvitz, E. (2018). Characterizing the Internet Research Agency's social media operations during the 2016 U.S. presidential election using linguistic analyses [Preprint]. PsyArXiv. https://doi.org/10.31234/osf.io/ajh2q.

Bozdag, E. and Van den Hoven, J. (2015). Breaking the filter bubble: Democracy and design. *Ethics and Information Technology, 17*(4), 249–65. https://doi.org/10.1007/s10676-015-9380-y.

Bruns, A. (2019). *Are filter bubbles real?* Polity Press.

Chadwick, A. (2017). *The hybrid media system: Politics and power.* Oxford University Press.

Comscore (2019). Comscore March 2019 top 50 multi-platform website properties (desktop and mobile). https://www.comscore.com/Insights/Rankings.

Conger, K. (2021). Twitter, in widening crackdown, removes over 70,000 QAnon accounts. *New York Times*. https://www.nytimes.com/2021/01/11/technology/twitter-removes-70000-qanon-accounts.html.

Delli Carpini, M.X. (2018). Alternative facts: Donald Trump and the emergence of a new U.S. media regime. In Z. Papacharissi and P. Boczkowski (Eds.), *Trump and the media* (pp. 17–23). MIT Press.

Dubois, E. and Blank, G. (2018). The echo chamber is overstated: The moderating effect of political interest and diverse media. *Information, Communication & Society, 21*(5), pp. 729–45. https://doi.org/10.1080/1369118X.2018.1428656.

Enli, G. (2017). Twitter as arena for the authentic outsider: Exploring the social media campaigns of Trump and Clinton in the 2016 U.S. presidential election. *European Journal of Communication, 32*(1), pp. 50–61. https://doi.org/10.1177/0267323116682802.

Fishkin, R. (2018). SparkToro's new tool to uncover real vs. fake followers on Twitter, SparkToro. https://sparktoro.com/blog/sparktoros-new-tool-to-uncover-real-vs-fake-followers-on-twitter/.

Groshek, J. and Koc-Michalska, K. (2017). Helping populism win? Social media use, filter bubbles, and support for populist presidential candidates in the 2016 U.S. Election Campaign. *Information, Communication & Society, 20*(9), 1389–407. https://doi.org/10.1080/1369118X.2017.1329334.

Jack, C. (2017). Lexicon of lies: Terms for problematic information. Data & Society Research Institute. https://datasociety.net/library/lexicon-of-lies/.

Karpf, D. Digital politics after Trump. *Annals of the International Communication Association, 41*(2), pp. 198–207. https://doi.org/10.1080/23808985.2017.1316675.

Kwak, H., Lee, C., Park, H. and Moon, S. (2010). What is Twitter, a social network or a news media? In *Proceedings of the 19th International Conference on World Wide Web* (pp. 591–600). ACM.

Meier, F., Elsweiler, D., and Wilson, M.L. (2014). More than liking and bookmarking? Towards understanding Twitter favouriting behaviour. In *Proceedings of ICWSM'14*. AAAI Press. http://www.aaai.org/ocs/index.php/ICWSM/ICWSM14/paper/view/8094.

NewsGuard (2020). NewsGuard Nutrition Label. https://www.newsguardtech.com.

Niederer, S. (2019). Networked content analysis: The case of climate change. Institute of Network Cultures. https://networkcultures.org/blog/publication/tod32-networked-content-analysis-the-case-of-climate-change/.

O'Hara, K. and Stevens, D. (2015). Echo chambers and online radicalism: Assessing the internet's complicity in violent extremism. *Policy & Internet, 7*(4), pp. 401–422. https://doi.org/10.1002/poi3.88.

Pariser, E. (2011). *The filter bubble: What the internet is hiding from you*. Penguin.

Peacock, C., Hoewe, J., Panek, E., and Willis, G. P. (2019). Hyperpartisan news use: Relationships with partisanship, traditional news use, and cognitive and affective involvement. Paper presented at the Annual Conference of the International Communication Association, Washington, DC.

Rogers, R. (2014). Debanalising Twitter: The transformation of an object of study. In Weller, K., Bruns, A., Burgess, J., Mahrt, M. and Puschmann, C. (Eds.), *Twitter and society* (pp. ix-xxvi). Peter Lang.

Rogers, R. (2020a). The scale of Facebook's problem depends upon how "fake news" is classified. *Harvard Kennedy School Misinformation Review, 1*(6). https://doi.org/10.37016/mr-2020-43.

Salenger, M. [meredthsalenger]. (2020, March 02). "Real quick: How are Republicans like Donald ok with 2% of people dying from coronavirus as if 2% is not a very high number. But when you discuss a 2-cent wealth tax on people making over 50 million they freak out like it's the worst thing that could ever happened to them" [tweet]. https://twitter.com/meredthsalenger/status/1234337053.

Shepherd, T., Harvey, A., Jordan, T., Srauy, S., and Miltner, K. (2015). Histories of hating. *Social Media + Society*. https://doi.org/10.1177/2056305115603997.

Silverman, C. (2016, November 16). This analysis shows how viral fake election news stories outperformed real news on Facebook. *Buzzfeed News*. https://www.buzzfeednews.com/article/craigsilverman/viral-fake-election-news-outperformed-real-news-on-facebook

Starbird, K. (2017). Examining the alternative media ecosystem through the production of alternative narratives of mass shooting events on Twitter. In *Proceedings of the 11th International AAAI Conference on Web and Social Media*. AAAI Press. http://faculty.washington.edu/kstarbi/Alt_Narratives_ICWSM17-CameraReady.pdf.

Sunstein, C. R. (2001). *Echo chambers: Bush v. Gore, impeachment, and beyond*. Princeton University Press.

Tate, R. (2009, 19 Nov.). Twitter's new prompt: A linguist weighs in. *Gawker*. https://gawker.com/5408768/twitters-new-prompt-a-linguist-weighs-in.

Wahl-Jorgensen, K. (2019). *Emotions, media and politics*. Polity.

Data availability

https://doi.org/10.7910/DVN/QIJQ3X

About the authors

Maarten Groen is a researcher and programmer at the Visual Methodologies Collective at the Amsterdam University of Applied Sciences. His research focuses on using data to empower citizens through participatory and digital methods and the analysis and visualization of the resulting data. His background is in Computer and Information Science.

Marloes Geboers, PhD, is a member of the Visual Methodologies Collective at the Amsterdam University of Applied Sciences and Postdoctoral Fellow in platform subcultures in Media Studies, University of Amsterdam. She researches the affective affordances of platforms, particularly how they shape the visualities and narratives of war and suffering. Her educational background is in political science and journalism.

6 Twitter as accidental authority

How a platform assumed an adjudicative role during the COVID-19 pandemic

Emillie de Keulenaar, Ivan Kisjes, Rory Smith, Carina Albrecht and Eleonora Cappuccio[1]

Abstract

This chapter explores Twitter's moderation of authoritative sources and their audience's claims concerning COVID-19 treatments, transmission and prevention techniques. It examines how they diverge over time, and how Twitter intervenes in resulting debates via content moderation guidelines and techniques. It argues that as public health organizations and heads of state struggle to maintain consensus among themselves and with their Twitter audiences on these issues Twitter exceptionally steps in as an authority in its own right. It does so by flagging, suspending and deleting contents, including those of authoritative sources that threaten to disrupt a common understanding of the virus and vital health information.

Keywords: Content moderation, platform rules, sensemaking, problematic information, COVID-19 treatment

Research questions

How did claims by authoritative sources (@realDonaldTrump, @CDC, @NIH, @WHO and @pahowho, the North American division of the World Health Organization) on COVID-19 transmission, prevention and treatments

1   The authors would like to acknowledge Jack Wilson and Carlo De Gaetano for their contributions to this research. Emillie de Keulenaar's participation has been supported by the UKRI-Canada ESRC grant, *Responsible AI for inclusive, democratic societies: A cross-disciplinary approach to detecting and countering abusive language online* (ESRC reference: ES/T012714/1).

Rogers. R. (ed.), *The Propagation of Misinformation in Social Media: A Cross-platform Analysis*. Amsterdam: Amsterdam University Press 2023
DOI: 10.5117/9789463720762_CH06

diverge from those of their audiences between March and October 2020? How did Twitter's content moderation guidelines and techniques for COVID-19 misinformation interfere in these divergences? How did COVID-19 affect Twitter's overall policies on misinformation?

Essay summary

As new information on the epidemiological nature of COVID-19 infections and its impact on public safety evolves, so do claims on which objective facts constitute it (Yong, 2020). Twitter has been tasked with ensuring that their users maintain a basic level of consensus around public safety guidelines and other information relative to personal and public health by, for example, centralizing access to local health organizations and representatives, flagging and at times deleting "misleading" tweets that contradict such sources (Skopeliti and John, 2020). But with diverging guidelines and facts occasionally opposing even authorities—notably ex-U.S. President Trump, the American Center for Disease Control, the National Institutes of Health and the World Health Organization—the platform has struggled to determine whom to attribute ultimate authority for reliable information about COVID-19 transmission, treatment and protection.

In this context, we find that English-speaking publics who interact with any of these authorities have at times been polarized around either Donald Trump or the World Health Organization. As these authorities contradict each other, we find that Twitter begins to moderate—and ultimately suspend—authorities that disrupt the general consensus over COVID-19, particularly Donald Trump. We conclude that Twitter's moderation of problematic information on the virus demonstrates how the platform relies less on specific guidelines over what constitute true and false information than on the general consensus between public health authorities.

These findings suggest two main implications. First, Twitter's moderation of authoritative sources renders the platform an authority in its own right, as it ultimately decides which of these authorities can and cannot govern on its platform. Second, COVID-19 has pushed platform moderation of misinformation from detecting and suppressing technically inauthentic contents to information that affects the overall consensus over what constitutes correct information, leading the platform to sanction outliers or "extremes," and shrink its size down to a more homogeneous (and thereby cohesive) public sphere. Both of these implications constitute a few emerging characteristics of a kind of "post-Trump" internet.

Implications

Heads of state, health organizations and the public have been frequently divided on claims around COVID-19, such as whether asymptomatic people and children can contaminate others, whether one should use a mask, or if children can be contagious (Iati et al., 2020; O'Leary, 2020). In this context, governments and public health authorities have struggled to maintain a consensus with their local publics and each other (Starbird, 2020), hurting public trust in their capacities as main references about the pandemic (Bordia and Difonzo, 2004; Bostrom et al., 2015; Starbird et al., 2016).

In response, social media, search engines and encyclopedic wikis have been tasked with ensuring that their users maintain consensus around public safety guidelines and other information relative to public health (Skopeliti and John, 2020). Since the early months of 2020, Google Web Search, YouTube, Facebook, Twitter and Reddit have set up centralized access points to information provided by local and global "authoritative sources" (Skopeliti and John, 2020). Though some stakeholders continue to demand more radical platform redesign (Dwoskin, 2020), more modest measures include prompting local guidelines on the virus whenever one searches or consults information about COVID-19 (Lee and Oppong, 2020), temporarily disabling the personalization of Newsfeeds (Lyons, 2020); flagging contents (tweets, posts, videos) that disseminate contested claims (Lyons, 2020), demoting "borderline" or suspicious contents like conspiracy theories and raising "authoritative content" to the top of search and recommendation results (De Keulenaar et al., 2021; YouTube, 2019), and altogether deleting materials that pose a danger to public health, such as anti-vaccination or alternative medication (De Keulenaar et al., 2021; YouTube, 2020).

But with information about the virus being uncertain in the early months of the pandemic, one wonders how a platform like Twitter has adapted its COVID misinformation policy to tolerate the relative contingency of knowledge and facts about the virus. Not only have authoritative guidance on treatments and protection frequently changed, but they have also contradicted each other. Guidance by the World Health Organization, favored by nearly all social media platforms, at times differed from what the Centers for Disease and Control Prevention, the NIH and then-U.S. President Donald Trump advised. While such discordances are to be expected, we assume that it has at times created a crisis of authority in the platform—a "state of exception" (Schmitt, 2005)—that has pushed Twitter to take exceptional measures to maintain a baseline of consensus in its platform.

Drawing partly from studies on collective sensemaking and rumors (Caplow, 1946; Dailey and Starbird, 2015; Krafft et al., 2017; Shibutani, 1966), we use close reading and natural language processing techniques to measure the relative divergence of authoritative and "audience" claims about COVID transmission, prevention and treatments. Authoritative sources include international and U.S. representatives and public health organizations, with claims released on Twitter and their respective websites, and their "audiences," defined here as the users who have at some point engaged with or referred to the former on Twitter. Our dataset contained 250 million tweets that mention #covid or #coronavirus between March and October of 2020. Authoritative sources include then-U.S. President Donald Trump, the Centers for Disease Control and Prevention, the National Institutes of Health, and the World Health Organization's International and Regional Office for the Americas. Using the Wayback Machine (Internet Archive, 2021), we then examine how Twitter adapted its content moderation techniques to moderate COVID-19 misinformation. We capture Twitter moderation data for each of the tweets in our dataset using Selenium, a web interface scraper, obtaining labels, suspensions and other removal disclaimers.

We find that the pandemic has pushed Twitter and its platform counterparts to delimit what "misinformation" or other problematic information is, be it in a technical, authoritative or even rhetorical sense. Determining the objective value of statements on COVID-19 treatments, prevention and transmission vehicles, however, is not a responsibility the platform initially embraces. Its preference is to relay that decision to "authoritative sources," a solution already set by other platforms to prioritize authoritative contents as "reputed" or "trustworthy" sources, despite mixed reactions from users suspicious of "political bias" in favor of left-wing American political culture (Economist, 2019). This study also shows mixed results. The absence of consensus among authoritative sources makes the 2020 U.S. (and international) crisis of authority on COVID-19 even more evident, with the WHO, CDC, NIV and the White House contradicting one another. The difference, we find, is that in the absence of authority, Twitter steps in as an authority itself.

Consensus and misinformation in the process of COVID-19 sensemaking: Conceptual implications

A number of misinformation policies and studies have focused on detecting and correcting misinformation by (for example) investing in media literacy and pinpointing factors that can "increase the chances of citizens to be exposed to correct(ive) information" (Scheufele and Krause, 2019, p. 7664). Strategies include removing false content and demoting false or "borderline" information in favor of authoritative sources (Scheufele and Krause, 2019, p. 7664).

A possible drawback of these strategies is the decontextualization of misinformed claims from the premises and info spheres that substantiate them. These spheres are frequently outside of misinformation-policed social media platforms (De Zeeuw et al., 2020), and their users may be unaware of the information needed to understand claims and directives from authoritative sources (Kou et al., 2017). In other instances, misinformative claims can come from more innocuous misunderstandings (De Zeeuw et al., 2020), or attempts at making sense of situations still unexplained by authorities (Krafft et al., 2017, p. 2976; Starbird et al., 2016). The inconsistency of official information is characteristic of the formation of rumors and other "improvised" sensemaking (Shibutani, 1966), which in themselves constitute an attempt to create consensus or a "common understanding" where there is none (Bordia and Difonzo, 2004).

In this sense, we join a field of study that approaches misinformation as a dynamic by-product of poor consensus between information providers and recipients—authoritative sources and their audiences—who must in crises "converge" around a common understanding of facts and the epistemic frameworks used to validate them (Scheufele and Krause, 2019, p. 7663; Starbird, 2012, p. 1). By pinpointing information that authoritative sources and their audiences mutually ignore and comparing diverging claims related to these terms,[2] we find that authoritative sources and their audiences do not always focus on the same aspects of COVID-19, nor do audiences always rely on the same authoritative sources.

From misinformative to misleading tweets: How COVID affected Twitter's moderation of "problematic information"

Over the course of 2020, Twitter adapted its anti-misinformation content moderation policies significantly. Twitter's initial approach to managing COVID-19 misinformation on its platform piggy-backed on existing policies that targeted inauthentic user behavior. In early February 2020, the platform targeted COVID misinformation as deceitful contents, or

---

2   For example, audiences mention "5G" and "food" as transmission vectors, while authoritative sources focus on "cough" and "touch."

disinformation: doctored footage or photography, or contents forged with the intention to mislead other users (Twitter, 2020). It uses the World Health Organization as a reference from which to determine whether a tweet is false or not. This requires heavy-handed, top-down measures to remove tweets that contradict such authorities before they can spread on the platform.

As the pandemic began to spread globally, however, it became clear that existing conceptions of disinformation do not capture the fact that COVID-19 is also the subject of widely diverging and contingent information. It becomes difficult, arguably impossible, for the "authoritative sources" Twitter recommends delivering stable facts and guidelines on the virus. On the one hand, this leads Twitter to fine-tune its definition of misinformation down to the level of the rhetoric of a tweet. This includes both *what* a tweet claims and *how* it claims it. On the other, Twitter also broadens its definition of misinformation as a problem of consensus. It recognizes that information about the virus, even when provided by authoritative sources, is subject to disagreements and change.

Rather than resorting merely to deletion, it seeks to reinforce a consensus on guidelines and facts about the virus by centralizing users' access to COVID information. It wants to ensure that users comment on the virus within delimited epistemic boundaries of what can and cannot be entrusted to be true. The delimitation of those perimeters is an arbitration outsourced to local, legislative and medical authorities: those tasked with deciding the truth about the virus. This means pointing users to local authoritative sources' websites on tweets that mention the virus or adding links to national or state-level guidelines on newsfeeds and homepages. These measures—exemplified by the early #KnowTheFacts prompt—would help fill in possible "data voids" (Golebiewski and boyd, 2019) between authoritative sources and their audiences.

Twitter as an accidental authority

Still, trouble comes when authoritative sources begin to contradict one another around mask usage, hydroxychloroquine treatments or airborne viral transmission. In such cases, Twitter does not favor one or another public health authority but does at times moderate authorities that disrupt their overall consensus. Ex-U.S. President Donald Trump's analogies of COVID and seasonal flu, or the merits of hydroxychloroquine-based treatments, contradict and confuse statements by the CDC and NIH. His tweets are flagged, counter-balanced by resources Twitter recommends users consult instead. Though the first tweet it suspended was sanctioned for violating its "glorification of violence" policy, Trump's tweets on COVID are nearly always labeled by default.

The decision to moderate authorities appears to mark a shift between redirecting users towards trust-worthy sources of information to curating such sources relative to their capacity to maintain a greater consensus amongst other relevant authorities. In this sense, Twitter is no longer moderating tweets individually, but as a larger ensemble of statements whose overall consensus constitutes the objective quality of COVID information. Technically, moderating consensus rather than single falsehoods grants Twitter significant institutional responsibilities. As it optimizes the relative proportion of public safety and consensus, Twitter accidentally becomes an "authoritative source"—or authority, for short—in its own right.

Twitter's moderation of existing authorities speaks to a number of foundational concepts of political theory, among which is Carl Schmitt's famed phrase that the "sovereign" is "that which decides the state of exception" (Schmitt, 1932). As consensus wanes among existing authorities in a given body politic and crisis sets in, the one who will hold ultimate authority is that who intervenes and decides for those in this sphere regardless of the legality of their actions. It is not so much Twitter's content moderation policies that legitimize its moderation of authoritative sources, but its very ability to do so regardless of existing conventions.

Findings

Finding 1: Authoritative sources and their audiences contradict each other most on undetermined facts, such as COVID-19 treatments. As may be expected, audiences and authoritative sources diverge most around unconfirmed information. There were no single, confirmed treatments for COVID-19 until the announcement of the Pfizer vaccine in August of 2020. Despite declaring that "no treatment" and "vaccines" were available by January, authoritative sources like the World Health Organization and the CDC fail to prevent their audiences from contemplating a plethora of treatments ranging from house-grown remedies and specialized medicines (see Figure 6.1), be it vitamin C, ethanol, zinc or remdesivir.

In this context, authoritative sources act primarily as debunkers of unconfirmed or false information. The World Health Organization opens a page dedicated to debunking false ingredients reported on social media. From January, it debunks nearly half of the ingredients discussed by their

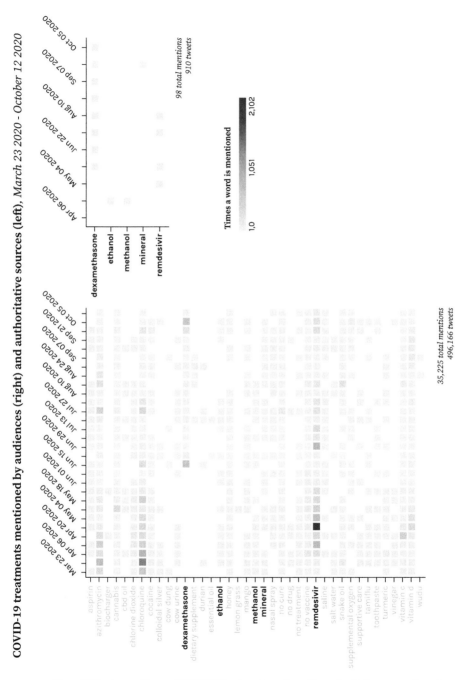

Figure 6.1 Heatmap of forms of COVID-19 treatment mentioned by authoritative sources (tweets and website data) and their Twitter audiences (tweet replies and mentions of website domains by authoritative sources, e.g., whitehouse.gov). Visualization by Emillie de Keulenaar and Eleonora Cappuccio.

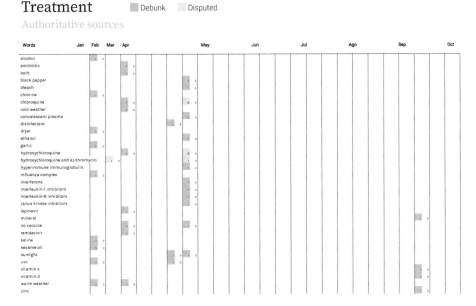

Figure 6.2 Heatmap of authoritative clams on COVID-19 treatments. Purple values count as authoritative debunks of audience claims; blue values indicate instances in which authoritative have framed a given treatment as disputed. Visualization by Carlo Gaetano.

audiences: ethanol, honey, lemon, cannabis, cocaine, colloidal silver, lopinavir and others (see Figure 6.2).

Elsewhere, authoritative claims also express uncertainty on transmission, treatments and prevention, stressing the uncertain nature of research on COVID-19 (Bostrom et al., 2015, p. 633). This can be said about chloroquine, hydroxychloroquine, remdesivir, dexamethasone, prednisolone and Tamiflu, about which authoritative sources mention ongoing research and testing. This does not prevent audiences from continuing to engage with these ingredients.

Finding 2: Audiences are divided around contradicting claims by authoritative sources. Zooming into authoritative and audience claims on the efficacy of hydroxychloroquine, we see that audiences (below, "users") appear to polarize around diverging authoritative statements. While some echo Donald Trump's claims that the ingredient is effective (including in combination with azithromycin), others relay the World Health Organization's claim that it is not. A small majority state the same claim as the CDC and the NIH who rule the matter as still "uncertain."

The same can be said about modes of transmission. In the early months of the pandemic, authoritative sources and their audiences usually referred

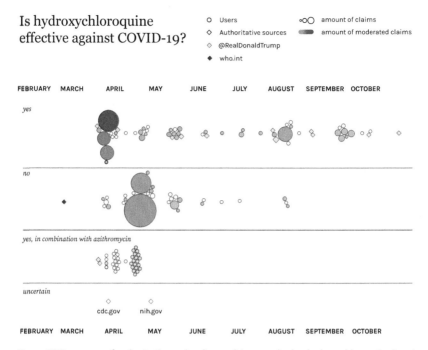

Figure 6.3 Bee swarm of authoritative and audience claims on whether hydroxychloroquine is or is not effective against COVID-19 infections. Visualization by Carlo de Gaetano.

to different modes of COVID-19 transmission. Audiences do focus on modes of transmission mentioned by authoritative sources: (respiratory) droplets, close contact, community spread, coughing, sneezing and touch. Here, too, authoritative sources act as debunkers: 5G is dismissed at least twice after gaining considerable traction among audiences in March.

The caveat, here, is that audiences continue to focus on modes of transmission disputed among authoritative sources (see Figure 6.4). With little scientific consensus on the minutiae of droplet transmissions, there is notable public confusion on the airborne nature of the virus (Achenbach and Johnson, 2020; Lewis, 2020; Mandavilli, 2020). The World Health Organization expresses uncertainty about airborne transmission throughout February, then later joins the U.S. Centers for Disease Control and Prevention in March to affirm that it spreads mainly via droplets. Only in April 2020 does the CDC offer a verdict: "according to experts," it says, "the virus can be transmitted by both droplets and smaller, 'aerosol' types of particles" (Centers for Disease Control and Prevention, 2020). While the World Health Organization rejects this claim, a slight majority of users echoes the CDC's statement well until October.

In this context, audiences express a relatively constant amount of uncertainty throughout, as well as conspiratorial suspicions in early March.

Types of transmission mentioned by authoritative sources (down) and their Twitter audiences (up), *March 23 2020 - October 12 2020*

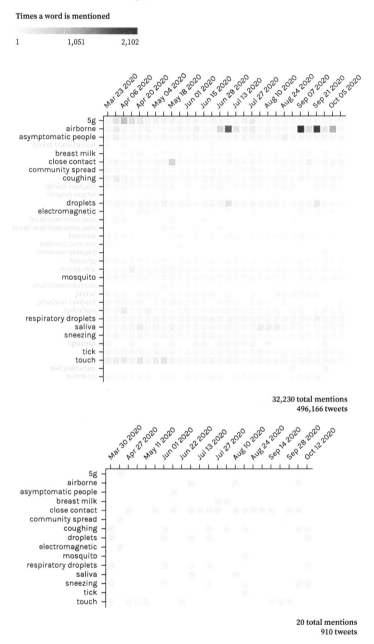

Figure 6.4 Heatmap of modes of transmission mentioned by authoritative sources (tweets and websites) and their Twitter audiences (tweet replies and mentions of website domains by authoritative sources, e.g., whitehouse.gov). Visualization by Emillie de Keulenaar and Eleonora Cappuccio.

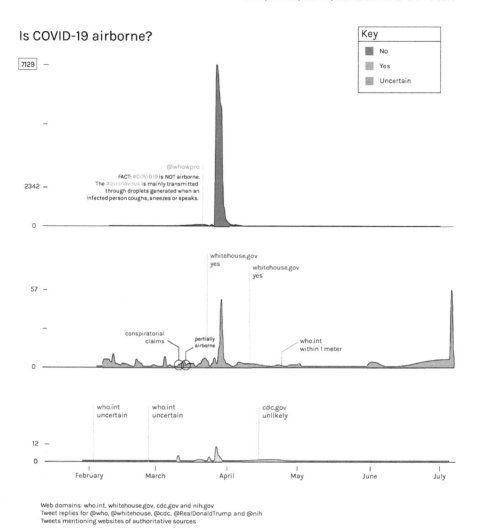

Figure 6.5 Line graph of audience and authoritative statements about whether COVID-19 is airborne or not. Visualization by Eleonora Cappuccio and Emillie de Keulenaar.

While this is especially applicable in the months of February and March, audiences appear to express a relatively constant amount of claims aligned with the majority of authoritative sources. This may suggest that more consensus *between* authoritative sources could foster consensus among their publics.

There is further disagreement on whether COVID-19 is transmitted through droplets or smaller aerosol particles (see Figure 6.5). While virtually all sources agree that the virus is transmitted by the former, some specify that aerosols may remain in the air for longer periods of time. The World

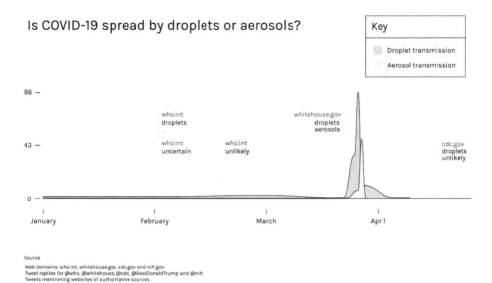

Figure 6.6 Line graph of claims on droplet or aerosol transmission by authoritative sources (web domains) and their Twitter audiences (tweet replies and mentions of website domains by authoritative sources, e.g., whitehouse.gov). Visualisation by Eleonora Cappuccio and Emillie de Keulenaar.

Health Organization's expressions of doubt regarding the latter claim is quickly contradicted by the White House. Audiences express an equally distributed amount of agreement with each claim, seemingly partitioned into groups that either rely on the word of the World Health Organization or that of the White House.

The debate on whether the virus is droplet or aerosol airborne shows how popular understandings of viral transmission appear to have evolved through discussions between authoritative sources and audiences. Early public doubts about whether the virus was airborne have prompted authorities to define and measure airborne transmission in increasingly concrete terms (see Figure 6.6). While the World Health Organization had stated earlier that airborne transmission is an exchange of infected droplets, recent findings on aerosol transmission substantiate earlier public conceptions of airborne transmission as a somewhat ubiquitous form of "air infection" (Mandavilli, 2020).

Finding 3: Twitter has adapted its content moderation policies to capture the disputed nature of COVID-19 information. In the face of such disputes, Twitter's "COVID-19 misleading information" policy underwent frequent changes throughout 2020 (see Figure 6.7). On February 4, 2020, Twitter's initial definition of COVID-19 misinformation is based on a conception of misinformation as deceit, be that in the intent of its author ("media shared in a deceptive manner") or in its technical composition ("synthetic or manipulated media" on the virus) (Chu and McDonald, 2020). This definition follows existing conceptions of misinformation as disinformation, or as semantically or technically inauthentic. Examples of the former include "a deliberate intent to deceive people about the nature or origin of the content," and for the latter, "content that has been substantially edited in a manner that fundamentally alters its composition, sequence, timing, or framing," "any visual or auditory information that has been added or removed," and "fabricated or simulated media depicting a real person" (Twitter, 2020a). Both of these types of information are subjected to an incremental type of moderation, where they are first labeled, demoted and altogether removed after infringing misinformation policies more than once (Roth and Pickels, 2020). Twitter's policy against COVID misinformation as "manipulated media" is sealed with a general "zero tolerance approach to platform manipulation," announced in March 4, 2020 (Twitter, 2020b).

As the virus disseminates outside of China in early March, Twitter broadens its conception of COVID-19 misinformation as contradicting local and international "authoritative sources" (Twitter, 2020b). The idea, then, is to establish a baseline of facts about the virus with which to moderate user-generated contents. Content moderation targets content that may contradict what is known and stated by authoritative sources. This includes "denial of global or local health authority recommendations to decrease someone's likelihood of exposure to COVID-19"; "denial of established scientific facts about transmission during the incubation period or transmission guidance from global and local health authorities"; and "alleged cures for COVID-19 that are not immediately harmful but are known to be ineffective" (Twitter, 2020b). To reinforce this policy, Twitter prioritizes posts by the World Health Organization and local health organizations in users' homepages and personal timelines. From January 29, 2020, Twitter also launches a series of labeling techniques to redirect users towards claims by authoritative sources on the transmission, protection and treatment of the virus. Contradictions to these claims are first labeled and then removed (see Figure 6.6) (Twitter, 2020b).

The fact that authoritative sources occasionally disagree with each other poses a new challenge to existing COVID policies. For this reason, content moderation guidelines adopt a two-fold strategy: they simultaneously restrict the kind of claims users can make about COVID-19 transmission, prevention and treatments, and highlight the disputed nature of such claims. The idea is to adapt moderation to the contingent and disputed nature of various information about the disease, be they international discrepancies in public health policies or diverging claims made by authoritative sources about the virus. As did other platforms (e.g., Google and Facebook), it also creates a flag prompt ("#KnowTheFacts") whenever users search or encounter information about the virus on the platform (Chu and McDonald, 2020). By May 11, it introduces new labeling and warning techniques intended to "provide additional context and information on some tweets containing disputed or misleading information related to COVID-19" (Twitter, 2020c).

Later, on December 16, 2020, Twitter goes as far as to specify the type of rhetoric that infringes upon its COVID-19 misinformation policy. It targets tweets that "advance a claim of fact, expressed in definite terms" and later "tweets that are an assertion of fact (not an opinion), expressed definitely, and intended to influence others' behavior" (Twitter, 2020d). Misleading statements on "vaccines" consist in spreading "preventative measures that are not approved by health authorities, or that are approved by health authorities but not safe to administer from home"; "the sale or facilitation of medicines or drugs that require a prescription or physician consultation"; or information on "adverse impacts or effects of receiving vaccinations, where these claims have been widely debunked" (Twitter, 2020d). It targets conspiratorial language, labeling tweets "which suggest that COVID-19 vaccinations are part of a deliberate or intentional attempt to cause harm or control populations" (Twitter, 2020d). It reinforces consent to local authoritative guidelines by targeting tweets that dispute "local or national advisories or mandates pertaining to curfews, lockdowns, travel restrictions, quarantine protocols, inoculations …," and even targets tweets about "research findings (such as misrepresentations of or unsubstantiated conclusions about statistical data) used to advance a specific narrative that diminishes the significance of the disease." Once again, all of the above is first labeled, and then removed (Twitter, 2020d).

Finding 4: Twitter acts as a debunking system. In practice, this means labeling almost every tweet that mentions a COVID-19 treatment ingredient disputed by authoritative sources (see Figure 6.8). Though some are deleted, most are simply flagged and redirected to a centralized reference page on local COVID-19 guidelines and information. This also applies to claims disputed amongst authoritative sources, such as whether hydroxychloroquine is or is not a safe drug.

Covid-19 misleading information policy
https://help.twitter.com/en/rules-and-policies/medical-misinformation-policy
https://blog.twitter.com/en_us/topics/company/2020/covid-19.html

January 29, 2020

COVID-19 #KnowTheFacts search prompt launched

⌁ #KNOWTHEFACTS LABEL

February 4, 2020

Media shared in a deceptive manner

Deliberate intent to deceive people about the nature or origin of the content;

⌁ LABEL
‼ WARNING
⬇ DEMOTION
✕ REMOVAL

Synthetic or manipulated media

Content that has been substantially edited in a manner that fundamentally alters its composition, sequence, timing, or framing;

Any visual or auditory information that has been added or removed;

Fabricated or simulated media depicting a real person;

⌁ LABEL
‼ WARNING
⬇ DEMOTION
✕ REMOVAL

March 4, 2020

Zero tolerance approach to platform manipulation

March 16, 2020

Broadened definition of "harm"

Content that goes directly against guidance from authoritative sources of global and local public health information;

Denial of global or local health authority recommendations to decrease someone's likelihood of exposure to COVID-19;

Alleged cures for COVID-19 that are not immediately harmful but are known to be ineffective;

Harmful treatments or protection measures that are known to be ineffective;

Denial of established scientific facts about transmission during the incubation period or transmission guidance from global and local health authorities;

⌁ LABEL
✕ REMOVAL

April 11, 2020

Unverified claims that have the potential to incite people to action, could lead to the destruction or damage of critical infrastructures, or cause widespread panic or social unrest

⚡ SUSPENSION

May 11, 2020

New labels and warning images

Provide additional context and information on some Tweets containing disputed or misleading information related to COVID-19.

⌁ LABEL

July 14, 2020

Information that may increase the likelihood of exposure to the virus

⌁ LABEL
✕ REMOVAL

Information that may have adverse effects on the public health system's capacity to cope with the crisis

⌁ LABEL
✕ REMOVAL

Tweets that are an assertion of fact (not an option), expressed definitely, and intended to influence others' behavior

The origin, nature, and characteristics of the virus;

Preventative measures, treatments/cures, and other precautions;

The prevalence of viral spread, or the current state of the crisis;

Official health advisories, restrictions, regulations, and public-service announcements;

How vulnerable communities are affected by/responding to the pandemic;

Significantly altered, manipulated, doctored or fabricated contents;

Claims presented improperly or out of context;

Claims shared in a Tweet widely accepted by experts to be inaccurate or false;

⌁ LABEL
✕ REMOVAL

Dec 16, 2020

Type of rhetoric

Advance a claim of fact, expressed in definite terms;

Be demonstrably false or misleading, based on widely available, authoritative sources;

Be likely to impact public safety or cause serious harm;

⌁ LABEL
✕ REMOVAL

False of misleading affiliation

Fake accounts which misrepresent their affiliation, or share content that falsely represents its affiliation to a medical practitioner, public health official or agency, research institution, or that falsely suggests expertise on COVID-19 issues.

⌁ LABEL
✕ REMOVAL

Strong commentary, opinions, and/or satire

☑ ALLOWED

Counterspeech

Direct responses to misleading information which seek to undermine its impact by correcting the record, amplifying credible information, and educating the wider community about the prevalence and dynamics of misleading information.

☑ ALLOWED

Personal anecdotes or first-person accounts

☑ ALLOWED

Public debate about the advancement of COVID-19 science and research

☑ ALLOWED

False or misleading information about the nature of the virus

Transmission of the virus;

Susceptibility of the virus;

Symptoms commonly associated with the virus;

The pandemic of COVID-19 vaccines;

⌁ LABEL
✕ REMOVAL

False or misleading information about the efficacy and/or safety of preventative measures, treatments, or other precautions to mitigate or treat the disease

The safety or efficacy of treatments or preventative measures that are not approved by health authorities, or that are approved by health authorities but not safe to administer from home;

The sale or facilitation of medicines or drugs that require a prescription or physician consultation;

Adverse impacts or effects of receiving vaccinations, where these claims have been widely debunked;

Vaccines and vaccination programs which suggest that COVID-19 vaccinations are part of a deliberate or intentional attempt to cause harm or control populations;

Personal protective equipment (PPE) such as claims about the efficacy and safety of face masks to reduce viral spread;

Preventative measures such as hand-washing, proper hygiene or sanitation methods, or social distancing;

Local or national advisories or mandates pertaining to curfews, lockdowns, travel restrictions, quarantine protocols, innoculations, including exemptions from such advisories or mandates;

How vaccines are developed, tested, and approved by official health agencies as well as information about government recommendations;

The prevalence of the virus or the disease, such as information pertaining to test results, hospitalizations, or mortality rates;

The capacity of the public health system to cope with the crisis, for example false information about the availability of PPE, ventilators, or doctors, or about hospital capacity;

Research findings (such as misrepresentations of or unsubstantiated conclusions about statistical data) used to advance a specific narrative that diminishes the significance of the disease.

⌁ LABEL
✕ REMOVAL

Figure 6.7 Timeline of Twitter's "COVID-19 misleading information policy." Source in image. Visualization by Emillie de Keulenaar, with previous contributions by Guilherme Appolinário.

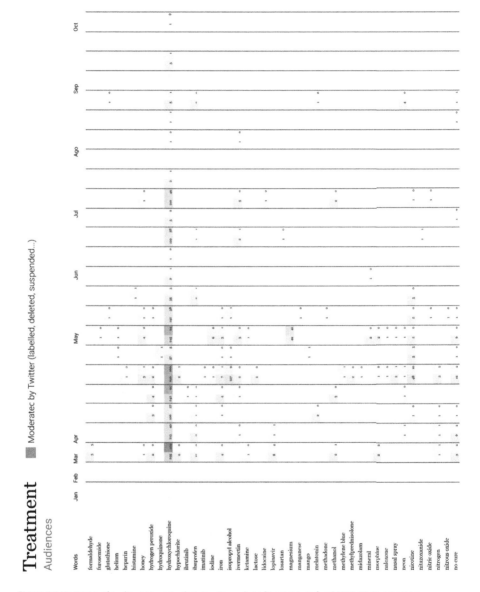

Figure 6.8 Heatmap of audience tweets that mention a list of treatments for COVID-19. In green are numbers of unmoderated tweets; in red, moderated tweets. Visualization by Carlo Gaetano.

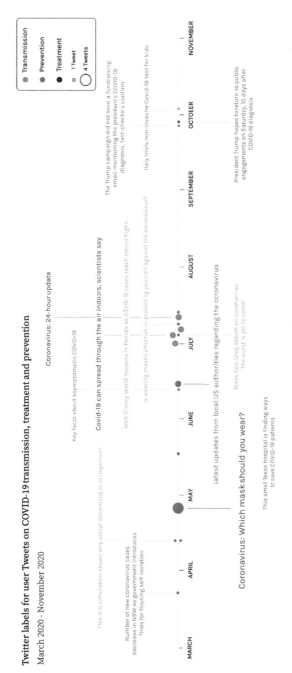

Figure 6.9 Bee swarm of Twitter labels for tweets mentioning COVID transmission, prevention and treatment. Visualization by Emillie de Keulenaar.

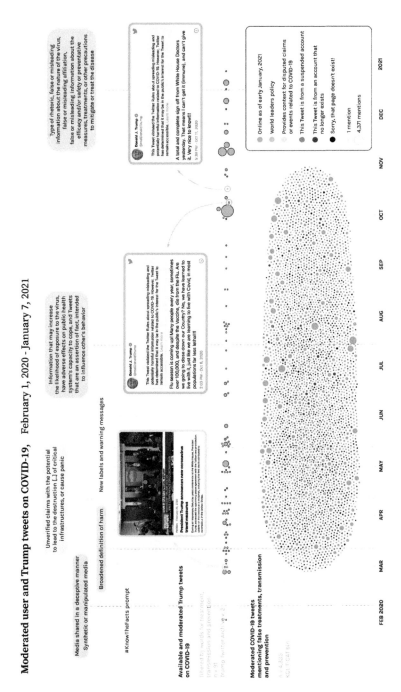

Figure 6.10 Bee swarm of moderated audience and Trump tweets mentioning words related to COVID-19 treatments, transmission and prevention. Every dot is one or many tweets posted in a given day. Visualization by Emillie de Keulenaar.

It also means supporting authoritative sources in their continuous debunking of user claims (Figure 6.9). Authoritative sources—the World Health Organization, in particular—repeatedly deny claims made on social media.

Finding 5: In the absence of consensus between authoritative sources, Twitter intervenes as an authority in its own right. At issue is that disagreements amongst authoritative sources create a crisis of authority on the platform. Twitter can no longer redirect users to one specific source. In the absence of consensus among authorities, Twitter begins to highlight the disputed nature of even authoritative claims (see Figure 6.10). This applies particularly to U.S. President Donald Trump's private account. While audience tweets are more severely moderated (suspended, deleted), Trump's tweets initially obtain the "#KnowTheFacts" prompt the platform introduced in January 29th (see Figure 6.7). Reuniting several other authoritative sources, this prompt is intended to display current consensus among a majority of authoritative sources, including "trusted news sources" (Twitter, 2020c). As Trump alleges that "sometimes over 100,000" people "die from the Flu" in October, Twitter flags it for violating "the Twitter Rules about spreading misleading and potentially harmful information related to COVID-19." The same happens to a later tweet claiming immunity from COVID-19.

Both of them do stay up, in accordance with Twitter's "World leaders" and "Public-interest exceptions" policies (Twitter, 2019), until Trump's account is permanently suspended for violating a separate policy designed to prevent "glorification of violence" (Twitter, 2021).

Methods

The methodology of this study is two-fold. Based on a collection of millions of tweets, we first parse, analyze and visualize diverging claims on COVID-19 transmission, prevention and treatments between U.S. authoritative sources and their respective audiences. We then look at how Twitter moderated disputed claims by first consulting content moderation policies designed for COVID-19 misinformation, and then obtaining moderation metadata from tweets containing disputed contents.

Definitions

The U.S. has at least two channels responsible for communicating authoritative information on COVID-19: its head of state and its health departments or disease prevention agencies (See Table 6.1 in Annex). Because Twitter prioritizes the World Health Organization as an authoritative source, we also captured data from that organization's international and American offices. We refer to heads of state and public health organizations as "authoritative sources," and the WHO, health ministries, departments and disease prevention agencies as "public health organizations." By "audiences," we refer to users who have at some point interacted with any one of the authoritative sources on our list, be it by replying, mentioning them or their website domains (e.g., whitehouse.org).

By "claims" about the coronavirus, we mean information that can be confirmed as true or refuted as false by governments and health organizations. We focused on how the virus is transmitted, available treatments, and preventive methods.

Data collection

For data collection on Twitter, we used Borra and Rieder's Twitter Capture and Analysis Toolkit, which collects tweets based on a chosen set of queries (Borra and Rieder, 2014). These queries were "covid," "coronavirus" and "WuhanVirus" and captured a total of 61,498,037 tweets from January 26 to October 2020. Of those, we extracted 910 tweets from government and public health organizations and 496,166 replies and mentions of official domains. In addition to tweets, we also collected claims on COVID-19 transmission, prevention and treatment by the CDC, NIV and Donald Trump's administration on their official websites (cdc.gov, nih.org, whitehouse.gov). Information on Twitter's COVID-19 misinformation moderation policies came primarily from two sources: Twitter's blog on COVID-19 and its "COVID-19 Misleading Information Policy." From these, we were able to note what information they target and how they moderate it (suspension, labeling, deletion, etc.). We then obtained moderation metadata from tweets that mentioned disputed claims by using Selenium, the web scraping application.

Parsing claims inductively and deductively

To map divergences in government, public health organization and "audience" statements about COVID-19, we sought to capture and compare the widest possible range of claims about the transmission, prevention and treatment of the virus. We captured both true and false statements with both deductive and inductive approaches. The deductive approach consisted in consulting secondary sources on COVID-19 misinformation, such as Wikipedia (Table 6.1 in Annex). The inductive approach consisted in manual and semi-automatic capture of claims. This involved reading tweets and (authoritative or official) websites that contained the words "transmission," "prevention" or "protection" and "treatment" or "cure." We also generated word embeddings and bigrams for the queries "transmission," "prevention" or "protection" and "treatments" or "cure" to find other relevant terms. We obtained a total of 48 words for transmission, 83 for treatments (2,739 with medications extracted from drugbank.ca) and 79 for prevention (Table 6.2 in Annex).

Coding and filtering claims in tweets and official websites

We split and detected sentences per topic as follows:
1. Transmission: sentences mentioning "infect," "transmi," "transfer," "contag," "contamin," "catch," or "spread";
2. Prevention: sentences mentioning "prevent," "protect"; and
3. Treatment: sentences mentioning "treatment," "cure" and "vaccine."

For more complex queries such as whether the virus is airborne or whether one should wear masks, we manually coded every sentence that mentioned both "wear" and "mask" for the masks query and "airborne" and either "aerosol" or "droplet" for the "airborne" query. For sentences mentioning COVID-19 transmission, coding meant annotating claims that (1) the virus is or is not airborne, and more specifically that (2) it spread through droplets or aerosols. For those mentioning protection, it implied annotating claims that (1) the general public should and should not wear masks ("should wear," "should not wear," respectively) and (2) who should be wearing masks (caregivers, essential workers, travelers...). In many cases, claims were far beyond simple binaries, and if frequent, required a category of their own.

We then manually coded the information retrieved from government and health authorities' official webpages on whether they provided any instructions or claims about transmission, treatments and use of masks that were inconsistent among them. We used the Internet Archive to track changes in the information in these webpages from January 2020 to July 2020. For each page with any information about transmission, treatments or use of masks, we coded them by date of change accordingly. For transmission, we coded if they agree if the transmission is possible through airborne or aerosol, contact, droplet, fluid or animals. For treatments, we coded if they recommend chloroquine, hydroxychloroquine or ibuprofen. For masks, we coded if they recommend wearing a mask or face-covering in public, wear a mask if one has symptoms, or wear a mask if around sick people.

Coding and filtering claims in social media textual data: Limitations

Twitter audience responses contain a large number of retweets of claims made by authoritative sources. Because of this, we also included tweets that do not necessarily reply or mention authoritative sources but are geolocated in the U.S. Geolocation is included in TCAT's tweet metadata.

Moderation data

Moderation status and labels for the 4.2 million relevant tweets (i.e., by authoritative sources or audiences, and containing any of our keywords) were gathered using web scraping (Selenium).

References

Achenbach, J. and Johnson, C. Y. (2020, April 30). Studies leave question of "airborne" coronavirus transmission unanswered. *Washington Post*. https://www.washingtonpost.com/health/2020/04/29/studies-leave-question-airborne-coronavirus-transmission-unanswered/.

Bordia, P. and Difonzo, N. (2004). Problem solving in social interactions on the internet: Rumor as social cognition. *Social Psychology Quarterly*, 67(1), pp. 33–49. https://doi.org/10.1177/019027250406700105.

Borra, E. and Rieder, B. (2014). Programmed method: Developing a toolset for capturing and analyzing tweets. *Aslib Journal of Information Management*, 66(3), pp. 262–278. https://doi.org/10.1108/AJIM-09-2013-0094.

Bostrom, A., Joslyn, S., Pavia, R., Walker, A. H., Starbird, K., and Leschine, T. M. (2015). Methods for communicating the complexity and uncertainty of oil spill response actions and tradeoffs. *Human and Ecological Risk Assessment: An International Journal*, 21(3), pp. 631–645. https://doi.org/10.1080/10807039.2014.947867.

Caplow, T. (1946). Rumors in war departmental contributions: Teaching and research in the social sciences. *Social Forces*, 25(3), pp. 298–302. https://heinonline.org/HOL/P?h=hein.journals/josf25andi=314.

Centers for Disease Control and Prevention. (2020, April 1). Healthcare professionals: Frequently asked questions and answers. Centers for Disease Control and Prevention. https://web.archive.org/web/20200401051025/https://www.cdc.gov/coronavirus/2019-ncov/hcp/faq.html.

Chu, J. and McDonald, J. (2020, January 29). Helping the world find credible information about novel #coronavirus. Twitter Blog. https://blog.twitter.com/en_us/topics/company/2020/authoritative-information-about-novel-coronavirus.

Dailey, D. and Starbird, K. (2015). "It's raining dispersants": Collective sensemaking of complex information in crisis contexts. In *Proceedings of the 18th ACM Conference Companion on Computer Supported Cooperative Work and Social Computing*, pp. 155–158. https://doi.org/10.1145/2685553.2698995.

De Keulenaar, E., Burton, A.G., and Kisjes, I. (2021). Deplatforming, demotion and folk theories of Big Tech persecution. *Fronteiras – Estudos Midiáticos*, 23(2), pp. 118–139. https://doi.org/10.4013/fem.2021.232.09.

De Zeeuw, D., Hagen, S., Peeters, S., and Jokubauskaite, E. (2020). Tracing normiefication: A cross-platform analysis of the QAnon conspiracy theory. *First Monday*, 25(11). https://doi.org/10.5210/fm.v25i11.10643.

Dwoskin, E. (2020, November 12). Trump's attacks on election outcome prolong tech's emergency measures. *Washington Post*. https://www.washingtonpost.com/technology/2020/11/12/facebook-ad-ban-lame-duck/.

Economist (2019, June 8). Google rewards reputable reporting, not left-wing politics. *The Economist*. https://www.economist.com/graphic-detail/2019/06/08/google-rewards-reputable-reporting-not-left-wing-politics.

Golebiewski, M. and boyd, d. (2019). Data voids: Where missing data can easily be exploited. Data & Society Research Institute. https://datasociety.net/wp-content/uploads/2019/11/Data-Voids-2.0-Final.pdf.

Iati, M., Kornfield, M., O'Grady, S., and Mellen, R. (2020, May 4). Trump says it's safe to reopen states, while Birx finds protesters with no masks or distancing "devastatingly worrisome." *Washington Post*. https://www.washingtonpost.com/world/2020/05/03/coronavirus-latest-news/.

Internet Archive. (2021). Internet archive: Digital library of free & borrowable books, movies, music & Wayback Machine [Web-based]. Internet Archive. https://archive.org/.

Kou, Y., Gui, X., Chen, Y., and Pine, K. (2017). Conspiracy talk on social media: Collective sensemaking during a public health crisis. In *Proceedings of the ACM on Human-Computer Interaction*, 1(CSCW), article no. 61. https://doi.org/10.1145/3134696.

Krafft, P., Zhou, K., Edwards, I., Starbird, K., and Spiro, E.S. (2017). Centralized, parallel, and distributed information processing during collective sensemaking. In *Proceedings of the 2017 CHI Conference on Human Factors in Computing Systems*, pp. 2976–2987. https://doi.org/10.1145/3025453.3026012.

Lee, L. and Oppong, F. (2020, September 1). Adding more context to trends. Twitter Blog. https://blog.twitter.com/en_us/topics/product/2020/adding-more-context-to-trends.

Lewis, D. (2020). Is the coronavirus airborne? Experts can't agree. *Nature*, 580(7802), p. 175. https://doi.org/10.1038/d41586-020-00974-w.

Lyons, K. (2020, October 11). Twitter flags, limits sharing on Trump tweet about being "immune" to coronavirus. *The Verge*. https://www.theverge.com/2020/10/11/21511682/twitter-disables-sharing-trump-tweet-coronavirus-misinformation.

Mandavilli, A. (2020, July 4). 239 experts with one big claim: The coronavirus is airborne. *New York Times.* https://www.nytimes.com/2020/07/04/health/239-experts-with-one-big-claim-the-coronavirus-is-airborne.html.

O'Leary, N. (2020, March 10). How Dutch false sense of security helped coronavirus spread. *Irish Times.* https://www.irishtimes.com/news/world/europe/how-dutch-false-sense-of-security-helped-coronavirus-spread-1.4199027.

Roth, Y. and Pickels, N. (2020, May 11). Updating our approach to misleading information. Twitter Blog. https://blog.twitter.com/en_us/topics/product/2020/updating-our-approach-to-misleading-information.

Scheufele, D. A. and Krause, N. M. (2019). Science audiences, misinformation, and fake news. *Proceedings of the National Academy of Sciences*, 116(16), pp. 7662–7669. https://doi.org/10.1073/pnas.1805871115.

Schmitt, C. (2005). *Political theology: Four chapters on the concept of sovereignty.* University of Chicago Press.

Shibutani, T. (1966). *Improvised news: A sociological study of rumor.* Ardent Media.

Skopeliti, C., and John, B. (2020, March 19). Coronavirus: How are the social media platforms responding to the "infodemic"? First Draft. https://firstdraftnews.org:443/latest/how-social-media-platforms-are-responding-to-the-coronavirus-infodemic/.

Starbird, K. (2012). Crowdwork, crisis and convergence: How the connected crowd organizes information during mass disruption events [PhD].

Starbird, K. (2020, April 27). How to cope with an infodemic. Brookings. https://www.brookings.edu/techstream/how-to-cope-with-an-infodemic/.

Starbird, K., Spiro, E., Edwards, I., Zhou, K., Maddock, J., and Narasimhan, S. (2016). Could this be true? I think so! Expressed uncertainty in online rumoring. In *Proceedings of the 2016 CHI Conference on Human Factors in Computing Systems*, pp. 360–371. https://doi.org/10.1145/2858036.2858551.

Twitter (2019, October 15). World leaders on Twitter: Principles & approach. Twitter Blog. https://blog.twitter.com/en_us/topics/company/2019/worldleaders2019.

Twitter (2020a, February 7). Synthetic and manipulated media policy. Twitter. https://web.archive.org/web/20200207000218/https://help.twitter.com/en/rules-and-policies/manipulated-media.

Twitter (2020b, April). Coronavirus: Staying safe and informed on Twitter. Twitter Blog. https://blog.twitter.com/en_us/topics/company/2020/covid-19.

Twitter (2020c, May 11). Coronavirus: Staying safe and informed on Twitter. Twitter Blog. https://blog.twitter.com/en_us/topics/company/2020/covid-19.

Twitter (2020d, December 16). COVID-19 misleading information policy. Twitter. https://web.archive.org/web/20201216200114/https://help.twitter.com/en/rules-and-policies/medical-misinformation-policy.

Twitter (2021, January 8). Permanent suspension of @realDonaldTrump. Twitter Blog. https://blog.twitter.com/en_us/topics/company/2020/suspension.

Yong, E. (2020, April 29). Why the coronavirus is so confusing. *The Atlantic.* https://www.theatlantic.com/health/archive/2020/04/pandemic-confusing-uncertainty/610819/.

YouTube (2019, January 25). Continuing our work to improve recommendations on YouTube. YouTube Blog. https://blog.youtube/news-and-events/continuing-our-work-to-improve/.

YouTube (2020). COVID-19 medical misinformation policy—YouTube Help. https://support.google.com/youtube/answer/9891785?hl=en.

About the authors

Emillie de Keulenaar is a PhD candidate at the University of Groningen, and a researcher at the University of Amsterdam's Open Intelligence Lab and the United Nations Department of Political and Peacebuilding Affairs. Her interests lie in the history and impact of speech moderation from a cross-platform perspective as well as the effects of deep disagreements in the production of online misinformation.

Ivan Kisjes is a scientific programmer at the CREATE lab at the University of Amsterdam, involved in computational research in various humanities domains.

Rory Smith is the Research Manager at First Draft, where he leads on the organization's digital investigations into mis- and disinformation around the world. Before joining First Draft, Rory worked for CNN, Vox and Vice, covering various topics from immigration and food policy to politics and organized crime.

Carina Albrecht is a doctoral candidate and SSHRC Canada Graduate Scholar in the School of Communication at Simon Fraser University, and SFU-Mellon Critical Data Studies fellow at the Digital Democracies Institute. Her dissertation project explores alternative network science models for recommendation systems and search engines.

Eleonora Cappuccio is a PhD student in the Italian National Doctoral Program in Artificial Intelligence. She completed her master's degree in Communication Design at the Polytechnic University of Milan, developing her thesis at the DensityDesign research lab.

Annex

Table 6.1 Sources of false and true COVID-19 information.

	Transmission (only vehicles)	Treatment (ingredients and medication)	Prevention (protective measures, gear and preventive medicine)
Secondary sources	Wikipedia (2020) "Transmission (medicine)," Wikipedia. https://en.wikipedia.org/w/index.php?title=Transmission_(medicine)&oldid=963983254. Wikipedia (2020) "Misinformation related to the COVID-19 pandemic," Wikipedia. https://en.wikipedia.org/w/index.php?title=Misinformation_related_to_the_COVID-19_pandemic&oldid=966340289. Wikipedia (2020) "Coronavirus disease 2019," Wikipedia. https://en.wikipedia.org/w/index.php?title=Coronavirus_disease_2019&oldid=966470660.	Wikipedia (2020a) "Coronavirus disease 2019," Wikipedia. https://en.wikipedia.org/w/index.php?title=Coronavirus_disease_2019&oldid=966470660. Wikipedia (2020b) "List of unproven methods against COVID-19," Wikipedia. https://en.wikipedia.org/w/index.php?title=List_of_unproven_methods_against_COVID-19&oldid=966515765.	Wikipedia (2020a) "Coronavirus disease 2019," Wikipedia. https://en.wikipedia.org/w/index.php?title=Coronavirus_disease_2019&oldid=966470660. Wikipedia (2020b) "List of unproven methods against COVID-19," Wikipedia. https://en.wikipedia.org/w/index.php?title=List_of_unproven_methods_against_COVID-19&oldid=966515765.
Primary sources	CDC (2020) Coronavirus Disease 2019 (COVID-19)—Transmission, Centers for Disease Control and Prevention. https://www.cdc.gov/coronavirus/2019-ncov/prevent-getting-sick/how-covid-spreads.html. Gov.us (2020) How it spreads – COVID-19 Answers, gov.us. https://faq.coronavirus.gov/spread/.	CDC (2020a) Coronavirus Disease 2019 (COVID-19)—Prevention & Treatment, Centers for Disease Control and Prevention. https://www.cdc.gov/coronavirus/2019-ncov/prevent-getting-sick/prevention.html. CDC (2020b) Coronavirus Disease 2019 (COVID-19)—Therapeutic Options, Centers for Disease Control and Prevention. https://www.cdc.gov/coronavirus/2019-ncov/hcp/therapeutic-options.html.	CDC (2020) Coronavirus Disease 2019 (COVID-19)—Prevention & Treatment, Centers for Disease Control and Prevention. https://www.cdc.gov/coronavirus/2019-ncov/prevent-getting-sick/prevention.html. Gov.uk (2020) Coronavirus (COVID-19): guidance, GOV.UK. https://www.gov.uk/government/collections/coronavirus-covid-19-list-of-guidance.

	Transmission (only vehicles)	Treatment (ingredients and medication)	Prevention (protective measures, gear and preventive medicine)
	NHS (2020) Coronavirus—Virus transmission, NHS. https://www.england.nhs.uk/coronavirus/primary-care/about-covid-19/virus-transmission/.	DrugBank (2020) Drugs—DrugBank, DrugBank. https://www.drugbank.ca/drugs.	Gov.us (2020) How it spreads—COVID-19 Answers, gov.us. https://faq.coronavirus.gov/spread/.
	Gov.uk (2020) Coronavirus (COVID-19): guidance, GOV.UK. https://www.gov.uk/government/collections/coronavirus-covid-19-list-of-guidance.	NHS (2020) Coronavirus—Virus transmission, NHS. https://www.england.nhs.uk/coronavirus/primary-care/about-covid-19/virus-transmission/.	
	World Health Organization (2020) Advice for the public, World Health Organization. https://www.who.int/emergencies/diseases/novel-coronavirus-2019/advice-for-public.	Nih.gov (2020) What's new	Coronavirus Disease COVID-19, COVID-19 Treatment Guidelines. https://www.covid19treatmentguidelines.nih.gov/whats-new/.	
		World Health Organization (2020) Advice for the public, WHO. https://www.who.int/emergencies/diseases/novel-coronavirus-2019/advice-for-public.	
Additional sources	Word embeddings and bigrams for "transmission" and "contagion"	Word embeddings and bigrams for "cure" and "treatment"	Word embeddings and bigrams for "protection" and "prevention"

Table 6.2   Dictionaries of types of COVID transmission, treatment and prevention.

Transmission (only vehicles)	Treatment (ingredients and medication)	Prevention (protective measures, gear and preventive medicine)
5g	ablution	1.5 m
airborne	alcohol	2 m
asymptomatic people	andrographis paniculata	6 ft
bath tissue	antihistamine	ablution
blood transfusion	aspirin	alcohol
breast milk	azithromycin	antibacterial soap
close contact	bitter gourd	avoid close contact
community spread	black pepper	avoid touching your eyes
coughing	cannabis	avoid touching your eyes, nose and mouth
direct contact	CBD oil	avoid touching your mouth
direct physical contact	chlorine dioxide	avoid touching your nose
droplet nuclei	chloroform	boiled ginger
droplets	chloroquine	carbolic soap
electromagnetic	cocaine	chlorine
fecal-oral routes	colloidal silver	clean and disinfect
fecal transmission	cow dung	cloth
fecal-oral transmission	cow urine	disinfect regularly
fomites	dietary supplement	disinfection
indirect contact	durian	dispose of tissues
indirect physical contact	essential oil	dryer
intimate contact	ethanol	environmental cleaning
kissing	fasting	facemask
microchip	fennel tea	fasting
mosquito	goose fat	gargling
oral transmission	honey	garlic
petrol	hot liquids	garlic, ginger and onion
physical contact	hot whiskey	ginger
radiation	hydroxychloroquine sulphate	good hygiene
respiratory droplets	influenza complex	high temperature
saliva	lemon	isolate
sneezing	mango	lemon
sputum	methanol	N95
tick	mineral	mask
touch	acetic acid	face mask
wet particles	amphetamine, cocaine and nicotine	2 arms' length
wireless	azithromycin	6 feet
	biocharger	arsenicum album
	boiled ginger	avoid being exposed

Transmission (only vehicles)	Treatment (ingredients and medication)	Prevention (protective measures, gear and preventive medicine)
	dexamethasone	cover your mouth
	Indian cow	cover your nose
	lemon grass	hand hygiene
	mechanical ventilatory support	hot liquids
	mint tea	limits for public gatherings
	miracle mineral supplement	physical distance
	mustard patch	physical distancing
	nasal spray	plain soap
	neem leave	red soap
	no cure	respiratory etiquette
	no drug	rum, bleach and fabric softener
	no treatment	salt water
	no vaccine	sauna
	plant sap	self-isolation
	remdesivir	sneeze in the crook of your elbow
	saline	soap and water
	salt water	social distance
	shuanghuanglian	surgical masks
	six deep breaths	throw used tissues
	snake oil	turmeric
	supplemental oxygen	UV-C
	supportive care	UVC
	Tamiflu	Virus Shut Out Protection
	tinospora crispa	warm water
	toothpaste	warm weather
	turmeric	wash hand
	vinegar	wash your hands
	vitamin C	water and soap
	vitamin D	cloth face cover
	wudu	hand sanitizer
	zitroneer	wet wipes
	all drugs mentioned in drugbank.ca	white handkerchief
		white tissue

7 The earnest platform

U.S. presidential candidates, COVID-19, and social issues on Instagram

Sabine Niederer and Gabriele Colombo

Abstract

Increasingly, Instagram is discussed as a site for misinformation, inauthentic activities, and polarization, particularly in recent studies about elections, the COVID-19 pandemic and vaccines. In this study, we have found a different platform. By looking at the content that receives the most interactions over two time periods (in 2020) related to three U.S. presidential candidates and the issues of COVID-19, healthcare, 5G and gun control, we characterize Instagram as a site of earnest (as opposed to ambivalent) political campaigning and moral support, with a relative absence of polarizing content (particularly from influencers) and little to no misinformation and artificial amplification practices. Most importantly, while misinformation and polarization might be spreading on the platform, they do not receive much user interaction.

Keywords: social media, Instagram, U.S. elections, COVID-19, disinformation, digital methods

Research questions

To what extent is ambivalent and divisive (or earnest and non-divisive) content present in the most interacted-with posts concerning political candidates and social issues on Instagram in the run-up to the 2020 U.S. presidential elections? Do the candidates control their own "name space," i.e., the (top) posts about them? Are there signs of artificial amplification (so-called fake or suspicious followers) among the candidates and their parties?

Rogers. R. (ed.), *The Propagation of Misinformation in Social Media: A Cross-platform Analysis.*
Amsterdam: Amsterdam University Press 2023
DOI: 10.5117/9789463720762_CH07

How do influencers and celebrities on "political Instagram" contribute to the information climate?

Essay summary

During the "fake news crisis" of 2016, false news sources and front groups spread divisive and ambivalent information and misinformation across social media—notably on Facebook but also on Twitter and Instagram—in the period leading up to the U.S. presidential election (Silverman, 2016; DiResta et al., 2018; Howard et al., 2018). In 2020, concerns about such misinformation and divisiveness heightened in the lead-up to the U.S. elections. These concerns hit the global stage in full force with the rise of the COVID-19 pandemic, in which misinformation about the disease, the necessity of the precautions taken to curb its spread, and the safety of its vaccinations could pose immediate public health threats.

Recent studies and reporting have demonstrated that Instagram is susceptible to problematic information related to elections. Prior to the 2016 U.S. elections, Instagram was a fertile ground for disseminating misinformation and divisive content (Jack, 2017; DiResta et al., 2018). Furthermore, an analysis of Netherlands-based news media accounts on Instagram surfaced a special affinity (in terms of shared followers) between mainstream news sources and so-called junk news providers (Colombo and De Gaetano, 2020). Additionally, recent studies have found that conspiracy theories and anti-vaccine content spread under the guise of lifestyle content (Bond, 2021; Tiffany, 2021; Maragkou, 2020; McNeal and Broderick, 2020). Such "pastel QAnon" accounts—conspiracy theories spread in sugar-coated messages by "mummy bloggers, wellness coaches and lifestyle influencers" (Gillespie, 2020)—are yet another addition to the "cacophony of voices and narratives" which "have coalesced to create an environment of extreme uncertainty" (Smith et al., 2020, p. 2).

A report by the Center for Countering Hate describes how users who follow anti-vax accounts are presented with other problematic information by the platform's recommendation systems. These include "recommendations for antisemitic content, QAnon conspiracy theories, and COVID misinformation" (Center for Countering Hate, 2021, p. 8). The study points out how the U.S. elections and the pandemic have fueled the disinformation problem (Bond, 2021). Not only has there been an increase in disinformation because of the divisive U.S. elections and the COVID-19 pandemic, the platform's recommendation systems further grow the problem by connecting health information to a diverse range of conspiracy theories.

Instagram has been studied for its role in spreading divisive and polarizing content and the amplification of hate speech or harmful content (Bradshaw and Howard, 2018). When other mainstream platforms successfully "deplatformed" accounts accused of sharing hateful messages and polarizing content, for a while, Instagram functioned as a refuge, dubbed as "internet's new home for hate" (Lorenz, 2019) or "alt-right's new favorite haven" (Sommer, 2018). With deplatforming recently on the rise, and extreme user accounts forced to move to "an alternative social media ecosystem" (Rogers, 2020b), this opens up the question of whether the characterization of Instagram as a safe place still holds and whether the platform has succeeded in cleaning up divisive and polarizing content, at least in high-engagement spaces.

Instagram is also the platform most known (and studied) for inauthentic behaviors, such as purchased followers or artificially inflated like and comments counts, obtained through "click farms and follower factories" (Lindquist, 2019), or by participating in "comment pods," where users convene to like and comment each other's posts to inflate their own engagement metrics (Ellis, 2019). Detecting and limiting such inauthentic activities is an increasing need of the marketing industry, as one can note from the deluge of audit tools to "examine the health" (Hypeauditor, 2021) of one account's follower base through scrutinizing various features such as following-follower ratios or number of posts. The platform itself periodically deploys new measures with the aim of "keeping Instagram authentic" (Systrom, 2014), deactivating "spammy accounts" (Systrom, 2014), deleting those using "third-party apps to boost their popularity" (Instagram, 2018), or, more recently, asking suspicious profiles to verify their identity (Instagram, 2020).

In this study, we focus on multiple topics, exploring the quality of information and the users active in those spaces as well as the authenticity of their follower bases. U.S. election-related posts are studied through the prism of the presidential candidates, Trump, Biden, and Sanders. We then identified much-discussed topics in these candidates' spaces and selected gun control, healthcare, COVID-19 and 5G as particularly salient. Where some studies choose to filter out verified Instagram accounts to capture "organic social media conversations as opposed to media reports" (Smith et al., 2020, p. 8), or look at the "twilight zone" (Shane, 2020) beyond highly engaged-with posts, for this study we focus on the most engaging content (in terms of user interactions) regardless of the source. Therefore, we do not filter out any user accounts, which allows us to include in the analysis celebrities and influencers, whose role in spreading misinformation and divisive content has been an object of scrutiny in multiple cases due to their high level of interactions and follower bases "predisposed to believe them and trust their messages" (Ahmadi and Chan, 2020).

This study considers the quality of information on Instagram about the U.S. presidential candidates of 2020, the COVID-19 pandemic, and a selection of social issues (healthcare, 5G, gun control). These topics are explored in the spring and fall of 2020, where the study zooms in on posts per period that receive the most user interactions. For the top 50 posts, the study combines content analysis with user activity analysis and includes a follower analysis to test for artificial amplification, as discussed in the methods section.

We developed a coding scheme for the content analysis that builds on Benkler et al. (2018) and distinguishes between divisive content (that might fuel polarization, conspiracy, or conflict) and non-divisive content. Following Phillips and Milner (2017), we term as ambivalent content (contrasted here with earnest content) posts that are not inflammatory but may still generate a lighter form of division by possibly excluding those who do not have the cultural references to decode it, laugh about it, and involuntary become "laughed at" (Phillips and Millner, 2017).

In applying these notions to the most interacted-with content concerning political candidates and social issues in 2020, we found, counter-intuitively, that most is earnest as well as non-divisive. In fact, throughout 2020, the political and issue spaces become even more earnest. There is also little to no misinformation encountered. In spring of 2020, influencers, including celebrities, mostly share responsible posts about the pandemic, while later in the year, they mainly encourage people to vote. Regarding COVID-19, there is an evolution from health warnings and supportive messages to posts about mental health during a pandemic and posts demonstrating that personal and professional *life goes on* despite COVID-19. Overall, our study finds a healthier platform than one might expect from one often associated with misinformation. While misinformation might be spreading on the platform, it does not receive much user interaction.

Implications

Increasingly, Instagram is discussed as a site for misinformation, inauthentic activities, and polarization, particularly in recent studies about elections, the COVID-19 pandemic and vaccines. Conspiracy and anti-vax content even have appeared as gradient pastel images under the guise of wellness and lifestyle posts. In this study, we have found a different platform. By looking at the content that receives the most interaction, we characterize Instagram as a site of earnest political campaigning and moral support, with a relative absence of polarizing content and little to no misinformation.

First, we analyze posts that receive the most user interactions over two time periods (the spring and fall of 2020) related to three U.S. presidential candidates and the issues of COVID-19, healthcare, 5G and gun control. To characterize these spaces, we adopt a two-fold coding scheme: Following Benkler et al. (2018), we distinguish between "divisive" and "non-divisive" posts, and from Phillips and Milner (2017), we identify "ambivalent content" (contrasted here with "earnest content"). These are posts that often through multiple layers of meanings and irony might subtly fuel division, excluding those who do not have the cultural references to decode them.

Second, in the same candidate and issues spaces, we perform a user activity analysis, examining the most active users and the number of interactions they generate with their posts. Third, in order to assess the authenticity of U.S. presidential candidates and parties' audiences, we analyze their follower bases, looking at suspicious behaviors (such as dubious geographical provenance) that might signal automation or artificial amplification practices. Fourth, we zoom in on the role of celebrities and influencers, characterizing through close reading the nature and content of their posts with an eye towards their role in spreading misinformation and divisive content.

Overall, our study finds a healthier space than one might expect from a platform often associated with polarization and misinformation. In fact, throughout 2020, the political and issue spaces become even more earnest. While misinformation and polarization might be spreading on the platform, they do not receive much user interaction.

Indeed, the findings show that while posts about political candidates may entail fierce campaigning, the overwhelming majority of the most engaged with content is earnest and non-divisive. The finding is significant given that research has shown how well divisive and false news and commentary often spread compared to more sincere content (Vosoughi et al., 2018; Klein and Robison, 2019).

For the posts concerning the three presidential candidates under study, each has an equal amount of divisive content (about 15%) in the top 50 posts. For that content, however, it was found that over half of it was posted by Trump or Trump, Jr. One implication is that the Trumps are a leading source of divisiveness and that they are rather alone in that role, at least in the top posts under study. It should be noted that Trump is also the main target of that content type. Of the remaining divisive content, most posts are about Trump or his administration. Engagement is an impact metric rather than a measure of sentiment. In other words, non-divisive, earnest posts may trigger positive but also negative comments, as we know from research into trolling and antagonistic behavior online (Phillips, 2015). Negativity in the comment space still leads to a high interaction score, so the findings do not imply the absence of toxicity.

The namespace analysis shows an uneven distribution of attention to the three candidates. Trump proved to be successful in dominating his own namespace, while Biden's space is occupied by a variety of users (mainly endorsing him). Sanders is the most successful of the three candidates in populating the others' namespaces. After losing the race to the presidential nomination in the fall, he is left alone in his space, and his language becomes more divisive.

In a further examination of the followers of the political candidates and parties, we find signs of light artificial amplification only for the accounts of the Republican Party and Donald Trump. The finding implies that the majority of the user interaction is not achieved through the purchasing of followers or likes, as was found in previous research, suggesting an apparent slowing of that practice (DiResta et al., 2018; Feldman, 2017).

Lastly, it is worthwhile to zoom in on the outsized role of particular users, apart from the Trumps and the National Rifle Association. On a platform known for its influencers, we can distinguish between at least two types of "issue celebrities" here. The one assumes a more traditional role of celebrity fundraising and awareness-raising, which we find mainly in healthcare posts by those who support front-line workers and hospitals during the pandemic (sometimes with financial donations). For the topic of COVID-19, we also see other, more commercially entangled celebrity engagement, where they sell their products and promise to donate a percentage of the profits to a COVID-related cause.

The study contributes to scholarly work that examines how visual practices on Instagram "are not just social media artifacts, isolated and individual, but are surrounded by debates and discussions that take on political, legal, economic, technological, and sociocultural dimensions" (Highfield and Leaver, 2016, p. 49). By selecting the political content with most interactions, we approach engagement on the platform in a more comprehensive way than content posted by influencers only. Indeed, the points of departure are the political debates and discussions. They take center stage rather than emerge as a byproduct of celebrity and influencer culture. In further assessing the content of top posts as earnest or ambivalent and divisive or non-divisive (Hedrick et al., 2018), it contributes to the discussions on online (mis)information, offering an analytical framework that is sensitive to critiques of thin ontologies as true or false content (Lazer et al., 2018; Marres, 2018). The work thereby has methodological implications for those categorizing contemporary social media content.

Findings

Finding 1: The top posts concerning political candidates and social issues on Instagram contain largely earnest and non-divisive content. Social media platforms such as Instagram have been described as sites of misinformation and divisiveness, particularly around elections. In this study, however, the political and issue coverage that has received the most user interactions on Instagram from January to mid-April 2020 and from September 2020 to January 2021 is primarily earnest and non-divisive, with scant ambivalent content.

Concerning the political candidates, in spring approximately 85% of the posts are non-divisive, and the vast majority is earnest. The amount of divisiveness in each of the different candidate's namespaces is more or less the same, but nearly half of such content is posted by Donald Trump or Donald Trump, Jr., and most of the remaining divisive posts are about Trump. In the fall, despite the U.S candidates' spaces remaining generally earnest and non-divisive, there are variations compared to the situation in spring, depending on the candidate. Biden's namespace has become much less divisive; both compared to that in spring and to the others. The namespaces of Trump and Sanders have instead become more divisive than in spring. Sanders' space is the one with more divisive posts in the top 50 among the three candidates. Examining the tone and wordings of his posts, we observe an increasingly more divisive language, with direct attacks to various opponents, including Joe Biden (see Figure 7.2), President Trump and Wall Street (e.g., "pathetic ... president" and "Wall Street crooks"). Posts about Trump also become slightly more divisive in spring. Trump's namespace has the most memes and jokes, some making fun of him and others of his opponents (sometimes both in one meme). Furthermore, many of the posts in the Trump space are labeled and fact-checked by Instagram (Figure 7.3), with banners, blurring covers and various notices.

The fact that Instagram overlays content moderation notices and disclaimers—not only on Trump's statements and videos but also on memes and fake screenshots posted by satirical accounts—generates an additional layer of messiness that contributes to the ambivalence of this space.

earnest non-divisive   November 3, 2020   ambivalent non-divisive   November 4, 2020

earnest divisive   October 6, 2020   ambivalent divisive   October 2, 2020

Figure 7.1 Example of Bernie Sanders' posts becoming more divisive in wording. Sources: https://www.instagram.com/p/B9X3SZOBxhX/; https://www.instagram.com/p/CH1Kx5IBsMN/.

March 6, 2020   November 21, 2020

Figure 7.2 Examples of fact-checking and content moderation notices found in Trump space in fall. Sources: https://www.instagram.com/p/CGrPpA-MKL1/; https://www.instagram.com/p/CHLS06FBufB/; https://www.instagram.com/p/CHNCRwwLI4f/.

October 23, 2020   November 4, 2020

Content moderation notice   Content moderation notice   November 5, 2020   Original post
in January 2021   in May 2021

Figure 7.3 Classification of the top 50 Instagram posts (receiving most interactions) in the political candidates' namespaces. Date ranges: January 1, 2020–April 20, 2020 and September 22, 2020–January 5, 2021. Data source: CrowdTangle.

Finding 2: While social issues are mostly discussed in earnest and non-divisive ways in the most engaging posts, some are more divisive than others. Moving from spring to fall, issue spaces remain largely earnest and non-divisive (except for gun control), but the content of the posts differs over time. Contrary to reports about online misinformation on social media, we find Instagram to be an earnest space of non-divisive content about the COVID-19 pandemic and healthcare, mostly posting in support of healthcare workers and encouraging users to stay safe. In the fall posts about the pandemic and health, in general, become even more earnest and non-divisive (with only one divisive post in the healthcare space), and the content of the posts changes. COVID-19 no longer dominates healthcare posts; instead, they address mental health and include well-wishing.

From the spring to the fall the COVID-19 space moves from posts supporting healthcare workers and encouraging users to stay safe to posts about activities that are taking place despite the pandemic. In the first period conspiracy is present in the 5G space, amidst mainly commercial content,

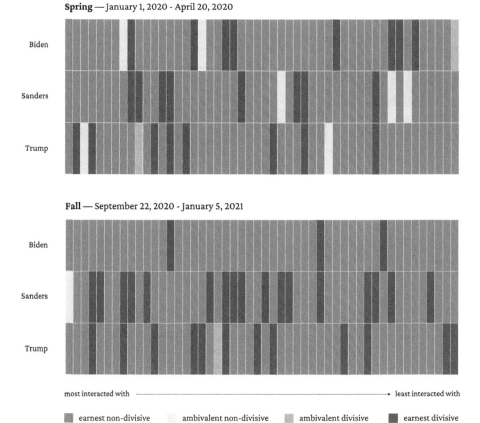

Figure 7.4 Classification of the top Instagram 50 posts (receiving most interactions) in the issues spaces. Date ranges: January 1, 2020–April 20, 2020 and September 22, 2020–January 5, 2021. Data source: CrowdTangle.

with the top post dismissive of the conspiracy theory that the coronavirus is spread through Chinese-made 5G towers. The 5G space becomes even more earnest in the second period under study, with a total absence of divisive or ambivalent content in the top posts, which are mainly commercial and with no signs of conspiracy-themed content in the top 50. We find one 5G conspiracy-related post well down in the results (#306). A post by Robert F. Kennedy, Jr., now removed from Instagram (Jett, 2021), references "deadly 5G radiation" together with "Big Pharma," "Big Data," "Bill Gates" and the "COVID vaccine project." Gun control is the most divisive of the issues we analyzed, and its top 50 posts are dominated by a single user, the National Rifle Association (with 30 out of the 50 posts), becoming even more divisive over time.

Finding 3: Trump performs well in his own namespace in the spring, while Biden is crowded out of his. In the fall, Sanders is left alone in his own namespace. For each candidate, we looked at their respective namespace, that is, the body of posts that @-mention the candidate. The rationale to do so is that when a presidential candidate holds control over his own namespace, this space is likely to be less divisive or ambivalent than when others mostly post about the candidate. For a candidate, controlling one's own namespace might mean being able to actively steer the discourse in their favor and reducing the level of divisiveness. In this next analytical step, we assess if and how the namespace is affected—in terms of its divisiveness and ambivalence—when the candidate occupies it.

Looking at the most active users in each candidate's namespace, Trump performs well in his namespace in both time frames analyzed. Trump's own Instagram content, likely run by his campaign, is not as negative as the insulting messages he is known for on Twitter (Quealy, 2017; Lee and Quealy, 2019). Many of his most engaging Instagram posts in the initial period are about his Super Tuesday wins in several states. However, of the earnestly divisive posts across all namespaces, many are by Trump or Trump, Jr. Compared to the spring, Trump still dominates his own namespace in the fall. His top posts in total receive fewer interactions than before, however, and there is a broader variety of users receiving interaction, including Snoop Dogg (with memes) as well as Kamala Harris, Michelle Obama, and Hillary Clinton (with critical posts).

In the spring Biden's account does not have a strong presence in the top posts about him. His namespace shows the most user diversity. Popular content posted about him by others varies from endorsements, the most popular of which was that by Barack Obama, to criticism and campaigning, for instance by Sanders in 1/5 of the top posts. Donald Trump, Jr. is also active in Biden's namespace, calling him out for his son's business in China and his views on gun control. In the next period, Biden's namespace remains crowded with diverse users, many of whom are non-political celebrities encouraging users to vote for him or congratulating him.

In the spring, Sanders is the most successful of the three candidates in populating the others' namespaces, posting much-interacted-with, campaign-style content about Trump and Biden. In second timeframe, Sanders is left alone in his own namespace, with the number of active users shrinking dramatically. Whereas in the first period, Sanders' namespace is populated by a variety of users, in the second, Sanders dominates his own namespace, with only six active users in the top 50, as expected after Biden became the democratic presidential candidate.

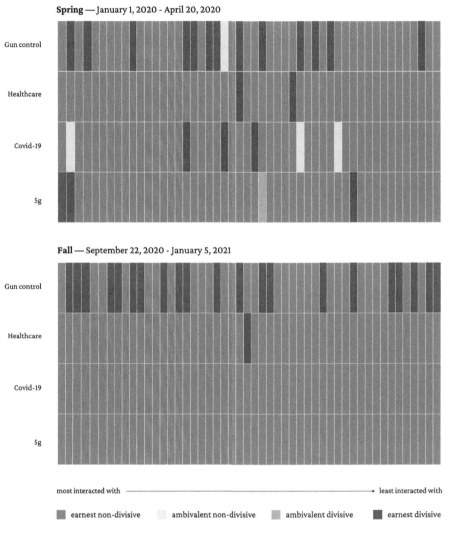

Figure 7.5 The most active Instagram users per political candidate's namespace. Date ranges: January 1, 2020–April 20, 2020 and September 22, 2020–January 5, 2021. Data source: CrowdTangle. The user accounts in our dataset not marked as "verified" public figures by Instagram are blurred in the visualization.

Finding 4: There are few signs of artificial amplification in the U.S. political space. In both time periods the accounts of U.S. presidential candidates and political parties on Instagram do not have suspicious follower bases, with almost 75% giving indications of being genuine followers, with some exceptions and slight differences between the periods. In the spring Donald Trump's account and, more prominently, the Republican party account, have

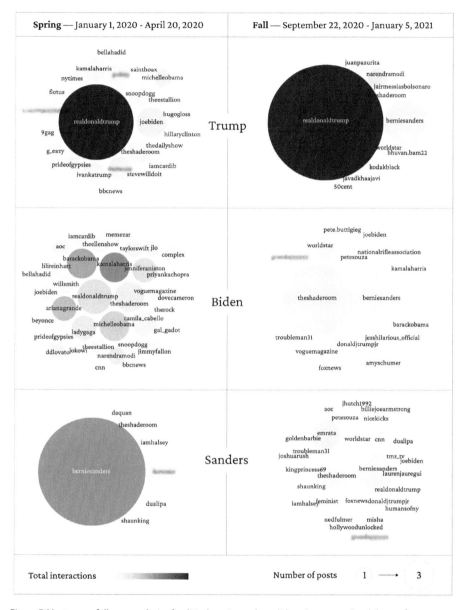

Figure 7.6 Instagram follower analysis of political parties and candidates' accounts. Breakdown of audience types into categories. Date ranges: January 1, 2020–April 20, 2020 and September 22, 2020–January 5, 2021. Data source: HypeAuditor.

slightly over 25% followers that the method considers suspicious (bots, or real accounts that use automatic tools for following or unfollowing other accounts). In the fall the composition of tool-suspected followers for the

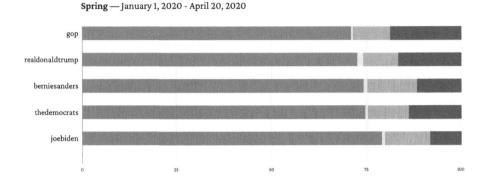

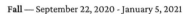

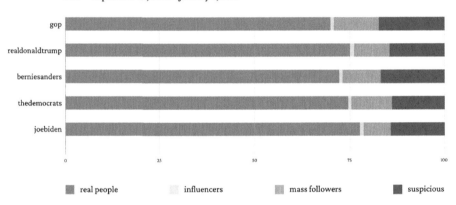

Figure 7.7 Instagram follower analysis of political parties and candidates' accounts. Breakdown of followers' countries of origin, showing the top 5 locations of users in the follower base of each account. Date ranges: January 1, 2020–April 20, 2020 and September 22, 2020–January 5, 2021. Data source: HypeAuditor.

accounts of Trump has slightly decreased, while that of both the Republican and Democratic parties remain largely the same. Contrariwise, the number of suspicious followers has risen slightly for Joe Biden (with a total of 21.4% mass and suspicious followers) and Bernie Sanders (who reaches nearly 27% of mass and suspicious followers).

Analyzing the geographical provenance of the followers of each account, which can also indicate artificial amplification practices, we found both timeframes the follower bases of the political candidates and parties to be overwhelmingly U.S.-based, with the exception of Donald Trump's. In the spring Trump's official account had 25% of followers from other locations than the U.S., including Iran, Brazil, and India.

In the fall we no longer find India-based users in the top 5 locations of Donald Trump followers.

Finding 5: Celebrities and influencers generally make responsible contributions to political Instagram. It is also worthwhile to zoom in on the role of celebrities and influencers on a platform known for their significance in influencing public opinion. Generally speaking, their posts fall into the category of earnest and non-divisive. They raise awareness, donate to causes, show support for a candidate, serve as role models, and debunk conspiracy theories. Indeed, some contributions fit into a longstanding tradition of "issue celebrity" fundraising and awareness-raising, particularly concerning healthcare, with posts by celebrities who support (sometimes with financial donations) healthcare workers and hospitals during the pandemic in spring. In the posts concerning COVID-19, we also witness celebrities promoting their products and promising to donate a percentage of the profits to COVID-19 related funds, as Kim Kardashian does in her four posts that make it into the top 50 on that issue. On healthcare, on top is Tom Hanks' message from Australia, reporting that he and his wife were infected and in self-isolation in Australia. In the 5G space, it is a repost of hip-hop artist 55Bagz making fun of the coronavirus-5G conspiracy that receives the most user interactions. On the issue of gun control, however, rapper Kevin Gates's post of his daughter posing with a gun receives a great deal of attention in a space otherwise dominated by the National Rifle Association (with 30 posts in the top 50). Concerning posts about political candidates, we see how candidate support messages by model and actress Emily Ratajkowski attract high amounts of user interactions.

In the fall we still observe the prominent role of celebrities both in the issue and candidate spaces, although the pool of most active ones in the top 50 posts changes slightly: new celebrities appear (such as athletes Cristiano Ronaldo and Virat Kohli), while others who reached the top in spring have disappeared (e.g., Tom Hanks). Kim Kardashian (present in the top 50 with multiple posts in Spring) remains at the top. For some issues, the tone and the content celebrities discuss change considerably compared to the previous period. Concerning COVID-19, messages of support and advice about the pandemic are replaced by posts that show how *life goes on* despite the pandemic (at least for celebrities who can afford it): film sets are moved to comply with travel restrictions, or "COVID-free" birthday parties are held on private islands. In the health space, support for healthcare workers is partly replaced with messages of awareness

Spring — January 1, 2020 - April 20, 2020

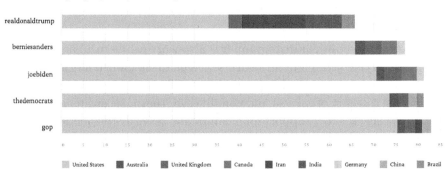

Fall — September 22, 2020 - January 5, 2021

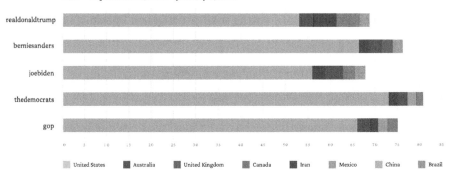

Figure 7.8 Examples of celebrities' posts in fall: Celebrities urging to vote in dedicated posts (Jennifer Aniston), or by inviting to vote (for Biden) in the caption of otherwise non-political posts (Ariana Grande); Celebrity personal life (Kim Kardashian) and professional life (The Rock) going on despite COVID-19. Sources: https://www.instagram.com/p/CGskEr_jE5d; https://www.instagram.com/p/CG5rtaaF8k_/; https://www.instagram.com/p/CG2zK7WgghF/; https://www.instagram.com/p/CHX3TvOFRfn/.

about mental health issues, specifically around World Mental Health Day on October 10th.

In the political spaces, more celebrities are active, calling on users to go and vote, both in dedicated posts (e.g., Jennifer Aniston) or by adding #voteforBiden to otherwise non-political posts. Indeed, among the candidates, Biden is the one receiving the most celebrity support. Together with celebrities, some famous politicians (e.g., Barack Obama) voice support for Biden, while others express criticism for Trump (e.g., Kamala Harris, Michelle Obama, and Hillary Clinton). In the Trump space, Snoop Dogg receives quite a lot of attention by posting memes about the president.

Celebrities urging users to vote

October 23, 2020   October 28, 2020

Celebrity life despite Covid-19

October 27, 2020   November 9, 2020

Figure 7.9 The most active Instagram users per issue space. Date ranges: January 1, 2020–April 20, 2020 and September 22, 2020–January 5, 2021. Source: CrowdTangle. The user accounts in our dataset not marked as "verified" public figures by Instagram are blurred in the visualization.

Methods

Content analysis of candidates and issues spaces

The Instagram data for this study is collected with CrowdTangle, Facebook's media monitoring tool that has been made available to academics through the Social Science One program. CrowdTangle allows users to collect Instagram posts that mention one or more keywords during a specific time frame. To create our dataset, we first compiled a list of keywords for each candidate, including candidate names, campaign slogans, and most-used hashtags. Then, we selected four of the most-mentioned topics in the candidate spaces: healthcare, COVID-19, 5G and gun control. For each of these topics, we compiled a list of relevant keywords intending to include official terms, vernacular words, and, if applicable, pro- and counter-terminology, e.g., including in the query both "gun control" and "gun ownership." (See Appendix for the full list of queries.) We used each query to collect Instagram posts shared in two timeframes: between January 1 and April 20, 2020 (we refer to this period as spring throughout this chapter) and between September 22, 2020, and January 5, 2021 (which we refer to as fall). For each query and each period, we selected the top 50 posts based on the total sum of interactions, which is the number of likes and comments by Instagram users that a post has received.

In this study, we focus on most engaged with posts, as well as most active users in high-engagement spaces, asking specifically whether the posts from highly visible accounts receiving the most user interactions are earnest or ambivalent and whether they are divisive or not. After having manually removed unrelated posts from the dataset, we conduct a close reading of the top 50 posts per space, taking into consideration both the visual elements (image or video) and the post captions, applying a four-category analytical scheme (see Figure 7.10).

We flag as divisive content posts that fuel conflict, polarization, or even radicalization (following Benkler et al., 2018), in contrast to more positive messages (e.g., supporting a candidate or sharing quarantine tips), which we label as non-divisive. We make a distinction between earnest content that is posted with clear intent and may be understood by many users and content that often through humor or (sub)cultural references lends itself to different interpretations, depending on those who receive it and what they read into it. Here, we keep in mind the possibility of encountering convincing yet "maliciously 'fake' content" (Highfield and Leaver, 2016, p. 52).

In opposition to "earnest and non-divisive" content, we categorized as "earnest and divisive" inflammatory posts that might fuel polarization, conspiracy, or conflict. We used "ambivalent and non-divisive" to categorize content that is not inflammatory but may still generate a lighter form of division by possibly excluding those who do not have the cultural references to decode it, laugh about it, and involuntary become "laughed at" as Phillips and Millner put it (2018). We subsequently tagged as "ambivalent and divisive" content that, while ambivalent (as above),

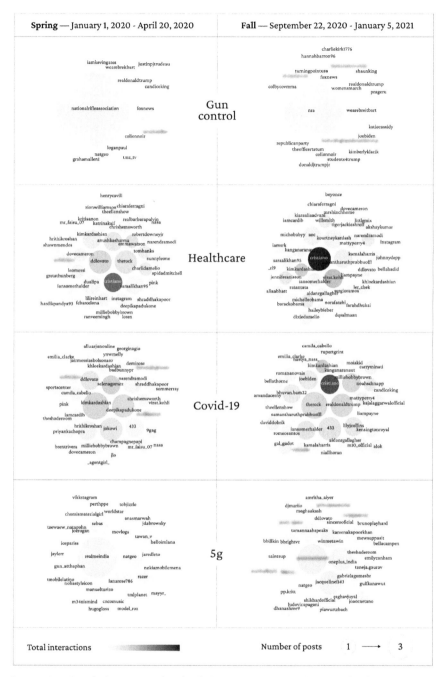

Figure 7.10 Analytical scheme. Examples of coded posts in earnest non-divisive, ambivalent non-divisive, earnest divisive, and ambivalent divisive. Sources: https://www.instagram.com/tv/CHImtYqHfO9/; https://www.instagram.com/p/CHKEGaNh_G3/; https://www.instagram.com/p/CGAn6KFsjDq/; https://www.instagram.com/p/CF1-vqonZJr/.

can be recognized as highly dismissive, polarizing, or otherwise geared towards division.

It is important to note that as we are analyzing content during a political campaign, and many posts were "campaigning" in terms of both their message and tone of voice. Here, we only coded such content as divisive when it was explicitly dismissive of a political opponent or another person or accusatory in incendiary terms. Not all critical posts were labeled as divisive, just as not all jokes were coded as ambivalent.

User activity analysis of candidates and issues spaces

For each of the presidential candidates and issue spaces, we analyzed the most active users. Here, we count how many times a user has posted and calculate the total number of interactions (likes and comments) received by each user for the total of his or her posts. User activity analysis tells us whether one or more very active users dominate a political or issue space and whether those who are the most vocal are also the most interacted with by other users. Concerning the political candidates, we also ask whether one candidate succeeds in "invading" another candidate's namespace. As one candidate mentions (often attacking or criticizing) another candidate, s/he may receive a high number of user interactions, therefore appearing in the top 50 posts of one of the opponents.

Artificial amplification and follower analysis

To assess the authenticity of candidates' and parties' audiences and detect signs of artificial amplification, we use the digital marketing tool, HypeAuditor. The tool provides a set of metrics for one Instagram account, which it compiles into an "audience report." For each candidate and party (Biden, Sanders, and Trump as well as the political party names), we collect the Instagram usernames and then use HypeAuditor to obtain an audience report. The report provides an audience type breakdown, dividing followers into four categories: real people, influencers (> 5,000 followers), mass followers (>1,500 followers), and suspicious followers, defined as "Instagram bots and people who use specific services for likes, comments and followers purchase" (Komok, 2020). From the Hypeauditor report, we also consider the followers' country analysis for each account, which breaks down followers by location and could also point to possible anomalies in the follower base.

Celebrities on Instagram

In the last part of the study, we zoom into the role of celebrities in the various political and issue spaces. In characterizing online celebrities, scholars have made the distinction between "social media natives," sometimes referred to as micro-celebrities to indicate the niche of their fame, whose "activities have been associated with social media from the beginning" (Giles, 2017), and established celebrities who become active on social media and employ the techniques of micro-celebrities to engage with their audience (Marwick and boyd, 2010). In our user activity analysis, rather than tracing where their fame originated from, we consider as celebrities all public figures whose user accounts are labeled as "verified" by the platform.

To obtain a verified account on Instagram, reviewers assess whether an account is "in the public interest" and (in addition to following the platform's terms of service) is "authentic, unique, complete and notable" (Instagram, n.d.). Verified accounts must also be famous outside of Instagram, as the platform "review(s) accounts that are featured in multiple news sources" (Instagram, n.d.) and assigns a verified badge only to those associated with a "well-known, highly searched for person, brand or entity" (Instagram, n.d.). Social media influencers who have not built up a public presence outside of the platform are not marked as verified. Once the badge of a verified account is earned, it is hardly revoked, and "there appear to be no consequences when authentic, verified accounts share lies and half-truths" (Ahmadi and Chan, 2020).

Appendix

Overview of queries used in CrowdTangle

Covid-19 [corona, covid_19, covid, coronaviruspandemic, coronavirus]
5G [5g]
Healthcare [healthinsurance, medicareforall, medicare, medicareforallnow, health, healthcare, lowerdrugcosts, protectourcare, obamacare, Abortion, Medicare]
Gun control [gun control, firearms regulation, gun restrictions, anti-gun, carry permit, 2nd amendment, second amendment, right to keep and bear arms, gun ownership]

Biden [biden, joebiden, biden2020]
Sanders [berniesanders, sanders, feelthebern, bernie2020, votebernie]
Trump [donaldtrump, trump, KAG2020, Trump2020, makeamericagreata-
gain, maga]

Instagram accounts that were part of the follower analysis with HypeAuditor

Political candidate accounts: @berniesanders, @joebiden, @realdonaldtrump
Political party accounts: @thedemocrats, @gop

References

Ahmadi, A.A., and Chan, E. (2020). Online influencers have become powerful vectors in promoting false information and conspiracy theories. First Draft. https://firstdraftnews.org/latest/influencers-vectors-misinformation/.

Benkler, Y., Faris, R., and Roberts, H. (2018). *Network propaganda: Manipulation, disinformation, and radicalization in American politics*. Oxford University Press.

Bond, S. (2021, March 9) Instagram suggested posts to users. It served up COVID-19 falsehoods, study finds. NPR. https://www.npr.org/2021/03/09/975032249/instagram-suggested-posts-to-users-it-served-up-covid-19-falsehoods-study-finds.

Bradshaw, S. and Howard, P.N. (2018). *Challenging truth and trust: A global inventory of organized social media manipulation*. Computational Propaganda Research Project. Oxford Internet Institute. https://demtech.oii.ox.ac.uk/wp-content/uploads/sites/93/2018/07/ct2018.pdf.

Burkhardt, J.M. (2017). Combating fake news in the digital age. *ALA Library Technology Reports*, 53(8): pp. 5–9. https://doi.org/10.5860/ltr.53n8.

Center for Countering Hate (2021, March 9). Malgorithm: How Instagram's algorithm publishes misinformation and hate to millions during a pandemic. https://252f2edd-1c8b-49f5-9bb2-cb57bb47e4ba.filesusr.com/ugd/f4d9b9_89ed644926aa4477a442b55afbeacooe.pdf.

Colombo, G. and De Gaetano, C. (2020). Dutch political Instagram. Junk news, follower ecologies and artificial amplification. In R. Rogers and S. Niederer (Eds.), *The politics of social media manipulation* (pp. 147–168). Amsterdam University Press.

DiResta, R., Shaffer, K., Ruppel, B., Sullivan, D., Matney, R., Fox, R., Albright, J., and Johnson, B. (2018). The tactics & tropes of the internet research agency, White Paper, New Knowledge. https://disinformationreport.blob.core.windows.net/disinformation-report/NewKnowledge-Disinformation-Report-Whitepaper.pdf.

Ellis, E. G. (2019, September 10). Fighting Instagram's $1.3 billion problem—Fake followers. *Wired*. https://www.wired.com/story/instagram-fake-followers/.

Feldman, B. (2017, June 8). In Russia, you can buy Instagram likes from a vending machine. *New York Times Magazine*, June 8. https://nymag.com/intelligencer/2017/06/you-can-buy-instagram-likes-from-a-russian-vending-machine.html.

Gillespie, E. (2020, September 30). "Pastel QAnon": The female lifestyle bloggers and influencers spreading conspiracy theories through Instagram. *The Feed*. https://www.sbs.com.au/news/the-feed/pastel-qanon-the-female-lifestyle-bloggers-and-influencers-spreading-conspiracy-theories-through-instagram.

Hedrick, A., Karpf, D., and Kreiss, D. (2018). The earnest internet vs. the ambivalent internet. *International Journal of Communication, 12*(8). https://ijoc.org/index.php/ijoc/article/view/8736/.

Highfield, T. and Leaver, T. (2016). Instagrammatics and digital methods: Studying visual social media, from selfies and GIFs to memes and emoji. *Communication Research and Practice, 2*(1), pp. 47–62. https://doi.org/10.1080/22041451.2016.1155332.

Howard, P.N., Ganesh, B., Liotsiou, D., Kelly, J., and François, C. (2018). The IRA, social media and political polarization in the United States, 2012–2018, Report, Computational Propaganda Research Project, Oxford Internet Institute. https://comprop.oii.ox.ac.uk/wp-content/uploads/sites/93/2018/12/The-IRA-Social-Media-and-Political-Polarization.pdf.

Instagram (n.d.). What are the requirements to apply for a verified badge on Instagram? Instagram Help Center. https://help.instagram.com/312685272613322.

Instagram. (2018). Reducing inauthentic activity on Instagram. Instagram Blog. https://about.instagram.com/blog/announcements/reducing-inauthentic-activity-on-instagram.

Instagram. (2020). Introducing new authenticity measures on Instagram. Instagram Blog. https://about.instagram.com/blog/announcements/introducing-new-authenticity-measures-on-instagram.

Jack, C. (2017). Lexicon of lies: Terms for problematic information. Data & Society Research Institute. https://datasociety.net/pubs/oh/DataAndSociety_LexiconofLies.pdf.

Jenkins, H. (2017, May 30). The ambivalent internet: An interview with Whitney Phillips and Ryan M. Milner (Part One). Confessions of an ACA-fan Blog. http://henryjenkins.org/blog/2017/05/the-ambivalent-internet-an-interview-with-whitney-phillips-and-ryan-m-milner-part-one.html.

Jett, J. (2021, February 11). Robert F. Kennedy, Jr. is barred from Instagram over false coronavirus claims. *New York Times*. https://www.nytimes.com/2021/02/11/us/robert-f-kennedy-jr-instagram-covid-vaccine.html.

Klein, E. and Robison, J. (2020). Like, post, and distrust? How social media use affects trust. *Political Communication, 37*(1), pp. 46–64. https://doi.org/10.1080 /10584609.2019.1661891.

Komok, A. (2020). What are suspicious accounts? HypeAuditor. https://help. hypeauditor.com/en/articles/2221742-what-are-suspicious-accounts.

Lazer, D. M., Baum, M.A., Benkler, Y., Berinsky, A.J., Greenhill, K.M., Menczer, F., ... and Schudson, M. (2018). The science of fake news. *Science, 359*(6380), pp. 1094–1096. https://doi.org/10.1126/science.aao2998.

Lee, J.C. and Quealy, K. (2019, May 24). The 598 people, places and things Donald Trump has insulted on Twitter: A complete list. *New York Times.* https://www. nytimes.com/interactive/2016/01/28/upshot/donald-trump-twitter-insults.html.

Lindquist, J. (2019). Illicit economies of the internet. *Made in China Journal, 3*(4), pp. 88–91. https://madeinchinajournal.com/2019/01/12/illicit-economies-of-the-internet-click-farming-in-indonesia-and-beyond/.

Lorenz. T. (2019, March 21) Instagram is the internet's new home for hate. *The Atlantic.* https://www.theatlantic.com/technology/archive/2019/03/ instagram-is-the-internets-new-home-for-hate/585382/.

Maragkou, E. (2020, December 8). The conspiracy theorist as influencer. Institute of Network Cultures Blog. https://networkcultures.org/blog/2020/12/08/ the-conspiracy-theorist-as-influencer/.

Marres, N. (2018). Why we can't have our facts back. *Engaging Science, Technology, and Society, 4*, 423–443. https://doi.org/10.17351/ests2018.188.

McNeal, S. and Broderick, R. (2020, April 4). Lifestyle influencers are now sharing some bogus far-right conspiracy theories about the coronavirus on Instagram. *Buzzfeed News.* https://www.buzzfeednews.com/article/stephaniemcneal/ coronavirus-lifestyle-influencers-sharing-conspiracy-qanon.

Oh, D. (2019). Review of *The ambivalent internet: mischief, oddity, and antagonism online. Information, Communication & Society, 22*(8), pp. 1189–1191. https://doi. org/10.1080/1369118X.2019.1606267.

Phillips, W. (2015). *This is why we can't have nice things: Mapping the relationship between online trolling and mainstream culture.* MIT Press.

Phillips, W. and Milner, R.M. (2017). *The ambivalent internet: Mischief, oddity, and antagonism online.* Polity.

Quealy, K. (2017, July 26). Trump is on track to insult 650 people, places and things on Twitter by the end of his first term. *New York Times.* https://www.nytimes. com/interactive/2017/07/26/upshot/president-trumps-newest-focus-discrediting-the-news-media-obamacare.html.

Rogers, R. (2020b). Deplatforming: Following extreme internet celebrities to Telegram and alternative social media. *European Journal of Communication, 35*(3). https://doi.org/10.1177/0267323120922066.

Shane, T. (2020, December 1). Searching for the misinformation "twilight zone." Nieman Lab. https://www.niemanlab.org/2020/12/searching-for-the-misinformation-twilight-zone/.

Silverman, Craig (2016, November 16) This analysis shows how viral fake election news stories outperformed real news on Facebook. *Buzzfeed News*. https://www.buzzfeednews.com/article/craigsilverman/viral-fake-election-news-outperformed-real-news-on-facebook.

Smith, R., Cubbon, S. and Wardle, C. (2020, November 12). Under the surface: Covid-19 vaccine narratives, misinformation and data deficits on social media. First Draft. https://firstdraftnews.org/long-form-article/under-the-surface-covid-19-vaccine-narratives-misinformation-and-data-deficits-on-social-media/.

Sommer, W. (2018). Instagram is the alt-right's new favorite haven. *The Daily Beast*. https://www.thedailybeast.com/instagram-is-the-alt-rights-new-favorite-haven.

Systrom, K. (2014). 300 million Instagrammers sharing real life moments. Instagram Blog. https://about.instagram.com/blog/announcements/300-million-instagrammers-sharing-real-life-moments.

Tiffany, K. (2020, August 18). How Instagram aesthetics repackage QAnon. *The Atlantic*. https://www.theatlantic.com/technology/archive/2020/08/how-instagram-aesthetics-repackage-qanon/615364/.

Van Driel, L. and Dumitrica, D. (2021). Selling brands while staying "authentic": The professionalization of Instagram influencers. *Convergence*, 27(1), pp. 66–84. https://doi.org/10.1177/1354856520902136.

Vosoughi, S., Roy, D., and Aral, S. (2018). The spread of true and false news online. *Science*, 359(6380), pp. 1146–1151. https://doi.org/10.1126/science.aap9559.

About the authors

Sabine Niederer, PhD, is Professor of Visual Methodologies at the Amsterdam University of Applied Sciences, where she heads the Visual Methodologies Collective, specializing in visual, digital, and participatory research of social issues. She is Program Manager of ARIAS, the platform for artistic research in Amsterdam and co-coordinator of the Digital Methods Initiative at the University of Amsterdam.

Gabriele Colombo, PhD, is a Research Associate at King's College London, Department of Digital Humanities, and collaborates with DensityDesign, a research lab at the Design Department of Politecnico di Milano. He is affiliated with the Visual Methodologies Collective at the Amsterdam University of Applied Sciences.

8   A fringe mainstreamed, or tracing antagonistic slang between 4chan and Breitbart before and after Trump

Stijn Peeters, Tom Willaert, Marc Tuters, Katrien Beuls, Paul Van Eecke and Jeroen Van Soest

Abstract

We studied whether the vernaculars of the extremely vitriolic, "politically incorrect" sub-forum of 4chan/pol/ have crossed over to the comment section of Breitbart News, a right-wing news website that was found in earlier research to have played a significant "agenda-setting" role in the 2016 U.S. presidential elections. We study if crossover exists around both the 2016 and 2020 elections. In our analysis, we find evidence suggestive of such crossover, centered around the presence first on 4chan and later Breitbart of a series of racist, antagonistic and otherwise extreme terms. This crossover of 4chan/pol/'s vitriolic vernacular marks an expansion of hyper-antagonistic "alt-right" politics to Breitbart's more mainstream right-wing populist audience.

Keywords: Alt-right, 4chan, Breitbart, vernacular crossover, extreme speech

Research questions

Can we find evidence of language originating on 4chan that propagates to the comment sections of Breitbart News around the time of the 2016 U.S. elections? How to characterize the words used on 4chan as compared to Breitbart around that time? Does the use and change in use of language on both platforms suggest a spread of extreme political thought? Can we observe similar dynamics of language propagation between both platforms around the 2020 U.S. presidential elections?

Rogers. R. (ed.), *The Propagation of Misinformation in Social Media: A Cross-platform Analysis.*
Amsterdam: Amsterdam University Press 2023
DOI: 10.5117/9789463720762_CH08

Essay summary

Over the past decade a diverse and increasingly influential far-right online media sphere has emerged. It has raised concerns that parts of this sphere may function as incubators for radicalization. In particular, the 2016 presidential elections in the United States were marked by the coarsening of the tone of political discourse, with candidate and eventual winner Donald Trump slandering his opponents, spreading conspiracy theories and provoking xenophobia. Alongside Trump's insurgent takeover of the Republican party, his election campaign during 2015 and 2016 marked the emergence of the "alt-right" political movement, which perceived Trump as an alternative to establishment conservatism.

As a libertarian movement with a strongly xenophobic, often racist stance towards immigration, the alt-right was also characterized by its use of antagonistic vernacular. We can think of this antagonistic slang as "memes," a concept typically used to refer to user-generated shared images that seem to spread across platforms and between communities, but which can also be used to refer to any "building blocks of complex cultures" online, including words and phrases (Shifman, 2011, p189). Indeed, in the analysis on offer here, we view specific phrases and tokens as such memetic building blocks that seem to propagate within and between distinct environments online. A platform of interest in this context is the far-right image board 4chan, which has been positioned as a "birthplace of memes" (Ludemann, 2018), an incubator of conspiracy theories like QAnon (De Zeeuw et al., 2020), and a place of rapid innovation of oftentimes antagonistic language (Peeters et al., 2021). It might therefore be expected that antagonistic alt-right slang incubated on the platform has the potential to spread to a wider audience, with 4chan acting as a breeding ground. To study this hypothesis, we look at 4chan as well as a more mainstream platform that has been associated with the alt-right, Breitbart News.

The questions are particularly relevant as the alt-right is a relatively unique, insurgent far-right political movement that rose to international attention in 2015 with remarkably little in the way of a centralized organizational structure, and for whom the circulation of memes and internet jargon was fundamental to its success (Hawley, 2017). Most emblematically, the memetic subcultural icon of "Pepe the Frog" became notoriously associated with this school of thought during the first half of the 2010s and achieved widespread attention (Lobinger et al., 2020). Arguably, however, among the alt-right's most significant accomplishments was the extent to which their antagonistic slang succeeded in framing political discussion.

Illustrative of this pattern was for example the expression "cuckservative" which emerged in early 2015 on (now deplatformed) alt-right websites such as My Posting Career, The Right Stuff as well as on 4chan's notorious /pol/ forum (Bernstein, 2015). In its original far-right subcultural usage the term referred to a genre of often racialized pornography thereby connecting a critique of establishment republicanism with the far-right's longstanding preoccupation with masculinity and miscegenation. By the end of the year, the prolific alt-right author Vox Day had self-published a track with the title *Cuckservative: How "conservatives" betrayed America*, and this alt-right meme had effectively worked its way into political discussion amongst mainstream Trump voters. It is this type of "propagation" of politically extreme vocabulary that is under study in this chapter.

Considering these recent events, there is a legitimate concern that the subculture associated with sites at the "bottom" of the internet could insinuate itself (or has already done so) with an extreme and conspiratorial discourse into the American political debate across a continually evolving range of platforms. There are indications that it has already transpired in the more recent 2020 U.S. election campaign. The QAnon persona, central to a right-wing conspiracy theory positing, among other things, that prominent members of the Democratic Party are part of a Satan-worshipping cannibalistic cult, started on 4chan but has since become a major factor in mainstream U.S. politics and as such is now discussed on a wide variety of platforms (De Zeeuw et al., 2020; Stanley-Becker, 2020). The polarized language we study reflects this rift in recent American political discourse.

An understanding of the internet as having a "bottom" implies the existence of further "layers." Along these lines, at the top we would find big media conglomerates, often rooted in "legacy media" such as major newspapers as the *New York Times*, cable broadcasters as CNN, and newer online-first outlets like Vox. As one moves "down," platforms grow more obscure, with a smaller reach and less clear editorial or content policies. At the bottom, one finds "fringe" sites, with obscure subcultures; this "deep vernacular web" (De Zeeuw and Tuters, 2020) can appear culturally baffling as well as offensive to the uninitiated. Sites in this stratum usually have a relatively small number of visitors, compared to mainstream sites. 4chan is particularly relevant here, as a fringe platform that has nevertheless been scrutinized for its production of internet memes (Bernstein et al., 2011), peculiar subcultural practices (Nissenbaum and Shifman, 2017) as well as language innovation (Tuters and Hagen, 2020; Peeters et al., 2021).

Our findings are based on datasets centered on the 2016 and 2020 U.S. elections, collected from 4chan/pol/ and from the comment section of

Breitbart News, a conservative, right-wing American news website especially popular during the first period as a staunch supporter of eventual winner Donald Trump. Although it has been described as "factually dubious" (Guess et al., 2018), Breitbart News occupied a crucial place in the political media ecosystem at the time. Benkler et al. (2018) offered an in-depth study of Breitbart's "agenda-setting" role in that election. Their analysis shows how Breitbart "anchored" a network of other similarly dubious right-wing news sites such as Daily Caller, Gateway Pundit and Infowars. Though no formal or editorial association between these sites exists, they provide a similar brand of content characterized as a mix of "paranoid conspiracy interpretations around a core of true facts" (Benkler, 2018, p. 34). Together they occupied a crucial position in the media ecology around the 2016 elections.

In this ecology Breitbart is a particularly interesting site for several reasons. One is that, at the time, Breitbart was the largest of these sites with approximately 10% of the entire general news audience according to one estimate (Malone, 2016). Founded by the deceased Andrew Breitbart, formerly a reporter for the Huffington Post, under the more recent editorship of Steve Bannon the site championed the right-wing libertarian Tea Party and a strongly American populist, civic nationalist agenda (cf. Burley, 2017). Receiving substantial financial support from the billionaire Mercer family, who initially backed Ted Cruz in the 2015 U.S. election campaigning, Breitbart would develop into a nakedly partisan branch of the Trump campaign while at the same time Bannon famously claimed that he considered the site to be a "platform for the alt-right" (Posner, 2016). With a background in both high finance and documentary filmmaking, Bannon is a self-styled public intellectual noted for his interest in an obscure branch of far-right political philosophy known as Traditionalism, which also had a readership on 4chan/pol/ (Teitelbaum, 2020; Tuters and OILab, 2020). Bannon would later join the Trump campaign as its chief strategist (Green, 2017). In 2016, Breitbart published an article entitled *An establishment conservative's guide to the alt-right*, co-authored by the notorious alt-right provocateur Milo Yiannopoulos. An investigative report later revealed it to have been written with the participation of known alt-right ideologues (Bernstein, 2017). As such, the site combines a clear, alt-right editorial position and explicit ties to the Trump campaign with a relatively wide reach.

Earlier analyses of Breitbart, including Benkler et al.'s, were limited to the editorial content of the site. We instead study the comment sections of Breitbart's articles that routinely receive thousands of comments, many only tangentially related to the article's subject. These appear to be moderated loosely, if at all. A 2017 report cites Disqus, which provides the technology on which Breitbart's comment section runs, promising that Breitbart "[wants] to work with us to figure out ways to minimize [hate speech]" (Captain, 2017). In this permissive setting, the comment section of Breitbart's London section was characterized as "a malignant swamp of race-baiting, nativism and antisemitic conspiracy," even accused of providing a platform for notorious alt-right celebrities (Mulhall et al., 2017). Appearing to function like a largely unmoderated discussion forum, the comment threads can thus serve to study the political views and discourse of the readership of a highly active element of far-right politics that moved increasingly to the center of the American Republican party around the 2016 elections.

In this same period /pol/, the self-described "politically incorrect" discussion board of anonymous imageboard 4chan, overtook /b/ (the "random" board) as the site's most active discussion forum. Previous quantitative research on /b/ has noted how the site was an "excellent venue for studying innovation diffusion," due in part to the fact that it was generally considered as "the source of many online memes" (Bernstein, 2011, p. 56). While in the earlier period in which /b/ had been more popular 4chan was the source of innocuous memes such as LOLcats, /pol/ memes were far more toxic, including offensive depictions of Pepe the Frog as well as the antisemitic triple parentheses phrasal meme (Tuters and Hagen, 2020). While there has been some quantitative research into the diffusion of toxic /pol/ memes to other web communities (Zannettou et al., 2018), to our knowledge there is no previous empirical work focused specifically on the crossover of vernacular language from /pol/ to another such threaded discussion forum.

This chapter, then, adds to a growing body of work focused on the "mainstreaming" of previously "fringe" web spaces like 4chan as the source of a "neoreactionary" style of political discourse (Nagle, 2017; Wendling, 2018; Beran, 2019; Woods, 2019). 4chan and Breitbart represent two parts of the media ecosystem that are particularly interesting to study in the context of the polarized and increasingly extreme U.S. political landscape. As such, we investigate whether 4chan's discourse resonates beyond its own borders around the time of the 2016 and 2020 U.S. presidential elections. Since so much of the discourse on 4chan's political discussion board, /pol/, can be characterized as conspiratorial, racist or otherwise extreme (cf. Tuters and Hagen, 2020), its later occurrence on other platforms is of great interest to those studying the mainstreaming of extremism and misinformation. While our analysis is primarily focused on the 2016 election campaign in which the alt-right movement first gained prominence, we also provide an initial analysis of the 2020 campaign for comparison.

We found that there are far more terms that appear only in the language of 4chan/pol/ than in the language of Breitbart comments. Additionally, of the terms that over time are prominent first in one dataset and later in both, those that first appear on 4chan are often highly political and furthermore can be characterized as anti-Muslim and xenophobic (e.g., "germanistan"), homophobic or transphobic (e.g., "xhe") or otherwise extreme (e.g., "shitlibs"). These extreme terms are then later observed on Breitbart. Though a direct relationship is difficult to ascertain, our initial findings suggested that 4chan, an active but non-mainstream niche site, had an outsized impact that reaches beyond its own confines.

We reflect on these findings, concluding that for the period 2015–2017 4chan/pol can be considered an originator or incubator of extreme discourse, where extreme idioms appear before propagating to the more mainstream discussion space of Breitbart News. Additionally, our observations indicate that this propagation of idioms between 4chan and Breitbart News seem to be less intense around the time of the 2020 U.S. presidential elections, and that consequently, studies of extreme discourse and misinformation should consider and monitor other platforms as the main sites of the mainstreaming of such terms. We end with a brief section on our data collection and analytical methods.

Implications

Our findings indicate that around the time of the 2016 U.S. elections antagonistic, highly political and problematic words that also can be characterized as xenophobic (e.g., "germanistan"); transphobic (e.g., "xhe") or otherwise extreme (e.g., "shitlibs") first observed on 4chan later entered the discourse in the comment section of Breitbart News, a more mainstream platform with important connections to the Trump presidential administration. While earlier research has investigated the crossing over of particular ideas (e.g., conspiracy theories), our study provides empirical data that suggests that this crossing-over also occurs on the level of language and is not bound only to specific theories or ideas. The findings further support previous observations about the sustained connection between 4chan/pol/ and Breitbart's comment section during this period.

One possible explanation for the propagation of extreme "chan" vernacular towards Breitbart around the 2016 elections is that some 4chan posters also frequent Breitbart's comment section. It would not be surprising if they used the language they were familiar with, which could explain their occurrence in both spaces. Tracing whether actors move between these platforms is difficult because 4chan is designed as an anonymous platform (Knuttila, 2011). 4chan posters are notoriously derisive of "mainstream media" and typically dismiss Breitbart as inadequately extreme. Although Breitbart has been described as having an "extreme right-wing bias" (Media Bias/Fact Check, 2021), it is seen as a place for "normies." In the vernacular, "normies" are those who follow mainstream media and otherwise adhere to common social norms (De Zeeuw et al., 2020). Nevertheless, it is possible that some 4chan posters may also frequent Breitbart News, which would be one explanation for the appearance of 4chan-like vernacular there. It would be the manner for both this vernacular as well as the extreme political positions to which it implicitly and explicitly refers to spread to a new "normie" audience.

Though a direct relationship between both platforms remains difficult to ascertain, our initial findings suggest that 4chan, the active but non-mainstream niche site, had an outsized impact that reaches beyond its own confines. As such, we conclude that for the period 2015–2017 4chan/pol can be considered an originator or incubator of extreme discourse, where extreme idioms appeared before they propagated to the more mainstream discussion space of Breitbart News. Additionally, our observations indicate that this propagation of idioms between 4chan and Breitbart News seems to be less intense around the time of the 2020 U.S. presidential elections, and that consequently studies of extreme discourse and misinformation should consider and monitor other platforms as the main sites of the mainstreaming of such terms.

A key implication of our work, then, is that 4chan /pol/ might give an early impression of problematic discourse that may become used by a wider audience at a later stage. As such, continued observation of the language disseminated through these fringe platforms—for which we offer one methodological blueprint by addressing its propagation towards Breitbart News—might benefit journalists, researchers and policy makers seeking to signal the emergence of new extreme discourses on emerging platforms such as Parler (cf. Floridi, 2021) and others that have more recently gained prominence in the 2020 U.S. election campaign.

More fundamentally, our findings speak to the much-debated relationship between the "bottom" of the internet—consisting of niche, often politically extreme sites—and more mainstream sites. The observation and study of this "bottom" has acquired urgency as ideas and vernacular that originate in these parts have been implicated in several far-right terrorist attacks in the United States, Canada and New Zealand. Furthermore, sites like

4chan serve as incubators for various impactful conspiracy theories, e.g., "Pizzagate" (Tuters et al., 2018) and the figure of QAnon (De Zeeuw et al., 2020). Indeed, while for many years the effects of the web were framed in terms of the democratic promise of participatory media (Jenkins, 2006; Benkler, 2006), the last half decade has shaken that narrative to its core with the emergence of "dark participation" in the context of online political discussion (Quandt, 2018). The role of the upstart Breitbart in anchoring a right-wing news ecosystem that set the agenda for the 2016 U.S. election may be seen as the fruition of earlier concerns over the fragmentation of the web into personalized spheres (Pariser, 2011), which continue apace with the emergence of the alt-tech ecosystem that has benefited from social media platforms' "deplatforming" of the Trump movement (Rogers, 2020b). Given the "fringe" quality of some of these sites we have good reason to believe that their vernacular subculture will overlap with that of 4chan, as this study showed for the "normie" website, Breitbart News, in the midst of the 2016 U.S. election.

Findings

For both the 2015–2017 and 2020–2021 periods, we split up the 4chan and Breitbart posts and comments in terms; each word, after filtering out hyperlinks and punctuation, is a term. For each term we can then classify on which of the platforms it occurs on a per-month basis, resulting in a propagation pattern for each term (see Figure 8.1).

Our findings suggest that around the 2016 U.S. presidential elections, the political vocabulary associated with extreme right-wing politics consistently appears on 4chan first, and then on the more mainstream Breitbart News later, potentially representing one strand of this propagation dynamic. We also observed that this dynamic becomes less prominent around the 2020 elections, suggesting that the locus for this extreme idiom's propagation from the "bottom" of the internet has again shifted. In particular, the analysis of these propagation patterns allows for the following observations:

Finding 1: Around the time of the 2016 U.S. presidential elections, the language of 4chan/pol/ contains more unique terms than that in the Breitbart comment sections. Our analysis shows that there are more terms unique to the /pol/ dataset than there are terms unique to the Breitbart dataset. Of the 67,605 terms, 19,346 (28.6%) were classified as occurring in the 4chan/pol/ dataset only, while 2,857 (4.2%) were classified as occurring only in the Breitbart dataset (see Figure 8.2). 4chan has previously been described as a

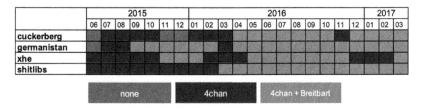

Figure 8.1 Visualization of the monthly occurrence of the terms "cuckerberg," "germanistan," "xhe," and "shitlibs" around the time of the 2016 U.S. presidential elections, between June 2015 and March 2017. For each month, terms are classified (color-coded) based on a comparison of their relative frequencies in 4chan/pol posts and in the comments on Breitbart News. These words represent the political vernacular found within the 4chan dataset.

source of subcultural and linguistic innovation (Nissenbaum and Shifman, 2017). This finding empirically confirms the observation, at least concerning the unique use of language on the forum. As English-language datasets, both are concerned with informal political discussion focused primarily on the United States context. Thus, while some variation may be expected; in principle, one might expect the language used to be similar between both, but this is only partially the case.

4chan's vernacular has been referred to as "chanspeak": "peculiar in-group misspellings" characterized by "shortening, simplifying and cutting down words" (Fiorentini, 2013; Herring, 2012). While this is perhaps true for the broader 4chan vernacular, the /pol/ slang we found is not adequately captured by this description. This can be attributed to the rapid linguistic innovation on this forum (Peeters et al., 2020). The terms we find are more adequately described as "phrasal memes," highly self-referential "remixes" of words, e.g., "cuckerberg" (a combination of "cuck" and "Zuckerberg"). While a proper linguistic analysis of this vernacular is outside the scope of this article, the dataset on offer here could in the case of /pol/ serve as a starting point for such a study.

Finding 2: During the same period, a substantial number of terms are first only observed in the language on 4chan, the fringe platform, but later also on Breitbart, the more mainstream platform, suggesting propagation of this vocabulary. Terms that occur on one platform first and later on another platform or both platforms can be observed in both "directions"; some occur first on Breitbart while others occur first on 4chan/pol/. In total, 2,043 terms (3%) follow such a pattern. Of these, 932 (45.6%) occur on 4chan first, while 1,111 (54.4%) occur on Breitbart first. This seems counterintuitive; it would imply that terms are first anchored in the language of Breitbart and only later in that of 4chan, which is difficult to reconcile with 4chan's reputation as a more innovative linguistic space as established in Finding

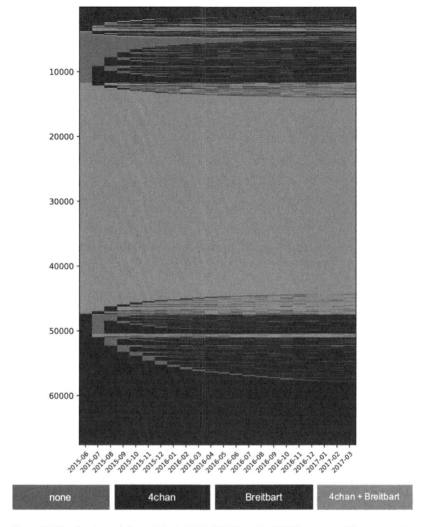

Figure 8.2 Classifications of all words in the 2015–2017 data (N = 67,605) over time. The consecutive occurrences of each word are represented as a single row of per-month squares that are color-coded for the occurrence of the word in 4chan/pol/ posts and Breitbart comments respectively.

1. On the other hand, Breitbart is a far larger and arguably more influential platform, and agenda-setting power may be attributed to it in that capacity. From this perspective, the fact that a substantial number of terms occur on 4chan first at all is significant and suggests that the terms might indeed "propagate," with language spreading—directly or indirectly—from 4chan eventually to Breitbart.

A closer look at these terms reveals that they can be divided into two broad categories—"named entities" and "neologisms." Linguistically, named entities refer to all terms that are proper names, for example, countries and people. The other category, "neologisms," are words that are neither common English nor otherwise used in "normal" discourse. In practice, these terms are mostly various slurs and part of a memetic vocabulary that is associated with 4chan discourse.

The named entities cannot reasonably be assumed to originate on either platform. Instead, the likely explanation for the occurrence of these terms is that they refer to people, places or organizations that were discussed because they were relevant to a current event or news item. This indicates that Breitbart users discussed these topics before 4chan, which is interesting insofar as it provides insight into the type of topics discussed by both forums and how rapidly they enter the discourse. The "neologisms" (including the examples in Figure 8.1) on the other hand are likely to originate in the vernacular of online platforms (Peeters et al., 2021). As such, the fact that they appear on 4chan and later on Breitbart suggests that they do propagate from the one to the other, either directly or via another intermediary platform.

Finding 3: Around the time of the 2016 U.S. presidential elections, many terms that seem to propagate from 4chan/pol/ to Breitbart reflect an extreme far-right politics. Of these terms that can be assumed to originate on 4chan/pol/, most are implicitly or explicitly related to far-right and conspiratorial theories or ideas. This is not surprising, since 4chan/pol/ itself has been associated with the "Pizzagate" political conspiracy (Tuters et al., 2018) and has been described as a "kind of petri dish for concocting extreme and extremely virulent forms of right-wing populist antagonism" (Tuters and Hagen, 2020, p. 2223). Of the words that appear first on 4chan (see also Figure 8.1) several are emblematic of an extreme political discourse, such as "cuckerberg" (a jab at Facebook owner Mark Zuckerberg combined with the slur "cuckold"; other variations found were "cuckservative(s)," "cucktard," "cucky," and "cuckery"), anti-Muslim terms such as "germanistan" and "britainistan," words like "xhe" (used mockingly to insult transgender people), and various slurs aimed at liberal U.S. voters like "shitlibs" and "berniebots."[1]

While 4chan/pol/ is well-known as a far-right discussion space (Hine et al., 2017; Ludemann, 2018), our data and analyses show that the vocabulary associated with this discourse is not contained to this "fringe" platform but after initial usage it also appears on more mainstream platforms. More specifically, the various xenophobic or otherwise extreme slurs and phrasal memes that are developed and incubated on 4chan/pol/ in some cases see

---

[1]   The full list of terms that propagate may be found in the dataset available from Zenodo at https://doi.org/10.5281/zenodo.5535341.

uptake in the comments on Breitbart News. As most of this language is unambiguous, and hard to mistake for anything else than derogatory, it raises concerns that not only the language but also the extreme political discourse associated with it is shared across sites.

Finding 4: Around the time of the 2020 U.S. presidential elections, the aforementioned mainstreaming of extreme chan vernacular seems to be less outspoken. Around the time of the 2020 U.S. presidential elections, some of the vernacular that propagated in 2015–2017 remains shared between 4chan and Breitbart, with notable examples including "cuck" and its derivatives, such as "cucked." Further analysis shows, however, that comparatively fewer new terms propagate from 4chan to Breitbart News around this time. As observed in our 2020–2021 dataset, only 347 terms out of 57,602 (or 0.6% compared to 3% for the 2015–2017 dataset) actually move from one platform to the other, and of those, only 124 were classified as moving from 4chan/pol to Breitbart (see Figure 8.3). Closer inspection of these moving terms reveals few original vernacular terms, even though the data suggest that during this period, 4chan in and of itself remains an incubator for extreme vernacular. Examples that do point towards a continued mainstreaming of 4chan terminology and memes concern the terms "coomer" (which refers to the 4chan meme of the "20-year-old coomer"), and "libshits" (an inversion of the previously discussed term "shitlibs"), but in comparison with the 2015–2017 period, the language propagation dynamics between both platforms seems much less outspoken.

Any comparison between the two datasets is necessarily tentative as we are yet to capture as much of the post-election period as we did for the 2016 elections. As such there remains a possibility that the propagation dynamic lags in this case, or that Breitbart's comment space has later become milder for other reasons—perhaps 4chan's interest in Breitbart has diminished, which may be found in a subsequent analysis. Nevertheless, the discourse around both elections may be assumed to reach its zenith in the months surrounding the election date. As such, the data gathered around the 2020 elections should provide a representative impression of the discourse around that election, even if it is quantitatively smaller and of a shorter duration than the earlier dataset.

These empirical observations strengthen previous assertions in the literature that the period 2015–2017 was one characterized by an intensified and salient "mainstreaming" of harmful vernacular between 4chan/pol and Breitbart News. Possible explanations for the relative decline in the propagation of idioms from 4chan to Breitbart around the 2020 U.S. presidential elections include the fact the site experienced a precipitous

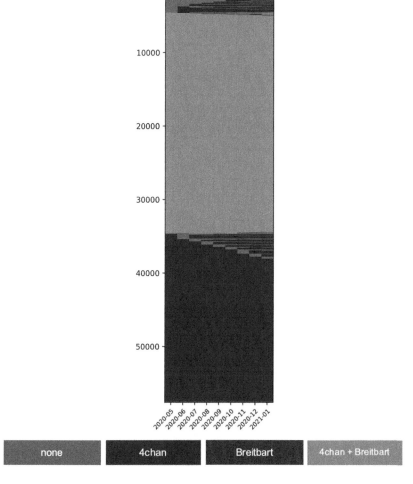

Figure 8.3 Classifications of all words in the 2020–2021 data (N = 57,603) over time. The consecutive occurrences of each word are represented as a single row of per-month squares that are color-coded for the occurrence of the word in 4chan/pol/ posts and Breitbart comments respectively.

decline after Trump took office, ultimately losing as much as three quarters of its total audience (Ellefson, 2019). According to Steve Bannon the site appears to have struggled financially following an advertiser boycott, which began in 2016 and was organized by Sleeping Giant to protest the site's bigotry and sexism (Klayman, 2019). The billionaire Mercer family sold their shares in the site in 2017 and are currently majority stakeholders of the alternative social media site Parler, connected to the 2021 storming of the DC Capitol (Lerman, 2021). The growth in significance of such "alt-tech sites" can be seen as one of the bi-products of the "deplatforming" of alt-right figureheads from social media—including eventually Trump himself (Rogers, 2020b).

Methods

4chan data was collected with 4CAT, a forum analysis toolkit (Peeters and Hagen, 2021) that contains a dataset comprising 4chan /pol/ data from 2013 to the present. This data is collected continuously (as it is posted on 4chan) by the tool itself and, for the period prior to 2018, supplemented with data from 4plebs.org, a third-party 4chan archive which publishes semi-regular data "dumps" on the Internet Archive, containing all posts made on a number of 4chan's boards, including /pol/. (Merged 4plebs' and 4CAT's datasets have been used in other research on 4chan, too (Tuters and Hagen, 2019; Voué et al., 2020; Jokubauskaitė and Peeters, 2020).) Notably, posts are included even if they are later deleted from the site, as all posts eventually disappear from 4chan itself, as threads are deleted after a period of inactivity.

The 2015–2017 Breitbart data was collected between September 2–9, 2019 using a custom scraper written in Python which first crawled breitbart.com for internal links to create an index of all articles posted on the site, and then collected all comments for all articles posted between June 2015 and March 2017, using the Disqus API. The resulting dataset reflects the state of the comment section as it was at the moment of scraping. There is a possibility that some comments were removed between the moment of posting and the moment of scraping, up to 4 years later; however, as mentioned earlier, Breitbart's moderation policy seems to have been lax during the period we study, and it is unlikely that later policies were enacted retroactively. We therefore assume that the data is a reasonably accurate reflection of what the comment threads would have looked like closer to the date the comments were posted. The 2020–2021 Breitbart data was collected with the same technique, between February 17 and March 3, 2021.

Our first dataset thus spans the period between the announcement of Donald Trump's candidacy for the U.S. presidential election (June 2015) and his first months in office, whereas the second dataset comprises a smaller interval around the 2020 U.S. elections in which Trump was again a candidate (and lost). As data capture of this nature is cumbersome, we were unable to gather a dataset comprising an equal timespan so shortly after the 2020 elections; a more direct comparison would be a fruitful avenue for future work.

Before analyzing the captured data, for both datasets we cleaned the scraped comments and posts by applying case folding and removing punctuation, URLs, HTML tags (in Breitbart comments) and comment referral numbers such as ">>280207128" (in /pol/ comments).

Analysis

This chapter addresses the questions of (1) whether we can empirically identify terms that are first prominent in the language on 4chan/pol/ and later also in the language of the Breitbart comment sections around the time of the 2016 U.S. presidential elections, (2) how to characterize the language used on 4chan/pol/ compared to that of Breitbart's comment sections at that time, (3) whether the nature of these identified terms indicates a spread of extreme political thought, and (4) whether we can identify similar dynamics between both platforms around the time of the 2020 U.S. presidential elections. We expect that we can observe this pattern for terms associated with far-right thought, and that it constitutes a mainstreaming of fringe, taboo or otherwise extreme political concepts.

Quantitative analysis

We investigate corpora of posts and comments using methods from natural language processing to empirically identify terms that occur first on one platform and then on another, and to quantify the propagation patterns of these terms between both platforms (Willaert et al., 2020; Willaert et al., 2021). We collected two datasets for both platforms, a first set comprising posts from June 2015 through March 2017, and a second set containing data from May 2020 through January 2021. These texts were then tokenized (split into individual terms). For both platforms, the monthly frequencies of each term were counted, and those terms with an absolute frequency of less than 200 were removed, as these were mostly less germane and included typos. Next, the relative monthly frequency of each term was calculated for both /pol/ and Breitbart. Relative frequencies were used because we are interested in the prominence of the terms in the language of each platform, and we aim to compare this prominence between platforms. We then compare these relative frequencies and classify each term into one of four classification bins, indicating whether for a given month the term:
- occurred neither on /pol/ nor on Breitbart,
- occurred on both /pol/ and Breitbart,

- occurred exclusively on /pol/, or
- occurred exclusively on Breitbart.

For each term, this analysis results in a sequence of classification bins. In order to reduce the influence of very low frequency terms, a term is only assigned to the Breitbart bin or /pol/ bin if it had a relative frequency of at least 0.00001%. If not, its frequency is considered to be 0 for that month. This filtering resulted in a classification sequence for each term, which was visualized using color coding (Figure 8.2).

Qualitative analysis

The initial quantitative approach yielded a subset of terms for both periods that warranted further scrutiny; we are particularly interested in those terms that were first observed as prominent on 4chan/pol/ and later also observed on Breitbart. Our approach here was to first remove any obvious named entities (people, countries, institutions) from the list as well as common English language. The remaining tokens could then be analyzed in more detail via a closer reading, in which the context and occurrence of the token on 4chan/pol/ as well as on other platforms is studied via 4plebs (the searchable archive of /pol/) and 4CAT (the modular web platform scraping tool). Here we retained words with a clear political (sub)text, similar to those shown in Figure 8.1.

As such, we have employed a quali-quantitative approach (Venturini and Latour, 2010), where we combine an initial computational analysis of a large dataset to extract a relevant subset of the corpora at hand, which we then analyze further with a more interpretative qualitative approach of this subset.

References

Benkler, Y. (2006). *The wealth of networks: How social production transforms markets and freedom.* Yale University Press.

Benkler, Y., Faris, R., and Roberts, H. (2018). *Network propaganda: Manipulation, disinformation, and radicalization in American politics.* Oxford University Press.

Beran, D. (2019). *It came from something awful: How a toxic troll army accidentally memed Donald Trump into office.* St. Martin's Publishing Group.

Bernstein, J. (2015, July 27). Behind the racist hashtag that is blowing up Twitter. *BuzzFeed News.* https://www.buzzfeednews.com/article/josephbernstein/behind-the-racist-hashtag-some-donald-trump-fans-love.

Bernstein, J. (2017, October 5). Here's how Breitbart and Milo smuggled Nazi and white nationalist ideas into the mainstream. *BuzzFeed News*. https://www.buzzfeednews.com/article/josephbernstein/heres-how-breitbart-and-milo-smuggled-white-nationalism.

Bernstein, M., Monroy-Hernández, A., Harry, D., André, P., Panovich, K., and Vargas, G. (2011). 4chan and /b/: An analysis of anonymity and ephemerality in a large online community. In *Proceedings of the International AAAI Conference on Web and Social Media*, *5*(1), Article 1. https://ojs.aaai.org/index.php/ICWSM/article/view/14134.

Burley, S. (2017). Disunite the right: The growing divides in the pepe coalition. Political Research Associates. https://www.politicalresearch.org/2017/09/19/disunite-the-right-the-growing-divides-in-the-pepe-coalition.

Captain, S. (2017, March 8). Disqus grapples with hosting toxic comments on Breitbart and extreme-right sites. *Fast Company*. https://www.fastcompany.com/3068698/disqus-grapples-with-hosting-toxic-comments-on-breitbart-and-extreme-right-sites.

Day, V. and Eagle, J. R. (2016). *Cuckservative: How "conservatives" betrayed America*. Castalia House.

De Zeeuw, D., Hagen, S., Peeters, S., and Jokubauskaite, E. (2020). Tracing normiefication. *First Monday*. https://doi.org/10.5210/fm.v25i11.10643.

De Zeeuw, D. and Tuters, M. (2020). Teh internet is serious business: On the deep vernacular web and its discontents. *Cultural Politics*, *16*(2), pp. 214–232. https://doi.org/10.1215/17432197-8233406.

Ellefson, L. (2019, August 7). Breitbart's audience has dropped 72% since Trump took office—As other right-wing sites have gained. *The Wrap*. https://www.thewrap.com/breitbart-news-audience-dropped-steve-bannon-72-percent/.

Fiorentini, I. (2013). "ZOMG! Dis is a new language": The case of lolspeak. *Newcastle Working Papers in Linguistics*, *13*(1), pp. 90–108.

Floridi, L. (2021). Trump, Parler, and regulating the infosphere as our commons. *Philosophy & Technology*, *34*(1), pp. 1–5. https://doi.org/10.1007/s13347-021-00446-7.

Green, J. (2017). *Devil's bargain: Steve Bannon, Donald Trump, and the nationalist uprising*. Penguin.

Guess, A., Nyhan, B., and Reifler, J. (2018). Selective exposure to misinformation: Evidence from the consumption of fake news during the 2016 U.S. presidential campaign [Working paper]. http://www.dartmouth.edu/~nyhan/fake-news-2016.pdf.

Hawley, G. (2017). *Making sense of the alt-right*. Columbia University Press.

Herring, S. (2012). Special internet language varieties: Culture, creativity & language change [Paper]. The II LETiSS Workshop Language Go Web: Standard and Nonstandard Languages on the Internet, Pavia.

Hine, G., Onaolapo, J., Cristofaro, E. D., Kourtellis, N., Leontiadis, I., Samaras, R., Stringhini, G., and Blackburn, J. (2017). Kek, cucks, and God emperor Trump: A measurement study of 4chan's politically incorrect forum and its effects on the web. *Proceedings of the International AAAI Conference on Web and Social Media*, *11*(1), Article 1. https://ojs.aaai.org/index.php/ICWSM/article/view/14893.

Jenkins, H. (2006). *Convergence culture: Where old and new media collide.* New York University Press.

Jokubauskaitė, E. and Peeters, S. (2020). Generally curious: Thematically distinct datasets of general threads on 4chan/pol/. In *Proceedings of the International AAAI Conference on Web and Social Media* (pp. 863–867), 14.

Klayman, A. (2019). The Brink [Feature documentary; Digital film]. https://alisonklayman.com/the-brink.

Knuttila, L. (2011). User unknown: 4chan, anonymity and contingency. *First Monday.* https://doi.org/10.5210/fm.v16i10.3665.

Lerman, R. (2021, February 24). Major Trump backer Rebekah Mercer orchestrates Parler's second act. *Washington Post.* https://www.washingtonpost.com/technology/2021/02/24/parler-relaunch-rebekah-mercer/.

Lobinger, K., Krämer, B., Venema, R., and Benecchi, E. (2020). Pepe—Just a funny frog? A visual meme caught between innocent humor, far-right ideology, and fandom. In B. Krämer and C. Holtz-Bacha (Eds.), *Perspectives on populism and the media* (pp. 333–352). Nomos. https://doi.org/10.5771/9783845297392-333.

Ludemann, D. (2018). /pol/emics: Ambiguity, scales, and digital discourse on 4chan. *Discourse, Context & Media*, *24*, pp. 92–98. https://doi.org/10.1016/j.dcm.2018.01.010.

Malone, C. (2016, August 18). Trump made Breitbart great again. *FiveThirtyEight.* https://fivethirtyeight.com/features/trump-made-breitbart-great-again/.

Media Bias/Fact Check. (2021). Breitbart. https://mediabiasfactcheck.com/breitbart/.

Nagle, A. (2017). *Kill all normies: Online culture wars from 4Chan and Tumblr to Trump and the alt-right.* Zero Books.

Nissenbaum, A. and Shifman, L. (2017). Internet memes as contested cultural capital: The case of 4chan's /b/ board. *New Media & Society*, *19*(4), pp. 483–501. https://doi.org/10.1177/1461444815609313.

Papasavva, A., Zannettou, S., Cristofaro, E. D., Stringhini, G., and Blackburn, J. (2020). Raiders of the lost kek: 3.5 years of augmented 4chan posts from the politically incorrect board. *Proceedings of the International AAAI Conference on Web and Social Media*, *14*, pp. 885–894.

Pariser, E. (2011). *The filter bubble: What the internet is hiding from you.* Penguin.

Peeters, S. and Hagen, S. (2021). The 4CAT Capture and Analysis Toolkit: A Modular Tool for Transparent and Traceable Social Media Research (SSRN Scholarly

Paper ID 3914892). *Social Science Research Network*. https://doi.org/10.2139/ssrn.3914892.

Peeters, S., Tuters, M., Willaert, T., and de Zeeuw, D. (2021). On the vernacular language games of an antagonistic online subculture. *Frontiers in Big Data*, *4*(65). https://doi.org/10.3389/fdata.2021.718368.

Quandt, T. (2018). Dark participation. *Media and Communication*, *6*(4), pp. 36–48. https://doi.org/10.17645/mac.v6i4.1519.

Rogers, R. (2020b). Deplatforming: Following extreme internet celebrities to Telegram and alternative social media. *European Journal of Communication*, *35*(3). https://doi.org/10.1177/0267323120922066.

Shifman, L. (2012). An anatomy of a YouTube meme. *New Media & Society*, *14*(2), pp. 187–203. https://doi.org/10.1177/1461444811412160.

Stanley-Becker, I. (2020, August 1). How the Trump campaign came to court QAnon, the online conspiracy movement identified by the FBI as a violent threat. *Washington Post*. https://www.washingtonpost.com/politics/how-the-trump-campaign-came-to-court-qanon-the-online-conspiracy-movement-identified-by-the-fbi-as-a-violent-threat/2020/08/01/ddoea9b4-d1d4-11ea-9038-af089b63ac21_story.html.

Teitelbaum, B. R. (2020). *War for eternity: The return of traditionalism and the rise of the populist right*. Penguin.

Tuters, M. and Hagen, S. (2020). (((They))) rule: Memetic antagonism and nebulous othering on 4chan. *New Media & Society*, *22*(12), pp. 2218–2237. https://doi.org/10.1177/1461444819888746.

Tuters, M., Jokubauskaitė, E., and Bach, D. (2018). Post-truth protest: How 4chan cooked up the Pizzagate bullshit. *M/C Journal*, *21*(3), Article 3. https://doi.org/10.5204/mcj.1422.

Tuters, M. and OILab. (2020). Esoteric fascism online: 4chan and the Kali Yuga. In L. D. Valencia-García (Ed.), *Far-right revisionism and the end of history: Alt/histories* (pp. 287–303). Routledge.

Venturini, T. and Latour, B. (2010). The social fabric: Digital footprints and quali-quantitative methods. *Proceedings of Futur En Seine 2009: The Digital Future of the City*. Futur en Seine 2009.

Voué, P., De Smedt, T., and De Pauw, G. (2020). 4chan & 8chan embeddings. *ArXiv:2005.06946 [Cs]*. http://arxiv.org/abs/2005.06946.

Wendling, M. (2018). *Alt-Right: From 4chan to the White House*. Pluto Press.

Willaert, T., Van Eecke, P., Beuls, K., and Steels, L. (2020). Building social media observatories for monitoring online opinion dynamics. *Social Media + Society*, *6*(2). https://doi.org/10.1177/2056305119898778.

Willaert, T., Van Eecke, P., Van Soest, J., and Beuls, K. (2021). A tool for tracking the propagation of words on Reddit. *Computational Communication Research*, *3*(1), pp. 117–132. https://doi.org/10.5117/CCR2021.1.005.WILL.

Woods, A. (2019). Cultural Marxism and the cathedral: Two alt-right perspectives on critical theory. In C. M. Battista and M. R. Sande (Eds.), *Critical theory and the humanities in the age of the alt-right* (pp. 39–59). Springer. https://doi.org/10.1007/978-3-030-18753-8_3.

Zannettou, S., Caulfield, T., Blackburn, J., De Cristofaro, E., Sirivianos, M., Stringhini, G., and Suarez-Tangil, G. (2018). On the origins of memes by means of fringe web communities. *ArXiv:1805.12512* [Cs]. http://arxiv.org/abs/1805.12512.

Funding

The authors received funding from the ODYCCEUS project within the European Union's Horizon 2020 program, grant agreement number 732942.

Data availability

Datasets with the monthly term counts for Breitbart comments and 4chan/pol/ counts for the periods under investigation are available from Zenodo at https://doi.org/10.5281/zenodo.5535341. The data do not contain any personal information or post-level metadata.

About the authors

Stijn Peeters, PhD, is Assistant Professor in Media Studies at the University of Amsterdam, Technical Director of the Digital Methods Initiative, and a co-investigator of the CAT4SMR project, where he has (co-)developed several research tools such as 4CAT. His research interests include the media-archaeological analysis of fringe communities on social media.

Tom Willaert, PhD, is a postdoctoral researcher in digital methods at the Vrije Universiteit Brussel. His research bridges methodological gaps between data science and humanities interpretative practice, with a focus on methods for the analysis of online (mis)information.

Marc Tuters, PhD, is a Senior Lecturer in Media Studies at the University of Amsterdam where his current research examines radical visual subcultures at the bottom of the Web together with colleagues at the Open Intelligence Lab as well as the Digital Methods Initiative.

Katrien Beuls, PhD, is Assistant Professor in artificial intelligence in the Faculty of Computer Science at the University of Namur. Her main research interests include emergent communication and language, and computational construction grammar.

Paul Van Eecke, PhD, is Assistant Professor in the Artificial Intelligence Laboratory at the Vrije Universiteit Brussel. His main research topics include the emergence and evolution of language through communicative interactions and computational construction grammar and its applications.

Jeroen Van Soest, MSc, is a developer and member of the Evolutionary and Hybrid AI team in the Artificial Intelligence Laboratory at the Vrije Universiteit Brussel (VUB). He has developed NLP tools and data science applications for the Horizon 2020 ODYCCEUS project and is VUB's lead developer on the imec-ICON Trendify project.

9 Political TikTok

Playful performance, ambivalent critique and event-commentary

Natalia Sánchez-Querubín, Shuaishuai Wang, Briar Dickey and Andrea Benedetti

Abstract

During the U.S. presidential election of 2020, TikTok, an app known for lip-synching and remixes of popular media, became a tool for ludic civic engagement, ambivalent critique and event-commentary. More specifically, TikTokers practiced types of engagement such as playful political performance, in which they express sentiments about a candidate by dancing or singing. They also practice remix as ambivalent critique by juxtaposing news clips and music to comment on current events. These examples evoke genres of ludic civic engagement such as flash mobs and tactical clowning while also exhibiting qualities specific to TikTok. The rhetorical power of playfulness and remix lies in distorting, exaggerating, and dramatizing; on TikTok, these practices are mainstream rather than fringe, raising questions about the contribution of the platform to political discourse.

Keywords: TikTok, remix video, playful engagement, ambivalent critique, event-commentary

Research questions

How are people using TikTok in the run-up to the 2020 U.S. presidential election, and how to characterize TikTokers' political engagement?

Rogers. R. (ed.), *The Propagation of Misinformation in Social Media: A Cross-platform Analysis.*
Amsterdam: Amsterdam University Press 2023
DOI: 10.5117/9789463720762_CH09

Essay summary

During the 2020 U.S. presidential election campaign season, TikTok, together with other social media platforms, served a great deal of political content in the form of short videos. In doing so, TikTok became "the default platform for millions of teenagers who want to educate themselves on issues, express their political ideologies and organize to take action" (Lorenz, 2020a). Journalists reported, for example, on the TikTok teenagers that "meme the vote" (Pardes, 2020), the activities of TikTok party-based coalitions or "hype houses" (Lorenz, 2020b) as well as the app's political misinformation problem.

These days people routinely use social media to engage with societal issues and events such as elections. For example, YouTube vloggers discuss politics and conspiracy theories. Some of them amass large audiences and become ideological (social media) influencers (Lewis, 2020; Creech and Maddox, 2020). Remixing news content is also a popular sense-making practice and form of cultural commentary (Geboers, 2019). Reactions to events circulate on Reddit, Twitter, Facebook, and 4Chan as memes and viral clips (Nagle, 2017; Tuters and Hagen, 2020). TikTok also assumed this role in the run-up to the elections through its well-known cultural practices of lip-synching and creating sketches involving audio clips from popular media. TikTok has been described as a "never-ending talent show" (Aroesti, 2019, para. 4), for which people create content by replicating, remixing, and adapting media and sounds.

Our research asks how people are using TikTok and its features politically. We analyze popular TikTok videos associated with the 2020 presidential candidates, Trump, Biden, and Sanders, using mixed methods. What we find supports the argument that TikTok is an emerging tool for ludic civic engagement, ambivalent critique, event-commentary as well as the main-streaming of polarizing satire. These findings are in line with the argument that online media can facilitate "participation through their performative, experimental, and creative affordances" (Glas et al., 2019, p. 11). Moreover, the practices that we explore in this chapter evoke ideas already familiar in media and political studies (e.g., using performance for political critique) while also exhibiting characteristics unique to TikTok as a medium. TikTok use during the elections is, in this way, a recent example of the convergence between "citizenship, media technologies, and play" (Glas et al., 2019, p. 11).

TikTok, we learn, remained "fresh" during the election cycle. The top videos associated with Trump, Biden, and Sanders returned by the app (1,000 videos per candidate), on two different dates, March 2020 and January 2021, showed little overlap. Also, each set of videos addressed events current when the queries were made, thus offering evidence that TikTok is an emergent event-commentary app.

Furthermore, two media practices were predominant amongst the most popular videos. On the one hand, people use TikTok to practice playful political performance. By "performance," we refer to how people use social media to stage a persona—in this case, a persona with a political stance—while dancing, acting, and singing. In addition, we differentiate three types of videos that involve this media practice. People "stage an opinion" about a candidate by acting and dancing, "document and share activities" like voting, and "give speeches." Medina et al. (2020) describe the politically engaged TikTok user in a similar way, namely, as a "performer who externalizes personal political opinion via an audio-visual act, with political communication becoming a far more interactive experience than on YouTube or Instagram" (2020, p. 264).

Secondly, we argue, TikTok users practice remix as ambivalent critique. That means they use the app to re-edit, modify, and juxtapose clips from the news and popular culture to comment on the elections. We see this practice in two types of videos. People "dramatize" news clips and remix each other's content to form counterarguments, which we call "partisan duetting and stitching." We add the term "ambivalent" to emphasize that the intent and tone of these remix videos is difficult to pinpoint. Humor and serious critique as well as engagement and disinterest appear to coexist in TikTok.

Fake news and conspiratorial narratives, we find, are mostly absent from the most popular content. However, the performative, playful, and ambiguous tone of the videos, as well as its hyperpartisan and humorous nature invite reflection about problematic behavior on the app and the contributions made to political discourse.

Implications

TikTok as an emerging app for event-commentary

Social media are described as "event-following machines" when content about an issue is fresh and aligns with current events. For instance, Twitter is the micro-blogging site where journalists, politicians, and lay people voice opinions about pressing matters and inform themselves about what is happening during and in the aftermath of protests, natural disasters, and cultural events (Rogers, 2014, 2020; Bruns and Weller, 2016; Rathnayake and Suthers, 2018). A "stale" social media, on the contrary, is no longer the go-to space to find information about what is happening or spread one's message. It is also not an ideal source of data for cultural analysis.

TikTok, we find, remained "fresh" during two different moments of the election cycle. The most popular videos associated with Donald Trump, Bernie Sanders, and Joe Biden, collected first in March 2020 and later, in January 2021, showed little overlap. Furthermore, each set of videos addressed events related to the elections that were important at the time the queries were made. For example, videos associated with Trump, collected in March 2020, featured clips from "Namaste Trump," a rally held in India in late February 2020. At the event, Trump was cheered by thousands of supporting Indians (Crowley, 2020). Throughout and after the event, people used TikTok to share their sentiment about the upcoming election and voting preferences. In February 2021, the most popular videos addressed, by contrast, the outcomes of the election and issues such as misinformation and the alleged voter fraud to which, according to Trump supporters, Biden owed his victory. These findings add weight to the emerging argument that TikTok is a platform for political communication, issue-formation, and event-commentary (Hautea, 2021).

Playful political performance: staging opinions, giving a speech, and documenting

In academic discussions, elections are theorized as theater, performance, and spectacles that depend on media coverage and are increasingly fashioned as entertainment (Chou and Roland, 2016). For example, politicians sit down for interviews on television shows. Magazines report on the holidays and fashion choices of presidential candidates, making them into spectacles. Public figures also promote themselves on social media like Twitter, a software platform, but also, metaphorically, a place from which to speak to one's followers (Gillespie, 2010). Conventions and rallies feature musical acts and guest artists that lend candidates an air of coolness.

Citizens also engage in political performance. Social media becomes a tool to stage a persona, with a political identity and stance. People use their social media accounts, for example, to share opinions about current issues, donate, and make public their political affiliations. Sharing news articles, posting selfies wearing campaign gear, creating memes, and recording videos talking about their experiences all can be forms of political performance.

TikTok is a space for citizen political performance, too, albeit of a particular playful nature. In the context of the U.S. elections, TikTokers, we find, combine political performance, in the sense of presenting a persona

Figure 9.1 "I voted for a man named Donald J. Trump" [video frames]. A TikTok user sings and dances to the pro-Trump song (and now, TikTok sound) "Great Again" by American musician James McCoy Taylor.

with a political stance online, with dancing, acting, and singing. When creating this content, they also experiment with video editing techniques such as zooming, soundtracks, filters, special effects, and greenscreens. We differentiate three types of TikTok videos that use playful political performance: "staging opinions," "giving a speech," and "documenting."

In Figure 9.1, a woman dances and sings along to the song "Great Again" by American musician James McCoy Taylor. The sound playing in the video features the verses, "I voted for a man named Donald J. Trump / 'Cause when they're playin' the anthem I stand up / I know that half of America will too / And we ain't scared of no Kim Jong-un." The video was posted as a response to a comment left on the woman's account, which is displayed also on the screen. It reads: "I followed you and now you lost me. No more Trump." In another video, a man sings along to the "Trump Theme Song." The song includes verses such as: "Racism / Bigotry / Lying / Polygamy / Immature asshole on God / Pride / Mediocrity / And how he handled Iran…" These two videos are examples of what we call "staging an opinion."

Scholarship on music and politics has observed that soundtracks create emotional intensity around political personas. According to musicologist James Deadville, specific sounds become associated with the different political camps and help "to create a collective identity and to construct consensus" (Deadville, 2015, p. 1). Songs are "written or modified for a specific candidate" and concerts become political spaces (Deadville, 2015, p. 1), like when the "Dixie Chicks lead singer Natalie Maines infamously dissed Bush at a 2003 concert in London" (Henwood, 2017). Likewise, at public appearances, conventions, and rallies, the public expects certain playlists. Organizers, Deadville (2015) explains, draw on new classics of patriotic and inspirational character such as Bruce Springsteen's song "Born in the U.S.A." for the Democrats. That "hardly any of the invited famous pop artists wanted to perform at [Donald Trump's] inauguration in January 2017" was reported extensively (Mehring, 2020, p. 22). Moreover, outside convention halls, "protesters staged their own media-driven spectacles replete with music (and speech)" (Deadville, 2015, p. 8).

The activity on TikTok offers a recent example of the role music plays during elections. When people "stage their opinions," not unlike during political rallies and conventions, the lyrics and mood of a song become proxies for their feelings about a candidate (Mehring, 2020; Deadville, 2015). Music also becomes a tool for contestation on TikTok. Trump supporters, for example, used clips from the song "Red Kingdom" as a soundtrack for their TikTok videos. Red Kingdom, however, was intended as an anthem for the Kansas City Chiefs, an American football team. Conservative TikTokers, according to a writer for the Kansas-based magazine *The Pitch*, "have trolled themselves into thinking that a song by a Black activist for a football team with a Black superstar quarterback was created for their hateful agenda" (Searles, 2020, para. 3). To address the misappropriation, liberal TikTokers "made videos to flood the sound 'tag' with positive, inclusive content to 'drown out' the hateful posts" (Searles, 2020). Luke Bryan's song "Country Girl (Shake It for Me)," similarly, was used by TikTokers as a nod to the "liberal cowboy," after it became public that the singer was not a Trump supporter (Lenzen, 2020). Also, YG and Nipsey Hussle's protest track "FDT" (F— Donald Trump) "made similar waves but never garnered as much TikTok fame as its conservative counterparts" (Konrad, 2021, para. 8).

The videos we discuss above were returned on top by TikTok's search engine when searching for the presidential candidates. They are successful examples of broader trends and thus linked to other videos on the app, both conceptually and technically by sounds and hashtags. Clicking on the hashtag "Red Kingdom" or the "Trump Theme Song" sound redirects users to other videos featuring these same auditory elements and engaging with the same video concept, for example, by replicating or parodying it. TikTok is, in this sense, an "evolving tapestr[y] of self-referential texts collectively created, circulated, and transformed by participants online" (Phillips and Miller, 2017, p. 30). On Facebook or Reddit, memes look like image macros annotated with text. There is scholarship that explores the role of these image-based memes in contemporary politics, uncovering fringe visual and textual cultures. TikTok meme behavior is, however, performative, in that "users replicate the same type of video or similar video concepts using a sound or effect over and over again" (Zulli and Zulli, 2020, p. 10). TikTok invites those interested in ludic civic engagement online to consider the role of music in a new light.

"Staging an opinion" on TikTok also resonates with practices of ludic civic engagement that make use not only of music but that also rely on theatrical and humorous interventions (Glas et al., 2019). Stunts, tactical clowning, critical play, the carnival, and flash mobs are examples of such ludic engagements. Majken Jul Sørensen (2016), a scholar specializing in the subject of humor in activism, argues that these genres "share a playful attitude towards expression of dissent and use various creative or artistic ways of communicating" (2016, p. 12). For example, in 2013, a Spanish radio show organized a flash mob in an unemployment office, at a time when Spain endured an unemployment rate of 26%. A small orchestra arrived unnoticed in the waiting room and played "Here Comes the Sun" by The Beatles (Urquhart, 2013). The intervention, while on the ground, aimed to spread awareness to Spain's growing economic crisis by going viral. On another occasion, students staged a flash mob by dancing to Michael Jackson's song "Thriller" in "full Zombie regalia to protest the death of public education in Chile" (Colquhounon, 2013, para. 4).

TikTok users also stage their opinions about the U.S. presidential elections using theatrical gestures evocative of flash mobs and clowning. In Figure 9.2, for instance, a man uses Kamala Harris and Joe Biden's heads as drums. The text on the video reads: "which of the two has the most hollow head?" In Figure 9.3, another man bops to the viral sound, *Bass Da Da Da*, which is a fragment from a song by the same name. The text on the screen reads: "Does anyone else hear 'thank God for Donald Trump?'" The critiques posed by the Spanish and Chilean flash mobs are clear—there is a discontent with current employment and education situations. Spectators may read into the symbology of a band of zombie dancing towards a public institution. In the TikTok videos we study there is, instead, ambiguity, a topic that we returned to in the next section. As a case in point, in Figure 9.2, the discontent with Biden and Harris is clear, however much one may not infer a stance or goal from the video.

Besides "staging an opinion," the two other types of videos that involve playful political performance are "giving a speech" and "documenting." Figure 9.4 is an example of "giving a speech"; in the video, a man turns the camera towards himself and warns viewers about the liberal party, without using dramatic embellishments such as music or the video editing capabilities of TikTok. "The hard left," he says, "throws not facts just slurs" and "doesn't care about facts or truth." Figure 9.5 is an example of "documenting." A man records himself from the inside of his car. The driver of the car beside him has stepped outside and is hitting his window with a metal bar.

Figure 9.2 "Hollow heads" [video frames]. In this TikTok video a man uses editing effects to play drums with the heads of the then presidential candidate, Joe Biden, and running mate, Kamala Harris. The text displayed on the video reads: "which of the two has the most hollow head?"

Figure 9.3 Thank God for Donald Trump? [video frames]. In this TikTok video, a man bops to the sound of *Bass Da Da Da*, a fragment from the song by the same name. The text on the screen reads: "Does anyone else hear 'thank God for Donald Trump?'"

Figure 9.4 "The left lies" [video frames]. A TikTok user turns the camera towards himself. He warns viewers about the liberal party. The hard left, he says, "throws not facts just slurs" and will avoid any facet of truth. According to him, the left "doesn't care about facts or truth."

Figure 9.5 "Is this what happens...?" [video frames]. A man records an alleged Trump supporter hitting his car window with a bar. The text "This is what happens when Trump supporters get mad. Someone identify him?" appears on the video.

Overlayed on the screen is the following text: "This is what happens when Trump supporters get mad. Someone identify him?"

"Giving a speech" and "documenting" are familiar online forms of political performance. We find examples of "documenting" on Twitter from instances of citizen journalism to call outs and requests to find the perpetrator of a transgression. On YouTube, Facebook Live, and Instagram Stories people talk politics and give speeches, albeit in longer form than on TikTok. "Staging an opinion" through TikTok speech-giving could be said to specific to TikTok.

Remix as ambivalent critique: Dramatization of media clips and partisan stitching and duetting

Remixing is a creative media practice. It involves reediting "television, movies, and news media for critical and political purposes" (McIntosh, 2012, para. 1). "Donald Duck Meets Glenn Beck in Right Wing Radio Duck," a remix video by artist Jonathan McIntosh, exemplifies the practice. Glenn Beck is an American conservative commentator, conspiracy theorist, and radio host. McIntosh edited audio from Beck's radio show with Disney cartoons, suggesting a narrative in which Donald Duck became radicalized. The aim of the piece was "to demonstrate how right-wing media paradoxically appears sympathetic while fear-mongering" (burrough and Dufour, 2018, p. 98).

Another example of remix is the parody video "Candidate Obama Debates President Obama on Government Surveillance." The creator juxtaposes clips from different interviews during Obama's career, "pointing out the inconsistencies in Obama's position on national security" (Nunes, 2018, p. 219–220). The video essay is yet another form of audio-visual criticism. Remixed footage has, indeed, been part of "experimental cinema and film criticism for a number of decades" (McWhirter, 2016, p. 372). Recently, also YouTube has seen an outburst of video essayists. These are all examples of what media scholar Henry Jenkins calls participatory politics, namely, instances of citizens having "the means of creating political commentary through the reuse and reappropriation of the media content that makes up the majority of our contemporary political discourse" (Nunes, 2018, p. 219).

Remixing is an important practice within TikTok. Users of the app tend to "comment on and rework existing cultural imaginaries and narratives by refashioning old media forms .... [T]his is immediately visible in TikTok users combining audio fragments from movies and TV news with mimicry to poke fun of current events" (Vijay and Gekker, 2021, p. 717). In line with these trends, in the context of the U.S. presidential elections, we found TikTokers practicing *remix as ambivalent critique*. That is to say, TikTokers are using the app to juxtapose, combine, and enhance audio-visual materials related to the elections. Amongst the most popular content are the videos we label as "dramatization of media clips" and "partisan duetting and stitching." We see them as medium-specific forms of remix and examples of participatory politics.

Figure 9.6. "Wait for it" [video frames]. The video is an example of "remix as ambivalent critique" and, specifically, of the "dramatization of media clips." A TikTok user edits together footage from the press conference when Trump insults Cecilia Vega, a journalist from ABC News, with images of a Trump look-a-like dancing before the slogan Trump 2020.

We labeled videos as "dramatization of media clips" when TikTok users juxtapose and re-edit news clips (e.g., fragments from a televised press conference) with other clips, text, sounds, and voiceover commentary. Bringing together news content with these new elements reframes and alters their meaning, often overstating, mocking, and exaggerating actions, or in other words, dramatizing them. Figure 9.6 is an example of this practice. The video includes footage from a press conference held in the White House, in October 2018. Donald Trump points to Cecilia Vega, a journalist from ABC News, signaling that she can ask him a question. The sentence "wait for it" appears on the video. Then, Trump says "she's shocked that I picked her... she's like in a state of shock... That's OK. I know you're not thinking. You never do." The video transitions into a Trump lookalike dancing in front of a background with the words Trump 2020—a visual punchline.

In another example of the "dramatization of media clips," a TikTok user records a segment from the late-night television show *Jimmy Kimmel Live!* and adds a laugh track (Figure 9.7). The show created a video including both real images of Trump's visit to Pope Francis and edited images of him allegedly taking Pope Francis's hand and then of Francis slapping it away. The sketch mocked Trump and the former first lady's cold relationship and a similar hand-slapping incident. The CNN logo is displayed on the video. This user seems to be in on the joke—the video is a parody. The *Jimmy Kimmel Live!* video, however, had to be debunked by fact-checker website Snopes (Evan, 2017), indicating that once outside the context of the television, not everyone was aware of its nature.

Similarly, a TikTok user records his television, where we see Joe Biden taking part in a *Wired* magazine "Autocomplete" interview in May 2020. During the segment, guests answer the most "Googled" questions about themselves (Figure 9.8). One of the questions for Biden is: Does Joe Biden have a brother? Biden responds by saying, "I got a sister who is the love of my life." The focus of the video shifts to a teenager, sitting in front of the television, playing "Sweet Home Alabama" on his guitar and tipping his hat. In this context, the song plays on the stereotype that incest abounds

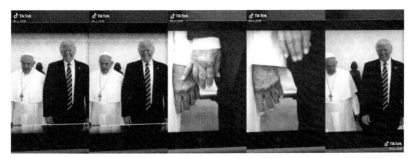

Figure 9.7 "Donald Trump and The Pope" [video frames]. A TikTok user records and overlaps with a laugh track a comedic sketch from the television show *Jimmy Kimmel Live!* where Trump appears to reach for Pope Francis's hand and the latter slapping it away.

Figure 9.8 **"Biden and his sister"** [video frames]. A TikTok user records his television as Joe Biden's *Wired* magazine "Autocomplete" interview plays. When asked if he has a brother, Joe Biden responds by saying, "I got a sister who is the love of my life." The focus of the video shifts to a teenager playing "Sweet Home Alabama" on his guitar and tipping his hat, joking that Biden's relationship with his sister might be inappropriate.

in the American South, hinting that Biden's relationship with his sister is inappropriate. This particular moment in the interview generated numerous memes.

Yet another memetic dynamic built into TikTok is the "duet" function. "Duet" means creating a split screen to display one's video side-by-side a video created by someone else. People "duet" to create a scene by bringing together two separate videos, dance parallel to someone else, or comment on content created by other TikTok users. If a person uses the "stitching" function, instead of having a split-screen, the videos are integrated into each other. It is often about re-using snippets of other people's video clips to create responses and remixes on the same theme. We find that these functions are used to engage with the elections and offer a TikTok-specific form of competition or contestation between political parties. We call this type of video "partisan duetting and stitching."

An example of duetting can be seen in Figure 9.9. The original video features a young Trump supporter, marching to the song "Kings & Queens" by Ava Max and lifting her hand towards the edge of the screen. The text on her screen reads, "let's start a chain of women for Trump." The invitation is for other women to post similar videos and to duet or stitch them together.

Figure 9.9 "Let's start a chain of women for Trump" [video frames]. A TikTok user invites women to record themselves marching to the song "Kings & Queens" by Ava Max and stitch them together to show support for Donald Trump. In the video, a man parodies the original video and mocks the content creator.

Figure 9.10 "When I can attract both genders" [video frames]. A TikTok user combs her eyebrows, while the sentence "when I can attract both genders" hovers on the screen. The video was stitched by a man wearing a Trump hat. He says "ahh, so there are only two genders. Thank you for proving my point sweetheart." He winks and tips his cap.

If they imitate the way the creator of the original video raises her hand, once the videos come together it would be like they were all holding hands. In Figure 9.9, however, it is a young man who responds and parodies the original video. He marches to the same song but when the time comes to join hands, he lifts an iron, even including a hissing sound. In yet another video, a Trump supporter uses a spray bottle to demonstrate how liquid goes through a mask. The video is "stitched" by a Biden supporter who conducts their own experiment, demonstrating that masks, indeed, work. In yet another example, in Figure 9.10, a young woman combs her eyebrows while the following text appears on the screen: "when I can attract both genders." The video is stitched by a man wearing a Trump hat. He says, "ahh, so there are only two genders. Thank you for proving my point sweetheart. He winks and tips his cap."

TikTok, one could argue, has popularized a new form of political remix video. Yet, this is not to say that the TikTok videos we study are the same as the work of artists as McIntosh, who are explicit about their political intent. TikTok videos are, instead, often ambivalent. We use the term ambivalent in similar fashion as Phillips and Milner (2017) and Tuters and Hagen (2020) do (see also Niederer and Colombo, this volume). These authors remark how online political communication (e.g., in forums as Reddit) is characterized by humor, absurdity, and a sense of detachment. It can be "antagonistic and social, creative and disruptive, humorous and barbed, the satirizing of products, antagonization of celebrities, and creation of questionable fan art" (Phillips and Milner, 2017, p. 10). Ambivalent can be understood in opposition to earnest or aligned with a clear agenda. TikTok, indeed, often leaves the viewer with the sensation that the absurdity of the current political reality is the object of critique. On TikTok, the lines between earnest and mocking entertainment and political engagement are constantly blurred—"sharing a 'funny' video that has a certain political stance does not mean committing or aligning to that politics" (Vijay and Gekker, 2021, p. 178).

TikTok's misinformation problem

We have presented three arguments so far. We first posit that TikTok remained "fresh" during the elections as evidence of its function as event-commentary medium. Then, we identified two media practices present in popular election-related videos: "playful political performance" and "remix as ambivalent critique." We also differentiate between types of videos that include these practices, such as "staging an opinion" and "dramatizing media clips." Furthermore, we discussed these videos and practices vis-à-vis playful activism, parody, and political remix videos. TikTok videos relate to these genres while also being medium-specific modes of ludic civic engagement. In this section, we revisit "playful political performance" and "remix as ambivalent critique" in relation to the issue of information disorders.

According to Claire Wardle (2017), co-founder of First Draft News, information disorders are types of content that raise concern in the context of issue-making and democratic process. Existing studies have already identified disorderly information on TikTok in the form of hyperpartisan, misleading content, manipulated content, and false context content about the U.S. presidential elections. For instance, Media Matters, a non-profit organization that scrutinizes right-leaning media, identified eleven examples of election conspiracies and misleading claims spreading on TikTok. These include videos with narratives about alleged voter fraud and a deceptively edited clip of Joe Biden, which accumulated hundreds of thousands of views (Little, 2020). To combat the problem, TikTok set up content guidelines for the elections and moderated "terms associated with hate speech, incitement to violence, or disinformation around voter fraud, such as ballot harvesting" (TikTok, 2021). Posting about conspiracies like QAnon and anti-vaccination narratives is now banned (TikTok, 2021). Media Matters reported that after their investigation, TikTok removed the flagged videos, reduced the discoverability of other problematic posts, and added banners linking suspicious content to authoritative sources about the election.

Among the most popular videos—from a subset of content returned in January 2021—there are no fake and conspiratorial videos, for example, associated with QAnon and other known, flagged topics. It is not entirely surprising given the app's information cleaning efforts. What we did find are videos in which misinformation is a topic. For example, in Figure 9.4 a man claims that the Democratic Party has no regard for the truth, a familiar argument amongst Trump supporters. This video is example of "playful political performance" and, specifically, "giving a speech." In another video, a TikToker duets an anti-mask video. They conduct an experiment that shows that masks actually block sprayed liquid. The parody clip created by *Jimmy Kimmel Live!* featured Pope Francis brushing of Trump's hand is fake and plays on rumors about Donald and Melania Trump's cold marriage. (As mentioned, the parody, nevertheless, had to be debunked by Snopes, the fact-checking organization.)

TikTok videos beyond the examples above invite yet another line of questioning. Playful performance, remix, and humor are dominant modes of expression on TikTok, and their meaning-making capacities depend on altering, juxtaposing, exaggerating, and dramatizing. The goal is not to correct remix and playfulness, or humor. These practices are not new and exist in forms of activism, political cartoon, and comedy shows. As we explored earlier in this chapter, they have important critical, civic, and political capacities to them by making "political issues into a piece of theater when their attacks on dominant discourses disrupt, subvert, oppose and transform business as usual" (Sørensen, 2016, p. 13). Yet a challenge TikTok poses, we argue, is considering playful performance, remix, and humor not as fringe critical practices but as mainstream modes for engaging with elections. Or, in other words, considering, for example, that one may learn about an event first through its parody or remix.

For example, *Ride It* by Regard is a viral sound for TikTokers to create finger dancing videos with word bubbles denoting cultural misunderstandings. These in-video texts usually display inaccurate representations of a culture, a nation or a minority group. In the Netherlands, for example, local creators use the sound to make videos indicating that not all Dutch people live in Amsterdam or the sunshine over the canals is a typical misrepresentation of Dutch life as wind and rain are a more common occurrence. For young voters in the U.S., the same sound is widely deployed to make dancing videos engaging with the "accusations" of being Trump supporters, which include "get called racist 24/7," "get yelled at for presenting facts," and "accused of not respecting women." Aligning with the study that finds sounds on TikTok functioning as a story builder to convey a specific message (Medina et al., 2020), Trump supporters employ the sound to suggest that these accusations are untrustworthy and even entertaining.

In another video, a young man wearing a "MAGA" hat performs a finger dance with the caption "not sorry if you're offended by facts," referring to "abortion is murder," "guns don't kill people, people do," and "taking away guns is unconstitutional." These are slickly produced videos, using creative tools at once to entertain and to put forward misunderstanding as the root of disagreement with Trump politics.

In the study of misinformation, parody or satire is said to sometimes fool the viewer, albeit unintentionally. Here we find that the sarcastic videos that parody candidates seem to be motivated by an intention to instill mistrust. Moreover, their lightheartedness could fool the viewers into thinking that it was just for fun. To consider here is how the "non-serious nature of TikTok further obscures its actions as a playfield for (political) persuasion" (Vijay and Gekker 2021, p. 714). TikTok has also raised concern "about its distorting impacts on political discourse and participation" (Vijay and Gekker, 2021, p. 714). Also challenging is the mainstreaming of ambivalence: what is labeled as "satire" is often hateful, polarizing and divisive content but it must not be taken seriously because it is a "joke."

Findings

Finding 1: TikTok is an event-commentary medium, active and topical during the election cycle. The hashtags linked to videos concerning the then-presidential candidates, Joe Biden (#biden2020), Donald Trump (#trump2020, #maga2020), and Bernie Sanders (#bernie2020), were active between March 2020 and February 2021. Comparing the 1,000 most engaged with videos on TikTok for each hashtag query in March 2020 and January 2021 revealed the most popular videos changed, an indication of activity. Popularity on TikTok is measured in terms of cumulative interactions, including the number of views, likes, comments, and shares that a video receives. The videos popular in 2020 and in 2021 have content that is highly topical. That is, it is connected to current events such as Trump's visit to India in 2020, the tensions with Iran, and Bernie Sanders dropping out of the race. They treat current events by way of remixing, dramatizing and in general manipulating or creating original media content based on those events. These digital activities are a key form of participating in the political discourse surrounding current events.

Finding 2: There are typical TikTok political engagement practices. The results of the coding of 120 TikTok videos collected in 2021 (30 per hashtag) resulted in 5 different types of videos, which were further subsumed under two media practices (see Table 9.1).

Table 9.1   Media practices and types of election-related TikTok videos.

Media practice	Video Concept	Description
Playful political performance	Staging an opinion	TikTok users engage in performative activities such as lip syncing, dancing or roleplaying to express their political ideas.
	Documenting/sharing	A pre-existing piece of media is reposted on TikTok with no meaning-altering embellishment.
	Giving a speech	TikTok users use only the video capacity of TikTok to record and share a short speech, with no editing or embellishment.
Remixing as ambivalent critique	Theatricalization of media	TikTok users add embellishments such as sounds, music, laugh tracks, dub dialogue or other editing techniques to existing media clips in a way that frames or alters the meaning of the original clip(s).
	Partisan stitching and duetting	TikTok users use the "stitching" tool, which places their own video next to another user's video, to create contrast with the latter. Often, the new video contests or mock's the content of the video it is stitched to.

Strategy	Count	Percentage
Theatricalization of media clips	48	40%
Documenting/ sharing	24	20%
Acting an opinion	19	15.8%
Stitching and duetting as contrast	5	4.2%
Giving a speech	2	1.7%
Other	22	18.3%

Methodology

The data was gathered using the TikTok-scraper (Drawrowfly, 2021), a software tool that uses TikTok's Web API to scrape media and related meta-information. We collected the 1,000 most popular videos associated with the hashtags #Trump2020, #maga2020, #biden, and #bernie2020 on March 23, 2020 and January 4, 2021. The scraper collected the video ID, username, date of creation, video URL, caption, hashtags, and engagement metrics such as view count for each of the videos. The dataset consists of 8,000 videos. We extracted the top 30 videos per hashtags, creating a subset of 120 videos. We answered the first research question by comparing the 1,000 videos collected for each of the hashtags on the two dates. Our goal was to determine if the most popular videos changed. The techniques used by TikTok users and the various types of political videos were identified through a qualitative exploration of the top 30 videos per hashtags. Each video from this sample was coded according to the performative and remix techniques used by its creator. This began with an open coding process to develop a consistent coding schedule which was then repeated several times. The four authors acted as coders and controlled for the consistency of the coding by employing an inter-researcher reliability test.

References

Aroesti, R. (2019, November 1). Why are teenagers on TikTok obsessed with an eerie 1950s song? *The Guardian*. https://www.theguardian.com/culture/2019/nov/01/why-are-teenagers-on-tiktok-obsessed-with-an-eerie-1950s-song.

Bruns, A. and Weller, K. (2016). Twitter as a first draft of the present: And the challenges of preserving it for the future. In *Proceedings of the 8th ACM Conference on Web Science (WebSci'16)* (pp. 183–189). ACM. https://doi.org/10.1145/2908131.2908174.

burrough, x. and Dufour, F. (2018). Creativity. In E. Navas, O. Gallagher, and x. burrough (Eds.) *Keywords in remix studies* (pp. 92–104). Routledge.

Caramanica, J. (2020, March 20). This "Imagine" cover is no heaven. *New York Times*. https://www.nytimes.com/2020/03/20/arts/music/coronavirus-gal-gadot-imagine.html.

Colquhoun, R. (2013, January 13). Political art and activism: Flash mob. National Collective. http://www.nationalcollective.com/2013/01/13/political-art-and-activism-flash-mob/.

Crowley, M. (2020, February 24) "America loves India," Trump declares at rally with Modi. *New York Times*. https://www.nytimes.com/2020/02/24/world/asia/trump-india.html.

De Zeeuw, D. and Tuters, M. (2020). Teh internet is serious business: On the deep vernacular web and its discontents. *Public Culture*, *16*(2), pp. 214–232. https://doi.org/10.1215/17432197-8233406.

Deadville, J. (2015). The sound of media spectacle: Music at the party conventions. *Music & Politics, 9*(2), pp. 1–24. https://doi.org/10.3998/mp.9460447.0009.205.

Drawrowfly. (2021). TikTok scraper [software]. https://github.com/drawrowfly/tiktok-scraper.

Evan, D. (2017, May 26). Did Pope Francis slap away President Trump's hand? *Snopes.* https://www.snopes.com/fact-check/pope-francis-trump-hand-slap/.

Geboers, M. (2019). "Writing" oneself into tragedy: Visual user practices and spectatorship of the Alan Kurdi images on Instagram. *Visual Communication.* https://doi.org/10.1177/1470357219857118.

Gekker, A. (2019). Playing with power: Casual politicking as a new frame for political analysis. In R. Glas, S. Lammes, M. de Lange, J. Raessens, and I. de Vries (Eds.) *The playful citizen: Civic engagement in a mediatized culture* (pp. 387–419). Amsterdam University Press.

Hautea, S., Parks, P., Takahashi, B., and Zeng, J. (2021). Showing they care (or don't): Affective publics and ambivalent climate activism on TikTok. *Social Media+ Society.* https://doi.org/10.1177/20563051211012344.

Konrad, C. (2021, January 28). Trump presidency permanently alters landscape of media. *The Maneater.* https://themaneater.com/trump-presidency-permanently-alters-landscape-of-media/.

Lenzen, C. (2020, November 9). This Luke Bryan song is an anti-Trump anthem on Tik-Tok. *The Daily Dot.* https://www.dailydot.com/irl/luke-bryan-anti-trump-tiktok/.

Lewis, R. (2020) "This is what the news won't show you": YouTube creators and the reactionary politics of micro-celebrity. *Television & New Media, 21*(2), pp. 201–217. https://doi.org/10.1177/1527476419879919.

Lorenz, T. (2020, November 4). Election night on TikTok: Anxiety, analysis and wishful thinking. *New York Times.* https://www.nytimes.com/2020/11/04/style/tiktok-election-night.html.

McIntosh, J. (2012). A history of subversive remix video before YouTube: Thirty political video mashups made between World War II and 2005. *Transformative Works and Cultures, 9.* https://doi.org/10.3983/twc.2012.0371.

McWhirter, A. (2015). Film criticism, film scholarship and the video essay. *Screen, 56*(3), pp. 369–377. https://doi.org/10.1093/screen/hjv044.

Medina Serrano, J.C., Papakyriakopoulos., O. and Hegelich S. (2020). Dancing to the partisan beat: A first analysis of political communication on TikTok. In *Proceedings of the 12th ACM Conference on Web Science,* pp. 257–266. https://doi.org/10.1145/3394231.3397916.

Nagle, A. (2017). *Kill all normies: Online culture wars from 4chan and Tumblr to Trump and the alt-right.* Zero Books.

Nunes, M. (2018). Parody. In E. Navas, O. Gallagher, and x. burrough (Eds.) *Keywords in remix studies* (pp. 217–229). Routledge.

Pardes, A. (2020, October 22). The TikTok teens trying to meme the vote. *Wired*. https://www.wired.com/story/tiktok-election-2020/.

Phillips, W. and Milner, R.M. (2017). *The ambivalent internet: Mischief, oddity, and antagonism online*. Polity.

Rathnayake, C., and Suthers, D.D. (2018). Twitter issue response hashtags as affordances for momentary connectedness. *Social Media+ Society*. https://doi.org/10.1177/2056305118784780.

Rogers, R. (2014). Debanalising Twitter: The transformation of an object of study. In K. Weller, A. Bruns, J. Burgess, M. Mahrt and C. Puschmann (Eds.), *Twitter and society* (pp. ix–xxvi). Peter Lang.

Rosenblatt, K. (2020, October 17). They can't vote, but they can meme: How these TikTokers are trying to get Biden elected. *NBC News*. https://www.nbcnews.com/pop-culture/viral/they-can-t-vote-they-can-meme-how-these-TikTokers-n1243555.

Salen, K. and Zimmerman, E. (2004). *Rules of play: Game design fundamentals*. MIT Press.

Searles, S. (2020, August 4). Republican Tik Tok thinks "Red Kingdom" by Tech N9ne is their new hype song; We're laughing. *The Pitch*. https://www.thepitchkc.com/republican-tik-tok-thinks-red-kingdom-by-tech-n9ne-is-their-new-hype-song-were-laughing/.

Schellewald, A. (2021). Communicative forms on TikTok: Perspectives from digital ethnography. *International Journal of Communication, 15*, pp. 1437–1457.

Smith Gale, S (2020, October 6). U.S. election 2020: TikTok gets pulled into the campaigns. *BBC News*. https://www.bbc.com/news/technology-54374710.

Tuters, M. and Hagen, S. (2020). (((They))) rule: Memetic antagonism and nebulous othering on 4chan. *New Media & Society, 22*(12), pp. 2218–2237. https://doi.org/10.1177/1461444819888746.

Urquhart, C. (2013, January 12). Here comes the sun flash mob cheers Spanish unemployment office. *The Guardian*. https://www.theguardian.com/world/2013/jan/12/here-comes-the-sun-spanish-unemployment-office.

Vijay, D. and Gekker, A. (2021). Playing politics: How Sabarimala played out on TikTok. *American Behavioral Scientist, 65*(5), pp. 712–734. https://doi.org/10.1177/0002764221989769.

Wardle, C. (2017, February 16). Fake news. It's complicated. First Draft. https://firstdraftnews.org/latest/fake-news-complicated/.

Zulli, D. and Zulli, D. J. (2020). Extending the internet meme: Conceptualizing technological mimesis and imitation publics on the TikTok platform. *New Media & Society*. https://doi.org/10.1177/1461444820983603.

About the authors

Natalia Sánchez-Querubín, PhD, is Assistant Professor at the University of Amsterdam. She works on digital media research and the intersection of social media with health stories and social issues.

Shuaishuai Wang, PhD, is Assistant Professor in the Department of Media and Communication at Xi'an Jiaotong – Liverpool University. His research lies at the intersection of platform studies, critical algorithm studies and digital culture.

Briar Dickey is a graduate of the Social and Cultural Science research master at Radboud University. His research takes an interdisciplinary, mixed methods approach to the examination of the far right, ontologies of gender, post-truth and identities online.

Andrea Benedetti is a PhD student in Design at the Politecnico di Milano, Italy. He works in the field of data visualization, studying the relationship between data, interfaces, and society from a designerly standpoint in order to find alternative ways to design technological artifacts.

Afterword: The misinformation problem and the deplatforming debates

The book arrives at the height of the "deplatforming" debates, which among other matters concern the editorial power of social media platforms, with questions about their authority and how they apply it in "arbitrating" sources, speech or truth. More specifically, the platforms' content moderation, as it is termed, includes warning, labeling, demoting as well as removing posts and users when they break platform rules. When a user is removed, it is called "deplatforming," but it may also refer to broader sanctioning such as suppression of content about multi-user movements such as QAnon, a wide-ranging conspiracy theory concerning the actions of operators inside government. Facebook, in particular, has sought to ban QAnon content, removing it from the platform.

The deplatforming debates also revolve around the extent to which the platforms are doing too much or too little moderation. They concern whether (and when) it is justified as well as effective (and for whom). While the volume authors do not address these questions directly, in the following I would like to take up what we have found when studying the "misinformation problem" and the contributions we can make to the debates, however indirectly.

In all, I touch on five points where the misinformation problem relates to the deplatforming discussion: the classification of problematic content (and its politics), platform privileging of certain content and users, the work put into establishing editorial authority, the difference in content moderation per platform as well as the methodological challenges (and opportunities) in studying content and user removal. Each is taken in turn, whereupon I conclude with a modest proposal to re-orient the discussion.

Especially in the Facebook chapter but also in others, we have taken a common approach to classifying sources as problematic or less so. The approach is both historicized as well as comparative. By historicized, I mean

Rogers. R. (ed.), *The Propagation of Misinformation in Social Media: A Cross-platform Analysis.* Amsterdam: Amsterdam University Press 2023
DOI: 10.5117/9789463720762_AFTER

that there has been an evolution in the definition and terminology of what was incipiently referred to as "fake news" in 2016 by Craig Silverman of *BuzzFeed News*, when writing up his findings concerning the types of sources that were performing well on Facebook in the run-up to the U.S. presidential elections (2016). When comparing engagement scores, or tallies of likes, shares and comments, he found that those from fly-by-night, imposter as well as "hyperpartisan" sources received more engagement than those he called mainstream. Subsequent scholarly work expanded the types of sources under study to "problematic information" as well as "junk news," adding (for example) satire as well as "computational propaganda" which includes amplification efforts such as fake followers and bot work (Jack, 2017; Bolsover & Howard, 2018). Facebook but also certain journalists, for their part, then narrowed the classification of problematic content to "false news," focusing on hoaxes and imposter sources and removing from the definition the "hyperpartisan," originally referring to "openly ideological web operations" (Herrman, 2016). Nowadays the term misinformation (which would include non-intentional falsehoods) is enjoying currency as an umbrella term. The evolution of the definitional led us to consider a comparative perspective where we found that an ample classification (including hyperpartisan) would enlarge the misinformation problem and a narrower definition (excluding hyperpartisan) would reduce its size, making it more ordinary. There is an accompanying political dimension, given that the hyperpartisan sources (receiving the highest engagement) are often more conservative in bent, at least at the time of writing. When classifying them as fake, junk or problematic, the adjectives become sectarian markers, and any content moderation along those definitional lines seems to take sides and invites backlash.

As related particularly in the Twitter studies, the second observation concerns which content as well as users are privileged by platforms. For some time during our work, a *New York Times* journalist would tweet the most engaged-with sources on Facebook, pointing out how they disproportionately favor hyperpartisan, conservative sources (Owen, 2021). A subsequent debate between the journalist and a Facebook representative took up whether those sources were enjoying as much exposure as the engagement metric might suggest, ultimately pointing to Facebook data in company transparency reports showing how the results of another metric—reach—indicate otherwise. In fact, that data seemed to show that Facebook has a problem with "spammy, clickbait" content, apart from that of the popularity of its "right-wing pages" (Warzel, 2021). The discussion points up the question of which users and content do well, metrically, both overall as well as per social media platform. It was at least partially answered in the exposé of Facebook's privileging mechanisms, made possible by the former Facebook employee, Frances Haugen, who presented news organizations with internal documents showing, among other things, that Facebook boosts posts which have received "angry" reactions over those who have been merely "liked." Thus, one is able to score higher or have greater impact with posts that make other users reply with anger. No similar whistle-blowing revelations have been made of other platforms, but on Twitter, we made a finding akin to the *New York Times* journalist's. Hyperpartisan sources receive a disproportionate amount of retweets, compared to other source types. Apart from the spammy or clickbait-like, driving engagement on major social media platforms are source types variously characterized as "misinformation, toxicity and low-quality news" (Merrill and Oremus, 2021). As platforms crack down on such content as misinformation and toxicity, it follows that they are moderating popular material, which attracts attention to such moderation rather than keeping it out of sight, as was the case with commercial content moderation from the beginning.

Prior to the fake news crisis of 2016 and beyond, the critique made of social media content moderation concerned the kind of "soul-crushing" labor behind it (Chen, 2014). Low-wage and outsourced, content moderation workers did not enjoy the status (and benefits) of company employees (Roberts, 2016). They also worked at a rapid pace, monitored for their capacity to decide accurately which disturbing content should be deleted or ignored. In our study we focus on the type of content that rises to the top when users engage with posts concerning national elections and the COVID-19 pandemic. Such material may intersect with the areas of conventional content moderation (such as violence and pornography) but are also moderated, rather exceptionally, for misinformation. The labor still could be called content moderation by the companies, but given the partnerships made with fact-checking organizations to undertake some of it, it more readily would be called editorial (Perez, 2021). We discuss those social media platforms and search engines specifically targeting misinformation around national elections and the pandemic (including, in our study, Facebook, Instagram, Twitter, TikTok as well as Google Web Search) as employing "editorial epistemologies," curating lists of authoritative sources returned for election- and pandemic-related queries and otherwise adjudicating content either automatically detected or flagged by users as problematic. It is arguably novel editorial work undertaken by the platforms and opens the questions of which other subject matters apart from elections and the pandemic should also deserve scrutiny and which expertise is required. For example, is climate change or another pressing social issue so deserving? The shift in moderation culture would put the platforms on a footing where authority for content demotion or deplatforming is achieved by editorial expertise and delivered as fact checks.

As has been pointed out, all platforms perform content moderation, and it could be considered at the heart of a platform's business model (Gillespie, 2018). The extent of its presence as well as its absence are objects of study, given how certain platforms have emerged known as "alt tech" that explicitly trade on low moderation or "free speech." They do not profess to the practice of deplatforming. For the platforms under study here, 4chan could be said to offer the least content moderation and Facebook (and Instagram) perhaps the most. Whether the platform has high or low content moderation is worthy of study, but also of interest is which actors platforms privilege. One could argue that platforms privilege their own "performers" rather than, say, news organizations. These performers may post hyperpartisan content, thereby making it more prominent on the platform. Indeed, as we reported in one of the Twitter chapters, mainstream news is marginalized not through a lack of content moderation per se but rather by virtue of the abundance of hyperpartisan sources present in the posts that perform well on the medium.

Finally, there are methodological challenges in studying deplatforming, and its connection to the misinformation problem, for the content is no longer available for scrutiny. It is also demanding to study demotion, especially if one relies on engagement metrics to surface pertinent content for study. Having been demoted, it is no longer ranked highly. One avenue is taken in the 4chan chapter, which ultimately deals with the extent to which an "alternative influence network" is influential there. The researchers extracted the links from a 4chan board and examined the extent to which they point to YouTube alt-influencers, especially on the right of the political spectrum. The approach may be called "platform perspectivism," whereby one uses the data available on one platform to study another. The approach previously was used to create a list of extreme YouTube videos linked from 4chan in order to check whether they are still available on the video sharing platform. Some had been deleted whereas others remained online, raising the question of the threshold for removal as well as the technique for identification. With respect to demotion, at the time of our study, TikTok introduced content removal or suppression policies which it later expanded to videos concerning the war in Ukraine. While not explicitly undertaken in the TikTok study, its approach offers a means to study demotion. Continually archiving of the results of a query (as ranked video URL lists) and graphing their ranked placement overtime would show whether there are any precipitous dips of single videos compared to the others in the list.

In conclusion, research on misinformation recalls debates about the quality of information on the internet more generally and content moderation discussions about approaches to make "relevant" sources rise to the top of search engine rankings (and what relevance means). The debates continued with the shift in emphasis to the effects of personalization as a "solution" to the relevance problem. Personalization brought with it the atomization or individualization of media exposure. Individual feeds on social media, optimized for one's interests but also for one's trigger points (so to speak), are in a sense a further extension of personalization together with a more evident affective component, with the canonical example now being how Facebook optimizes for "angry" content or "angertainment." When we find that social media, which dominates as an informational medium, is marginalizing the mainstream and mainstreaming the fringe, we are returning to the question of how to address the quality of information online but also how to handle the affective dimension. These are somewhat different points of departure from the question of whether or when to deplatform misinformation, but they could be re-introduced to guide the discussions.

Richard Rogers
Amsterdam, November 2022

References

Bolsover, G. and Howard, P. (2019). Chinese computational propaganda: Automation, algorithms and the manipulation of information about Chinese politics on Twitter and Weibo. *Information, Communication & Society*, 22(14). https://doi.org/10.1080/1369118X.2018.1476576.

Chen, A. (2014, October 23). The laborers who keep dick pics and beheadings out of your Facebook feed. *Wired*. https://www.wired.com/2014/10/content-moderation/.

Gillespie, T. (2018). *Custodians of the internet: Platforms, content moderation, and the hidden decisions that shape social media*. Yale University Press.

Herrman, John (2016, August 28). Inside Facebook's (totally insane, unintentionally gigantic, hyperpartisan) political-media machine. *New York Times*. https://www.nytimes.com/2016/08/28/magazine/inside-facebooks-totally-insane-unintentionally-gigantic-hyperpartisan-political-media-machine.html.

Jack, C. (2017). Lexicon of lies: Terms for problematic information. Data & Society Research Institute. https://datasociety.net/library/lexicon-of-lies/.

Merrill, J. B. and Oremus, W. (2021, October 26). Five points for anger, one for a "like": How Facebook's formula fostered rage and misinformation. *Washington Post*. https://www.washingtonpost.com/technology/2021/10/26/facebook-angry-emoji-algorithm/.

Owen, L. H. (2021, July 14). At first, Facebook was happy that I and other journalists were finding its tool useful...but the mood shifted. NiemanLab. https://www.niemanlab.org/2021/07/at-first-facebook-was-happy-that-i-and-other-journalists-were-finding-its-tool-useful-but-the-mood-shifted/.

Perez, S. (2021, August 2). Twitter partners with AP and Reuters to address misinformation on its platform. *TechCrunch*. https://techcrunch.com/2021/08/02/twitter-partners-with-ap-and-reuters-to-address-misinformation-on-its-platform/.

Roberts, S. T. (2016). Commercial content moderation: Digital laborers' dirty work. In S. U. Noble and B. Tynes (Eds.) *The intersectional internet: Race, sex, class and culture online* (pp. 147–160), Peter Lang.

Silverman, C. (2016, November 16) This analysis shows how viral fake election news stories outperformed real news on Facebook. *Buzzfeed News*. https://www.buzzfeednews.com/article/craigsilverman/viral-fake-election-news-outperformed-real-news-on-facebook.

Warzel, C. (2021, November 11). Facebook's vast wasteland. *The Atlantic Monthly*. https://newsletters.theatlantic.com/galaxy-brain/618ad9942e822d00205a26b3/facebooks-vast-wasteland/.

Bibliography

Achenbach, J. and Johnson, C. Y. (2020, April 30). Studies leave question of "airborne" coronavirus transmission unanswered. *Washington Post*. https://www.washingtonpost.com/health/2020/04/29/studies-leave-question-airborne-coronavirus-transmission-unanswered/.

Adams, A. (2016, August 25). SHOCKING: Joe Biden discusses the left's globalist agenda. https://www.youtube.com/watch?v=KaCBYrVsic4.

Adams, A. (2020, November 20). KRAKEN UNLEASHED: The press conference they don't want you to see... https://www.youtube.com/watch?v=_u34jhCKT2U.

AFP. (2021). AFP Factcheck Nederland, Agence France-Presse. https://factchecknederland.afp.com/list.

Ahmadi, A.A. and Chan, E. (2020). Online influencers have become powerful vectors in promoting false information and conspiracy theories. First Draft. https://firstdraftnews.org/latest/influencers-vectors-misinformation/.

Alba, D. (2020, June 1). Misinformation about George Floyd protests surges on social media. *New York Times*. https://www.nytimes.com/2020/06/01/technology/george-floyd-misinformation-online.html.

Allcott, H., Gentzkow, M. and Yu, C. (2019). Trends in the diffusion of misinformation on social media. *Research & Politics*, April–June 2019: 1–8. https://doi.org/10.1177/2053168019848554.

AllSides (2020). Media Bias Ratings. https://www.allsides.com/media-bias/media-bias-ratings#ratings.

Alter, J. [jonathanalter]. (2021, Jan 01). "If we 'move on', the GOP will refuse to concede future elections, then judge-shop until they steal one. There must be a price paid for sedition or we will lose our democracy. This is critically important work in the next couple of years" [tweet]. https://twitter.com/jonathanalter/status/1345074521561292800.

American Military News (2016, May 23). Article removed—Here's why. *American Military News*, https://americanmilitarynews.com/2016/05/donald-trump-sent-his-own-plane-to-transport-200-stranded-marines/.

Annany, M. (2018, April 4). The partnership press: Lessons for platform-publisher collaborations as Facebook and news outlets team to fight misinformation. *Columbia Journalism Review*. https://www.cjr.org/tow_center_reports/partnership-press-facebook-news-outlets-team-fight-misinformation.php.

Aroesti, R. (2019, November 1). Why are teenagers on TikTok obsessed with an eerie 1950s song? *The Guardian*. https://www.theguardian.com/culture/2019/nov/01/why-are-teenagers-on-tiktok-obsessed-with-an-eerie-1950s-song.

Bail, C.A., Argyle, L.P., Brown, T.W., Bumpus, J.P., Chen, H., Hunzaker, M.B.F., Lee, J., Mann, M., Merhout, F., and Volfovsky, A. (2018). Exposure to opposing views on social media can increase political polarization. *Proceedings of the National Academy of Sciences*, *115*(37), pp. 9216–9221. https://doi.org/10.1073/pnas.1804840115.

Barkun, M. (2016). Conspiracy theories as stigmatized knowledge. *Diogenes*, *62*(3–4). https://doi.org/10.1177/0392192116669288.

Barnidge, M. (2017). Exposure to political disagreement in social media versus face-to-face and anonymous online settings. *Political Communication*, *34*(2), pp. 302–321. https://doi.org/10.1080/10584609.2016.1235639.

Barnidge, M. and Peacock, C. (2019). A third wave of selective exposure research? The challenges posed by hyperpartisan news on social media. *Media and Communication*, 7(3), pp. 4–7. https://doi.org/10.17645/mac.v7i3.2257.

Bartlett, J. and Krasodomski-Jones, A. (2015). Counter-speech: Examining content that challenges extremism online. Demos. http://www.demos.co.uk/wp-content/uploads/2015/10/Counter-speech.pdf.

Bauman, Z. (2013). *Does the richness of the few benefit us all?* Polity.

Bengani, P. (2019, December 18). Hundreds of "pink slime" local news outlets are distributing algorithmic stories and conservative talking points. Tow Center for Journalism, Columbia University. https://www.cjr.org/tow_center_reports/hundreds-of-pink-slime-local-news-outlets-are-distributing-algorithmic-stories-conservative-talking-points.php.

Benkler, Y. (2006). *The wealth of networks: How social production transforms markets and freedom*. Yale University Press.

Benkler, Y., Faris, R. and Roberts, H. (2018). *Network propaganda: Manipulation, disinformation, and radicalization in American politics*. Oxford University Press.

Benkler, Y., Faris, R., Roberts, H. and Zuckerman, E. (2017, March 3). Study: Breitbart-led right-wing media ecosystem altered broader media agenda. *Columbia Journalism Review*. https://www.cjr.org/analysis/breitbart-media-trump-harvard-study.php.

Beran, D. (2019). *It came from something awful: How a toxic troll army accidentally memed Donald Trump into office*. St. Martin's Publishing Group.

Berger, J. and Milkman, K. L. (2012). What makes online content viral? *Journal of Marketing Research,* *49*(2), 192–205. https://doi.org/10.1509/jmr.10.0353

Bernstein, J. (2015, July 27). Behind the racist hashtag that is blowing up Twitter. *BuzzFeed News*. https://www.buzzfeednews.com/article/josephbernstein/behind-the-racist-hashtag-some-donald-trump-fans-love.

Bernstein, J. (2017, October 5). Here's how Breitbart and Milo smuggled Nazi and white nationalist ideas into the mainstream. *BuzzFeed News*. https://www.

buzzfeednews.com/article/josephbernstein/heres-how-breitbart-and-milo-smuggled-white-nationalism.

Bernstein, M., Monroy-Hernández, A., Harry, D., André, P., Panovich, K., and Vargas, G. (2011). 4chan and /b/: An analysis of anonymity and ephemerality in a large online community. *Proceedings of the International AAAI Conference on Web and Social Media*, 5(1), Article 1. https://ojs.aaai.org/index.php/ICWSM/article/view/14134.

Berry, J. and Sobieraj, S. (2014). *The outrage industry*. Oxford University Press.

Blackburn, J. (2018, February 16). *How 4chan and The_Donald influence the fake news ecosystem*. FIC Observatory. https://observatoire-fic.com/en/how-4chan-and-the_donald-influence-the-fake-news-ecosystem-by-jeremy-blackburn-university-of-alabama-at-birmingham/.

Bolsover, G. and Howard, P. (2019). Chinese computational propaganda: Automation, algorithms and the manipulation of information about Chinese politics on Twitter and Weibo. *Information, Communication & Society*, 22(14).

Boltanski, L. (1999). *Distant suffering: Morality, media and politics.* Cambridge University Press.

Bond, S. (2021, March 9) Instagram suggested posts to users. It served up COVID-19 falsehoods, study finds. NPR. https://www.npr.org/2021/03/09/975032249/instagram-suggested-posts-to-users-it-served-up-covid-19-falsehoods-study-finds.

Bordia, P. and Difonzo, N. (2004). Problem solving in social interactions on the internet: Rumor as social cognition. *Social Psychology Quarterly*, 67(1), pp. 33–49. https://doi.org/10.1177/019027250406700105.

Borra, E. and Rieder, B. (2014). Programmed method: Developing a toolset for capturing and analyzing tweets. *Aslib Journal of Information Management*, 66(3), pp. 262–278. https://doi.org/10.1108/AJIM-09-2013-0094.

Bostrom, A., Joslyn, S., Pavia, R., Walker, A. H., Starbird, K., and Leschine, T. M. (2015). Methods for communicating the complexity and uncertainty of oil spill response actions and tradeoffs. *Human and Ecological Risk Assessment: An International Journal*, 21(3), pp. 631–645. https://doi.org/10.1080/10807039.2014.947867.

Bounegru, L., Gray, J., Venturini, T. and Mauri, M. (2018). *A field guide to "fake news" and other information disorders*. Public Data Lab.

Bovet, A. and Makse, H.A. (2019). Influence of fake news in Twitter during the 2016 U.S. presidential election. *Nature Communications*, 10(1), p. 7. https://doi.org/10.1038/s41467-018-07761-2.

Boxell, L., Gentzkow, M., and Shapiro, J. (2017). Is the internet causing political polarization? Evidence from demographics. National Bureau of Economic Research. http://www.nber.org/papers/w23258.

Boxell, L., Gentzkow, M., and Shapiro, J. M. (2020). Cross-country trends in affective polarization. National Bureau of Economic Research. https://www.nber.org/papers/w26669.

Boyd, R. L., Spangher, A., Fourney, A., Nushi, B., Ranade, G., Pennebaker, J., and Horvitz, E. (2018). *Characterizing the Internet Research Agency's social media operations during the 2016 U.S. presidential election using linguistic analyses* [Preprint]. PsyArXiv. https://doi.org/10.31234/osf.io/ajh2q.

Bozdag, E. and Van den Hoven, J. (2015). Breaking the filter bubble: Democracy and design. *Ethics and Information Technology, 17*(4), 249–65. https://doi.org/10.1007/s10676-015-9380-y.

Bradshaw, S. and Howard, P. N. (2018). Challenging truth and trust: A global inventory of organized social media manipulation. Computational Propaganda Research Project. Oxford Internet Institute. https://demtech.oii.ox.ac.uk/wp-content/uploads/sites/93/2018/07/ct2018.pdf.

Bruns, A. (2019). *Are filter bubbles real?* Polity Press.

Bruns, A. and Weller, K. (2016). Twitter as a first draft of the present: And the challenges of preserving it for the future. In *Proceedings of the 8th ACM Conference on Web Science (WebSci'16)* (pp. 183–189). ACM. https://doi.org/10.1145/2908131.2908174.

Bruns, A., Harrington, S. and Hurcombe, E. (2020) Corona? 5G? Or both?: The dynamics of COVID-19/5G conspiracy theories on Facebook. *Media International Australia, 177*(1). https://doi.org/10.1177/1329878X20946113.

Burkhardt, J.M. (2017). Combating fake news in the digital age. *ALA Library Technology Reports*, 53(8): pp. 5–9. https://doi.org/10.5860/ltr.53n8.

Burley, S. (2017). Disunite the right: The growing divides in the pepe coalition. Political Research Associates. https://www.politicalresearch.org/2017/09/19/disunite-the-right-the-growing-divides-in-the-pepe-coalition.

burrough, x. and Dufour, F. (2018). Creativity. In E. Navas, O. Gallagher, and x. burrough (Eds.) *Keywords in remix studies* (pp. 92–104). Routledge.

Burton, A. and Koehorst, D. (2020). The spread of political misinformation on online subcultural platforms. *Harvard Kennedy School Misinformation Review, 1*(6). https://doi.org/10.37016/mr-2020-40.

Buyukozturk, B., Gaulden, S. and Dowd-Arrow, B. (2018). Contestation on Reddit, Gamergate, and movement barriers. *Social Movement Studies, 17*(5), pp. 592–609. https://doi.org/10.1080/14742837.2018.1483227

BuzzSumo. (2020). Buzzsumo media monitoring. https://buzzsumo.com.

Callery, A. and Proulx, D.T. (1997) Yahoo! cataloging the web. *Journal of Internet Cataloging, 1*(1). https://doi.org/10.1300/J141v01n01_06.

Caplow, T. (1946). Rumors in war departmental contributions: Teaching and research in the social sciences. *Social Forces*, *25*(3), pp. 298–302. https://heinonline.org/HOL/P?h=hein.journals/josf25andi=314.

Captain, S. (2017, March 8). Disqus grapples with hosting toxic comments on Breitbart and extreme-right sites. *Fast Company*. https://www.fastcompany.com/3068698/disqus-grapples-with-hosting-toxic-comments-on-breitbart-and-extreme-right-sites.

Caramanica, J. (2020, March 20). This "Imagine" cover is no heaven. *New York Times*. https://www.nytimes.com/2020/03/20/arts/music/coronavirus-gal-gadot-imagine.html.

Center for Countering Hate (2021, March 9) Malgorithm: How Instagram's algorithm publishes misinformation and hate to millions during a pandemic. https://252f2edd-1c8b-49f5-9bb2-cb57bb47e4ba.filesusr.com/ugd/f4d9b9_89ed644926aa4477a442b55afbeac00e.pdf.

Centers for Disease Control and Prevention. (2020, April 1). Healthcare professionals: Frequently asked questions and answers. Centers for Disease Control and Prevention. https://web.archive.org/web/20200401051025/https://www.cdc.gov/coronavirus/2019-ncov/hcp/faq.html.

Cernovich, M. (2016, September 14). Un/Convention: Exposing fake news at the RNC and DNC. YouTube video. https://www.youtube.com/watch?v=cNwgKR88UD0.

Chadwick, A. (2017). *The hybrid media system: Politics and power.* Oxford University Press.

Chen, A. (2014, October 23). The laborers who keep dick pics and beheadings out of your Facebook feed. *Wired*. https://www.wired.com/2014/10/content-moderation/.

Chu, J. and McDonald, J. (2020, January 29). Helping the world find credible information about novel #coronavirus. Twitter Blog. https://blog.twitter.com/en_us/topics/company/2020/authoritative-information-about-novel-coronavirus.

Coleman, E.G. (2014). *Hacker, hoaxer, whistleblower, spy: The many faces of Anonymous.* Verso.

Coleman, K. (2021). Introducing Birdwatch, a community-based approach to misinformation. https://blog.twitter.com/en_us/topics/product/2021/introducing-birdwatch-a-community-based-approach-to-misinformation.html.

Colley, T. and Moore, M. (2020). The challenges of studying 4chan and the Alt-Right: "Come on in the water's fine." *New Media & Society*. https://doi.org/10.1177/1461444820948803.

Colombo, G. and De Gaetano, C. (2020). Dutch political Instagram. Junk news, follower ecologies and artificial amplification. In R. Rogers and S. Niederer (Eds.), *The politics of social media manipulation* (pp. 147–168). Amsterdam University Press.

Colquhoun, R. (2013, January 13). Political art and activism: Flash mob. National Collective. http://www.nationalcollective.com/2013/01/13/political-art-and-activism-flash-mob/.

Comscore (2019). Comscore March 2019 top 50 multi-platform website properties (desktop and mobile). https://www.comscore.com/Insights/Rankings.

Conger, K. (2021). Twitter, in widening crackdown, removes over 70,000 QAnon accounts. *New York Times*. https://www.nytimes.com/2021/01/11/technology/twitter-removes-70000-qanon-accounts.html.

Cooper, Sara (2020). How to medical, TikTok video. https://www.tiktok.com/@whatchugotforme/video/6819061413877763334.

Coppins, M. (2020, March). The billion-dollar disinformation campaign to reelect the president. *The Atlantic*. https://www.theatlantic.com/magazine/archive/2020/03/the-2020-disinformation-war/605530/.

Courtois, C., Slechten, L., and Coenen, L. (2018). Challenging Google Search filter bubbles in social and political information: Disconforming evidence from a digital methods case study. *Telematics and Informatics, 35*(7), pp. 2006–2015. https://doi.org/10.1016/j.tele.2018.07.004.

Crowley, M. (2020, February 24) "America loves India," Trump declares at rally with Modi. *New York Times*. https://www.nytimes.com/2020/02/24/world/asia/trump-india.html.

Dailey, D. and Starbird, K. (2015). "It's raining dispersants": Collective sensemaking of complex information in crisis contexts. In *Proceedings of the 18th ACM Conference Companion on Computer Supported Cooperative Work and Social Computing*, pp. 155–158. https://doi.org/10.1145/2685553.2698995.

Dan, O. and Davison, B. D. (2016). Measuring and predicting search engine users' satisfaction. *ACM Computing Surveys, 49*(1), pp. 1–35. https://doi.org/10.1145/2893486.

Daniels, J. (2018). The algorithmic rise of the "alt-right." *Contexts, 17*(1). https://doi.org/10.1177/1536504218766547.

Day, V. and Eagle, J. R. (2016). *Cuckservative: How "conservatives" betrayed America*. Castalia House.

De Keulenaar, E., Burton, A.G., and Kisjes, I. (2021). Deplatforming, demotion and folk theories of Big Tech persecution. *Fronteiras – Estudos Midiáticos, 23*(2), pp. 118–139. https://doi.org/10.4013/fem.2021.232.09.

De Zeeuw, D. and Tuters, M. (2020). Teh internet is serious business: On the deep vernacular web and its discontents. *Cultural Politics, 16*(2), pp. 214–232. https://doi.org/10.1215/17432197-8233406.

De Zeeuw, D., Hagen, S., Peeters, S., and Jokubauskaite, E. (2020). Tracing normiefication. *First Monday*. https://doi.org/10.5210/fm.v25i11.10643.

Deadville, J. (2015). The sound of media spectacle: Music at the party conventions. *Music & Politics, 9*(2), pp. 1–24. https://doi.org/10.3998/mp.9460447.0009.205.

Dean, J. (1998). *Aliens in America*. Cornell University Press.

Delli Carpini, M.X. (2018). Alternative facts: Donald Trump and the emergence of a new U.S. media regime. In Z. Papacharissi and P. Boczkowski (Eds.), *Trump and the media* (pp. 17–23). MIT Press.

Diakopoulos, N., Trielli, D., Stark, J., and Mussenden, S. (2018). I Vote For—How Search Informs Our Choice of Candidate. In M. Moore and D. Tambini (Eds.), *Digital dominance: The power of Google, Amazon, Facebook and Apple* (pp. 320–341). Oxford University Press.

Digital Methods Initiative. (n.d.). *Search Engine Scraper*. https://wiki.digitalmethods.net/Dmi/ToolSearchEngineScraper.

DiResta, R., Shaffer, K., Ruppel, B., Sullivan, D., Matney, R., Fox, R., Albright, J. and Johnson, B. (2018). The tactics & tropes of the Internet Research Agency. New Knowledge. https://disinformationreport.blob.core.windows.net/disinformation-report/NewKnowledge- Disinformation-Report-Whitepaper.pdf.

Donovan, J. (2019). How memes got weaponized: A short history. *MIT Technology Review*. https://www.technologyreview.com/2019/10/24/132228/political-war-memes-disinformation/.

Donovan, J. and boyd, d. (2018, June 1). The case for quarantining extremist ideas. *The Guardian*. http://www.theguardian.com/commentisfree/2018/jun/01/extremist-ideas-media-coverage-kkk.

DPA. (2021). DPA fact-checking. Deutsche Presse-Agentur. https://dpa-factchecking.com/netherlands/.

Drawrowfly. (2021). TikTok scraper [software]. https://github.com/drawrowfly/tiktok-scraper.

Dubois, E. and Blank, G. (2018). The echo chamber is overstated: The moderating effect of political interest and diverse media. *Information, Communication & Society* 21 (5): 729–745. https://doi.org/10.1080/1369118X.2018.1428656.

Dwoskin, E. (2020, November 12). Trump's attacks on election outcome prolong tech's emergency measures. *Washington Post*. https://www.washingtonpost.com/technology/2020/11/12/facebook-ad-ban-lame-duck/.

Economist. (2019, June 8). Google rewards reputable reporting, not left-wing politics. *The Economist*. https://www.economist.com/graphic-detail/2019/06/08/google-rewards-reputable-reporting-not-left-wing-politics.

Einwiller, S.A. and Kim, S. (2020). How online content providers moderate user-generated content to prevent harmful online communication: An analysis of policies and their implementation. *Policy & Internet*, 12(2), pp. 184–206. https://doi.org/10.1002/poi3.239.

Ellefson, L. (2019, August 7). Breitbart's audience has dropped 72% since Trump took office—As other right-wing sites have gained. *The Wrap*. https://www.thewrap.com/breitbart-news-audience-dropped-steve-bannon-72-percent/.

Ellis, E.G. (2019, September 10). Fighting Instagram's $1.3 billion problem—Fake followers. *Wired*. https://www.wired.com/story/instagram-fake-followers/.

Enli, G. (2017). Twitter as arena for the authentic outsider: Exploring the social media campaigns of Trump and Clinton in the 2016 U.S. presidential election. *European Journal of Communication*, *32*(1), pp. 50–61. https://doi.org/10.1177/0267323116682802.

Evan, D. (2017, May 26). Did Pope Francis slap away President Trump's hand? *Snopes*. https://www.snopes.com/fact-check/pope-francis-trump-hand-slap/.

Facebook (2018, December 6). Coordinated inauthentic behavior. Facebook Newsroom. https://about.fb.com/news/2018/12/inside-feed-coordinated-inauthentic-behavior/.

Facebook (2021a, February 9). January 2021 coordinated inauthentic behavior report. Facebook Newsroom. https://about.fb.com/news/2021/02/january-2021-coordinated-inauthentic-behavior-report/.

Facebook (2021b, May 25). False news, Facebook Transparency Center. https://transparency.fb.com/policies/community-standards/false-news/.

Feldman, B. (2017, June 8). In Russia, you can buy Instagram likes from a vending machine. *New York Times Magazine*, June 8. https://nymag.com/intelligencer/2017/06/you-can-buy-instagram-likes-from-a-russian-vending-machine.html.

Fiorentini, I. (2013). "ZOMG! Dis is a new language": The case of lolspeak. *Newcastle Working Papers in Linguistics*, *13*(1), pp. 90–108.

Fishkin, R. (2018). SparkToro's new tool to uncover real vs. fake followers on Twitter, SparkToro. https://sparktoro.com/blog/sparktoros-new-tool-to-uncover-real-vs-fake-followers-on-twitter/.

Floridi, L. (2021). Trump, Parler, and regulating the infosphere as our commons. *Philosophy & Technology*, *34*(1), pp. 1–5. https://doi.org/10.1007/s13347-021-00446-7.

Gadde, V. and Roth, Y. (2018, October 17). Enabling further research of information operations on Twitter. Twitter Blog. https://blog.twitter.com/en_us/topics/company/2018/enabling-further-research-of-information-operations-on-twitter.html.

Gagliardone, I. (2019). Defining online hate and its "public lives": What is the place for "extreme speech"? *International Journal of Communication*, *13*. https://doi.org/1932–8036/20190005.

Gallucci, N. (2016, November 22). 8 ways to consume news without using Facebook. *Mashable*. https://mashable.com/2016/11/22/consume-news-without-facebook/.

Geboers, M. (2019). "Writing" oneself into tragedy: Visual user practices and spectatorship of the Alan Kurdi images on Instagram. *Visual Communication*. https://doi.org/10.1177/1470357219857118.

Gekker, A. (2019). Playing with power: Casual politicking as a new frame for political analysis. In R. Glas, S. Lammes, M. de Lange, J. Raessens, and I. de Vries (Eds.)

The playful citizen: Civic engagement in a mediatized culture (pp. 387–419). Amsterdam University Press.

Gibbs, S. (2016, December 5). Google alters search autocomplete to remove "are Jews evil" suggestion. *The Guardian*. https://www.theguardian.com/technology/2016/dec/05/google-alters-search-autocomplete-remove-are-jews-evil-suggestion.

Gillespie, E. (2020, September 30). "Pastel QAnon": The female lifestyle bloggers and influencers spreading conspiracy theories through Instagram. *The Feed*. https://www.sbs.com.au/news/the-feed/pastel-qanon-the-female-lifestyle-bloggers-and-influencers-spreading-conspiracy-theories-through-instagram.

Gillespie, T. (2018). *Custodians of the internet: Platforms, content moderation, and the hidden decisions that shape social media*. Yale University Press.

Gillespie, T. (2020). Content moderation, AI, and the question of scale. *Big Data & Society*, July–December: 1–5, https://doi.org/10.1177/2053951720943234.

Goforth, C. (2021, January 21). Notorious pro-Trump forum rebrands as "patriots" after post-Capitol riot infighting. *The Daily Dot*. https://www.dailydot.com/debug/pro-trump-site-renamed-internal-conflict/.

Golebiewski, M. and boyd, d. (2019). Data voids: Where missing data can easily be exploited. Data & Society Research Institute. https://datasociety.net/wp-content/uploads/2019/11/Data-Voids-2.0-Final.pdf.

Google. (2019a). How Google Fights Misinformation. Google Blog. https://www.blog.google/documents/37/How_Google_Fights_Disinformation.pdf.

Google. (2019b). Search Quality Evaluator Guidelines. https://static.googleusercontent.com/media/guidelines.raterhub.com/en//searchqualityevaluatorguidelines.pdf.

Gray, J., Bounegru, L., and Venturini, T. (2020). "Fake news" as infrastructural uncanny. *New Media & Society*, 22(2), pp. 317–341. https://doi.org/10.1177/1461444819856912.

Green, J. (2017). *Devil's bargain: Steve Bannon, Donald Trump, and the nationalist uprising*. Penguin.

Groshek, J. and Koc-Michalska, K. (2017). Helping populism win? Social media use, filter bubbles, and support for populist presidential candidates in the 2016 U.S. Election Campaign. *Information, Communication & Society, 20*(9), 1389–407. https://doi.org/10.1080/1369118X.2017.1329334.

Guess, A., Nyhan, B., and Reifler, J. (2018). Selective exposure to misinformation: Evidence from the consumption of fake news during the 2016 U.S. presidential campaign [Working paper]. http://www.dartmouth.edu/~nyhan/fake-news-2016.pdf.

Hagen, S. and Jokubauskaite, E. (2019). Dutch junk news on 4chan and Reddit / pol/. In R. Rogers and S. Niederer (Eds.), *The politics of social media manipulation* (pp. 115–151). Dutch Ministry of the Interior and Kingdom Relations.

Hagen, S., Burton, A., Wilson, J., and Tuters, M. (2019, September 8). Infinity's Abyss: An Overview of 8chan. *OILab*. https://oilab.eu/infinitys-abyss-an-overview-of-8chan/.

Haim, M., Graefe, A., and Brosius, H.-B. (2018). Burst of the filter bubble?: Effects of personalization on the diversity of Google News. *Digital Journalism*, *6*(3), pp. 330–343. https://doi.org/10.1080/21670811.2017.1338145.

Harris, S. (2019, February 5). #148 – Jack Dorsey. Sam Harris Podcast. https://samharris.org/podcasts/148-jack-dorsey/.

Hassell, H. J. G., Holbein, J. B., and Miles, M. R. (2020). There is no liberal media bias in which news stories political journalists choose to cover. *Science Advances*, *6*(14), eaay9344. https://doi.org/10.1126/sciadv.aay9344.

Hautea, S., Parks, P., Takahashi, B., and Zeng, J. (2021). Showing they care (or don't): Affective publics and ambivalent climate activism on TikTok. *Social Media+ Society*. https://doi.org/10.1177/20563051211012344.

Hawley, G. (2017). *Making sense of the alt-right*. Columbia University Press.

Hedrick, A., Karpf, D., and Kreiss, D. (2018). The earnest internet vs. the ambivalent internet. *International Journal Of Communication*, *12*(8). https://ijoc.org/index.php/ijoc/article/view/8736/.

Herring, S. (2012). Special internet language varieties: Culture, creativity & language change [Paper]. The II LETiSS Workshop Language Go Web: Standard and Nonstandard Languages on the Internet, Pavia.

Herrman, John (2016, August 28) Inside Facebook's (totally insane, unintentionally gigantic, hyperpartisan) political-media machine. *New York Times*. https://www.nytimes.com/2016/08/28/magazine/inside-facebooks-totally-insane-unintentionally-gigantic-hyperpartisan-political-media-machine.html.

Heuts, F. and Mol, A. (2013). What is a good tomato? A case of valuing in practice. *Valuation Studies*, *1*(2), pp. 125–146. https://doi.org/10.3384/vs.2001-5992.1312125.

Highfield, T. and Leaver, T. (2016). Instagrammatics and digital methods: Studying visual social media, from selfies and GIFs to memes and emoji. *Communication Research and Practice*, *2*(1), pp. 47–62. https://doi.org/10.1080/22041451.2016.1155332.

Hine, G., Onaolapo, J., Cristofaro, E. D., Kourtellis, N., Leontiadis, I., Samaras, R., Stringhini, G., and Blackburn, J. (2017). Kek, cucks, and God emperor Trump: A measurement study of 4chan's politically incorrect forum and its effects on the web. In *Proceedings of the International AAAI Conference on Web and Social Media*, *11*(1), Article 1. https://ojs.aaai.org/index.php/ICWSM/article/view/14893.

Hines, N. (2018, April 22). Alex Jones' protegé, Paul Joseph Watson, is about to steal his crackpot crown. *The Daily Beast*. https://www.thedailybeast.com/alex-jones-protege-paul-joseph-watson-is-about-to-steal-his-crackpot-crown.

Holt, K., Figenschou, T.U. and Frischlich, L. (2019). Key dimensions of alternative news media. *Digital Journalism*, *7*(7), pp. 860–869. https://doi.org/10.1080/2167 0811.2019.1625715.

Howard, P. (2020). *Lie machines*. Yale University Press.

Howard, P. N., Bolsover, G., Kollyani, B., Bradshaw, S., and Neudert, L.-M. (2017). Junk news and bots during the U.S. election: What were Michigan voters sharing over Twitter? Data Memo 2017.1, Project on Computational Propaganda, Oxford Internet Institute. http://blogs.oii.ox.ac.uk/politicalbots/wp- content/uploads/sites/89/2017/03/What-Were-Michigan-Voters-Sharing-Over-Twitter-v2.pdf.

Howard, P. N., Ganesh, B., Liotsiou, D., Kelly, J., and François, C. (2018). The IRA, social media and political polarization in the United States, 2012–2018, Report, Computational Propaganda Research Project, Oxford Internet Institute. https://comprop.oii.ox.ac.uk/wp-content/uploads/sites/93/2018/12/The-IRA-Social-Media-and-Political-Polarization.pdf.

HypeAuditor. (2020). Instagram reports. https://hypeauditor.com/reports/instagram/.

Iati, M., Kornfield, M., O'Grady, S., and Mellen, R. (2020, May 4). Trump says it's safe to reopen states, while Birx finds protesters with no masks or distancing "devastatingly worrisome." *Washington Post.* https://www.washingtonpost.com/world/2020/05/03/coronavirus-latest-news/.

If Americans Knew. (2017, February 3). Senator Schumer says God made him a guardian of Israel. YouTube video. https://web.archive.org/web/20210417224317/https://www.youtube.com/c/IfAmericansKnew-Video/about. Accessed August 2, 2020.

Ingram, D. and Collins, B. (2020, June 29). Reddit bans hundreds of subreddits for hate speech including Trump community. *NBC News.* https://www.nbcnews.com/tech/tech-news/reddit-bans-hundreds-subreddits-hate-speech-including-trump-community-n1232408.

Instagram (n.d.). What are the requirements to apply for a verified badge on Instagram? Instagram Help Center. https://help.instagram.com/312685272613322.

Instagram. (2018). Reducing inauthentic activity on Instagram. Instagram Blog. https://about.instagram.com/blog/announcements/reducing-inauthentic-activity-on-instagram.

Instagram. (2020). Introducing new authenticity measures on Instagram. Instagram Blog. https://about.instagram.com/blog/announcements/introducing-new-authenticity-measures-on-instagram.

Internet Archive. (2021). Internet archive: Digital library of free & borrowable books, movies, music & Wayback Machine [Web-based]. Internet Archive. https://archive.org/.

Introna, L. and Wood, D. (2004). Picturing algorithmic surveillance: The politics of facial recognition systems. *Surveillance & Society,* 2(2/3), pp. 177–198.

Jack, C. (2017). Lexicon of lies: Terms for problematic information. Data & Society Research Institute. https://datasociety.net/library/lexicon-of-lies/.

Jansen, B.J. and Spink, A. (2006). How are we searching the World Wide Web? A comparison of nine search engine transaction logs. *Information Processing & Management*, *42*(1), pp. 248–263. https://doi.org/10.1016/j.ipm.2004.10.007.

Jenkins, H. (2006). *Convergence culture: Where old and new media collide*. New York University Press.

Jenkins, H. (2017, May 30). The ambivalent internet: An interview with Whitney Phillips and Ryan M. Milner (Part One). Confessions of an ACA-fan Blog. http://henryjenkins.org/blog/2017/05/the-ambivalent-internet-an-interview-with-whitney-phillips-and-ryan-m-milner-part-one.html.

Jett, J. (2021, February 11). Robert F. Kennedy, Jr. is barred from Instagram over false coronavirus claims. *New York Times*. https://www.nytimes.com/2021/02/11/us/robert-f-kennedy-jr-instagram-covid-vaccine.html.

John, N.A. (2019). Social media bullshit: What we don't know about facebook.com/peace and why we should care. *Social Media + Society*, January-March: 1–16. https://doi.org/10.1177/2056305119829863.

Jokubauskaitė, E. and Peeters, S. (2020). Generally curious: Thematically distinct datasets of general threads on 4chan/pol/. *Proceedings of the International AAAI Conference on Web and Social Media*, *14*, pp. 863–867.

Kaplan Sommer, A. (2017, October 19). White nationalist Richard Spencer gives Israel as example of ethno-state he wants in U.S. *Haaretz*. https://www.haaretz.com/us-news/richard-spencer-gives-israel-as-example-of-ethno-state-he-wants-in-u-s-1.5459154.

Karpf, D. Digital politics after Trump. *Annals of the International Communication Association*, *41*(2), pp. 198–207. https://doi.org/10.1080/23808985.2017.1316675.

Kelemen, M. (2005). *Managing quality: Managerial and critical perspectives*. Sage. https://doi.org/10.4135/9781446220382.

Kist, R. and Zantingh, P. (2017, March 6). Geen grote rol nepnieuws in aanloop naar verkiezingen. *NRC Handelsblad*. https://www.nrc.nl/nieuws/2017/03/06/fake-news-nee-zo-erg-is-het-hier-niet-7144615-a1549050.

Klayman, A. (2019). The Brink [Feature documentary; Digital film]. https://alisonklayman.com/the-brink.

Klein, E. and Robison, J. (2020). Like, post, and distrust? How social media use affects trust. *Political Communication*, *37*(1), pp. 46–64. https://doi.org/10.1080/10584609.2019.1661891.

Knuttila, L. (2011). User unknown: 4chan, anonymity and contingency. *First Monday*. https://doi.org/10.5210/fm.v16i10.3665.

Komok, A. (2018). How to check Instagram account for fake followers. HypeAuditor. https://hypeauditor.com/blog/how-to-check-instagram-account-for-fake-followers/.

Komok, A. (2020). What are suspicious accounts? HypeAuditor. https://help.hypeauditor.com/en/articles/2221742-what-are-suspicious-accounts.

Konrad, C. (2021, January 28). Trump presidency permanently alters landscape of media. *The Maneater*. https://themaneater.com/trump-presidency-permanently-alters-landscape-of-media/.

Kou, Y., Gui, X., Chen, Y., and Pine, K. (2017). Conspiracy talk on social media: Collective sensemaking during a public health crisis. In *Proceedings of the ACM on Human-Computer Interaction*, 1(CSCW), article no. 61. https://doi.org/10.1145/3134696.

Krafft, P., Zhou, K., Edwards, I., Starbird, K., and Spiro, E.S. (2017). Centralized, parallel, and distributed information processing during collective sensemaking. In *Proceedings of the 2017 CHI Conference on Human Factors in Computing Systems*, pp. 2976–2987. https://doi.org/10.1145/3025453.3026012.

Kwak, H., Lee, C., Park, H. and Moon, S. (2010). What is Twitter, a social network or a news media? In Proceedings of the 19th International Conference on World Wide Web (pp. 591–600). ACM.

Langville, A.N. and Meyer, C.D. (2006). *Google's PageRank and beyond: The science of search engine rankings*. Princeton University Press.

Lazer, D. M., Baum, M. A., Benkler, Y., Berinsky, A. J., Greenhill, K. M., Menczer, F., ... and Schudson, M. (2018). The science of fake news. *Science, 359*(6380), pp. 1094–1096. https://doi.org/10.1126/science.aao2998.

Lee, J.C. and Qualey, K. (2019, May 24). The 598 people, places and things Donald Trump has insulted on Twitter: A complete list. *New York Times*. https://www.nytimes.com/interactive/2016/01/28/upshot/donald-trump-twitter-insults.html.

Lee, L. and Oppong, F. (2020, September 1). Adding more context to Trends. Twitter Blog. https://blog.twitter.com/en_us/topics/product/2020/adding-more-context-to-trends.

Lenzen, C. (2020, November 9). This Luke Bryan song is an anti-Trump anthem on TikTok. *The Daily Dot*. https://www.dailydot.com/irl/luke-bryan-anti-trump-tiktok/.

Lerman, R. (2021, February 24). Major Trump backer Rebekah Mercer orchestrates Parler's second act. *Washington Post*. https://www.washingtonpost.com/technology/2021/02/24/parler-relaunch-rebekah-mercer/.

Lewis, D. (2020). Is the coronavirus airborne? Experts can't agree. *Nature, 580*(7802), p. 175. https://doi.org/10.1038/d41586-020-00974-w.

Lewis, R. (2018). Alternative influence: Broadcasting the reactionary right on YouTube. Data & Society Research Institute. https://datasociety.net/library/alternative-influence/.

Lewis, R. (2020). "This is what the news won't show you": YouTube creators and the reactionary politics of micro-celebrity. *Television & New Media, 21*(2), pp. 201–217. https://doi.org/10.1177/1527476419879919.

Lindquist, J. (2019). Illicit economies of the internet. *Made in China Journal, 3*(4), pp. 88–91. https://madeinchinajournal.com/2019/01/12/illicit-economies-of-the-internet-click-farming-in-indonesia-and-beyond/.

Lobinger, K., Krämer, B., Venema, R., and Benecchi, E. (2020). Pepe—Just a funny frog? A visual meme caught between innocent humor, far-right ideology, and fandom. In B. Krämer and C. Holtz-Bacha (Eds.), *Perspectives on populism and the media* (pp. 333–352). Nomos. https://doi.org/10.5771/9783845297392-333.

Lorenz. T. (2019, March 21) Instagram is the internet's new home for hate. *The Atlantic*. https://www.theatlantic.com/technology/archive/2019/03/instagram-is-the-internets-new-home-for-hate/585382/.

Lorenz, T. (2020, November 4). Election night on TikTok: Anxiety, analysis and wishful thinking. *New York Times*. https://www.nytimes.com/2020/11/04/style/tiktok-election-night.html.

Lubbers, E. (2016, November 5). There is no such thing as the Denver Guardian, despite that Facebook post you saw. *The Denver Post*. https://www.denverpost.com/2016/11/05/there-is-no-such-thing-as-the-denver-guardian/.

Ludemann, D. (2018). /pol/emics: Ambiguity, scales, and digital discourse on 4chan. *Discourse, Context & Media*, 24, pp. 92–98. https://doi.org/10.1016/j.dcm.2018.01.010.

Lyons, K. (2020, October 11). Twitter flags, limits sharing on Trump tweet about being "immune" to coronavirus. *The Verge*. https://www.theverge.com/2020/10/11/21511682/twitter-disables-sharing-trump-tweet-coronavirus-misinformation.

Mahendran, L. and Alsherif, N. (2020, January 8) Adding clarity to our Community Guidelines. TikTok newsroom. https://newsroom.tiktok.com/en-us/adding-clarity-to-our-community-guidelines.

Malone, C. (2016, August 18). Trump made Breitbart great again. *FiveThirtyEight*. https://fivethirtyeight.com/features/trump-made-breitbart-great-again/.

Mandavilli, A. (2020, July 4). 239 experts with one big claim: The coronavirus is airborne. *New York Times*. https://www.nytimes.com/2020/07/04/health/239-experts-with-one-big-claim-the-coronavirus-is-airborne.html.

Maragkou, E. (2020, December 8). The conspiracy theorist as influencer. Institute of Network Cultures Blog. https://networkcultures.org/blog/2020/12/08/the-conspiracy-theorist-as-influencer/.

Marres, N. (2018). Why we can't have our facts back. *Engaging Science, Technology, and Society, 4*, pp. 423–443. https://doi.org/10.17351/ests2018.188.

Massanari, A. (2017). #Gamergate and the fappening: How Reddit's algorithm, governance, and culture support toxic technocultures. *New Media & Society, 19*(3), pp. 329–346. https://doi.org/10.1177/1461444815608807.

McIntosh, J. (2012). A history of subversive remix video before YouTube: Thirty political video mashups made between World War II and 2005. *Transformative Works and Cultures, 9*. https://doi.org/10.3983/twc.2012.0371.

McNeal, S. and Broderick, R. (2020, April 4). Lifestyle influencers are now sharing some bogus far-right conspiracy theories about the coronavirus on Instagram.

Buzzfeed News. https://www.buzzfeednews.com/article/stephaniemcneal/ coronavirus-lifestyle-influencers-sharing-conspiracy-qanon.

McWhirter, A. (2015). Film criticism, film scholarship and the video essay. *Screen, 56*(3), pp. 369–377. https://doi.org/10.1093/screen/hjv044.

Media Bias/Fact Check. (2020). Filtered search. https://mediabiasfactcheck.com.

Media Bias/Fact Check. (2021). Breitbart. https://mediabiasfactcheck.com/breitbart/.

Medina Serrano, J.C., Papakyriakopoulos., O. and Hegelich S. (2020). Dancing to the partisan beat: A first analysis of political communication on TikTok. In *Proceedings of the 12th ACM Conference on Web Science,* pp. 257–266. https://doi.org/10.1145/3394231.3397916.

Meier, F., Elsweiler, D., and Wilson, M.L. (2014). More than liking and bookmarking? Towards understanding Twitter favouriting behaviour. In *Proceedings of ICWSM'14.* AAAI Press. http://www.aaai.org/ocs/index.php/ICWSM/ICWSM14/paper/view/8094.

Merrill, J. B. and Oremus, W. (2021, October 26). Five points for anger, one for a "like": How Facebook's formula fostered rage and misinformation. *Washington Post.* https://www.washingtonpost.com/technology/2021/10/26/facebook-angry-emoji-algorithm/.

Mosseri, A. (2017, April 6). Working to stop misinformation and false news. Facebook Newsroom. https://about.fb.com/news/2017/04/working-to-stop-misinformation-and-false-news/.

Nagle, A. (2017). *Kill all normies: Online culture wars from 4chan and Tumblr to Trump and the alt-right.* Zero Books.

NewsGuard (2020). NewsGuard nutrition label. https://www.newsguardtech.com.

Niederer, S. (2019). Networked content analysis: The case of climate change. Institute of Network Cultures. https://networkcultures.org/blog/publication/tod32-networked-content-analysis-the-case-of-climate-change/

Nissenbaum, A. and Shifman, L. (2017). Internet memes as contested cultural capital: The case of 4chan's /b/ board. *New Media & Society, 19*(4), pp. 483–501. https://doi.org/10.1177/1461444815609313.

Noble, S. U. (2018). *Algorithms of oppression: How search engines reinforce racism.* New York University Press.

Nunes, M. (2018). Parody. In E. Navas, O. Gallagher, and x. burrough (Eds.) *Keywords in remix studies* (pp. 217–229). Routledge.

O'Hara, K. and Stevens, D. (2015). Echo chambers and online radicalism: Assessing the internet's complicity in violent extremism. *Policy & Internet, 7*(4), pp. 401–422. https://doi.org/10.1002/poi3.88.

O'Leary, N. (2020, March 10). How Dutch false sense of security helped coronavirus spread. *Irish Times.* https://www.irishtimes.com/news/world/europe/how-dutch-false-sense-of-security-helped-coronavirus-spread-1.4199027.

Oh, D. (2019). Review of *The ambivalent internet: mischief, oddity, and antagonism online. Information, Communication & Society*, 22(8), pp. 1189–1191. https://doi. org/10.1080/1369118X.2019.1606267.

Olmsted, K. (2009) *Real enemies: Conspiracy theories and American democracy, World War I to 9/11.* Oxford University Press.

Otero, V. (2017). The chart, version 3.1, ad fontes media. https://www.adfontesmedia. com/the-chart-version-3-0-what-exactly-are-we-reading/.

Owen, L. H. (2021, July 14) At first, Facebook was happy that I and other journalists were finding its tool useful...but the mood shifted. NiemanLab. https://www. niemanlab.org/2021/07/at-first-facebook-was-happy-that-i-and-other-journalists-were-finding-its-tool-useful-but-the-mood-shifted/.

Papasavva, A., Zannettou, S., Cristofaro, E. D., Stringhini, G., and Blackburn, J. (2020). Raiders of the lost kek: 3.5 years of augmented 4chan posts from the politically incorrect board. *Proceedings of the International AAAI Conference on Web and Social Media*, 14, pp. 885–894.

Pardes, A. (2020, October 22). The TikTok teens trying to meme the vote. *Wired.* https://www.wired.com/story/tiktok-election-2020/.

Pariser, E. (2011). *The filter bubble: What the internet is hiding from you.* Penguin.

Parks, L. (2019). Dirty data: Content moderation, regulatory outsourcing and The Cleaners. *Film Quarterly*, 73(1). https://doi.org/10.1525/fq.2019.73.1.11.

Peacock, C., Hoewe, J., Panek, E., and Willis, G. P. (2019). Hyperpartisan news use: Relationships with partisanship, traditional news use, and cognitive and affective involvement. Paper presented at the Annual Conference of the International Communication Association, Washington, DC.

Peeters, S. (2020, May 15). Normiefication of extreme speech and the widening of the Overton window. Open Intelligence Lab. https://oilab.eu/ normiefication-of-extreme-speech-and-the-widening-of-the-overton-window/.

Peeters, S. and Hagen, S. (2018). 4CAT: 4chan Capture and Analysis Toolkit [software]. https://4cat.oilab.eu.

Peeters, S. and Hagen, S. (2021). The 4CAT Capture and Analysis Toolkit: A Modular Tool for Transparent and Traceable Social Media Research (SSRN Scholarly Paper ID 3914892). Social Science Research Network. https://doi.org/10.2139/ssrn.3914892.

Peeters, S., Tuters, M., Willaert, T., and de Zeeuw, D. (2021). On the vernacular language games of an antagonistic online subculture. *Frontiers in Big Data*, 4(65). https://doi.org/10.3389/fdata.2021.718368.

Pepp, J., Michaelson, E. and Sterken, R. (2019). Why we should keep talking about fake news. *Inquiry.* https://doi.org/10.1080/0020174X.2019.1685231.

Perez, S. (2021, August 2). Twitter partners with AP and Reuters to address misinformation on its platform. *TechCrunch.* https://techcrunch.com/2021/08/02/twitter-partners-with-ap-and-reuters-to-address-misinformation-on-its-platform/.

Peterson, J. (2016, November 8). Jordan Peterson: The right to be politically incorrect. National Post. https://nationalpost.com/opinion/jordan-peterson-the-right-to-be-politically-incorrect.

Phillips, W. (2015). *This is why we can't have nice things: Mapping the relationship between online trolling and mainstream culture.* MIT Press.

Phillips, W. (2018). The oxygen of amplification. Data & Society Research Institute. https://datasociety.net/output/oxygen-of- amplification/.

Phillips, W. and Milner, R.M. (2017). *The ambivalent internet: Mischief, oddity, and antagonism online.* Polity.

Porter, J. (2020, May 29). Twitter restricts new Trump tweet for "glorifying violence." *The Verge.* https://www.theverge.com/2020/5/29/21274323/trump-twitter-glorifying-violence-minneapolis-shooting-looting-notice-restriction.

Quandt, T. (2018). Dark participation. *Media and Communication*, 6(4), pp. 36–48. https://doi.org/10.17645/mac.v6i4.1519.

Quealy, K. (2017, July 26). Trump is on track to insult 650 people, places and things on Twitter by the end of his first term. *New York Times.* https://www.nytimes.com/interactive/2017/07/26/upshot/president-trumps-newest-focus-discrediting-the-news-media-obamacare.html.

Rathnayake, C. and Suthers, D.D. (2018). Twitter issue response hashtags as affordances for momentary connectedness. *Social Media + Society.* https://doi.org/10.1177/2056305118784780.

Reider, B. (2015). YouTube Data Tools [software]. https://tools.digitalmethods.net/netvizz/youtube/index.php.

Rheingold, H. (1994). *The millennial whole earth catalog.* HarperCollins.

Roberts, S. T. (2016). Commercial content moderation: Digital laborers' dirty work. In S. U. Noble and B.M. Tynes (Eds.), *The intersectional internet: Race, sex, class and culture online* (pp. 147–160). Peter Lang.

Robertson, R. E., Lazer, D., and Wilson, C. (2018). Auditing the personalization and composition of politically related search engine results pages. *Proceedings of the 2018 World Wide Web Conference on World Wide Web*, pp. 955–965. https://doi.org/10.1145/3178876.3186143.

Roeder, O. (2018, August 8). We gave you 3 million Russian troll tweets. Here's what you've found so far. FiveThirtyEight. https://fivethirtyeight.com/features/what-you-found-in-3-million-russian-troll-tweets/.

Rogers, R. (2004). *Information politics on the web.* MIT Press.

Rogers, R. (2013). *Digital methods.* MIT Press.

Rogers, R. (2014). Debanalising Twitter: The transformation of an object of study. In K. Weller, A. Bruns, J. Burgess, M. Mahrt and C. Puschmann (Eds.), *Twitter and society* (pp. ix–xxvi). Peter Lang.

Rogers, R. (2017). Digital methods for cross-platform analysis. In J. Burgess, A. Marwick and T. Poell (Eds.) *The SAGE handbook of social media* (pp. 91–108). Sage.

Rogers, R. (2019). *Doing digital methods*. Sage.

Rogers, R. (2020a). The scale of Facebook's problem depends upon how "fake news" is classified. *Harvard Kennedy School Misinformation Review, 1*(6). https://doi.org/10.37016/mr-2020-43.

Rogers, R. (2020b). Deplatforming: Following extreme internet celebrities to Telegram and alternative social media. *European Journal of Communication, 35*(3). https://doi.org/10.1177/0267323120922066.

Rogers, R. (2021) Marginalizing the mainstream: How social media privilege political information. *Frontiers in Big Data.* https://doi.org/10.3389/fdata.2021.689036.

Rogers, R. and Hagen, S. (2020). Epilogue: After the tweet storm. In R. Rogers and S. Niederer (Eds.) *The politics of social media manipulation* (pp. 253–256). Amsterdam University Press.

Rogers, R. and Niederer, S. (Eds.) (2020). *The politics of social media manipulation*. Amsterdam University Press.

Romm, T. and Stanley-Becker, I. (2019, December 21). Facebook, Twitter disable sprawling inauthentic operation that used AI to make fake faces. *Washington Post.* https://www.washingtonpost.com/technology/2019/12/20/facebook-twitter-disable-sprawling-inauthentic-operation-that-used-ai-make-fake-faces/.

Rosenblatt, K. (2020, October 17). They can't vote, but they can meme: How these TikTokers are trying to get Biden elected. *NBC News.* https://www.nbcnews.com/pop-culture/viral/they-can-t-vote-they-can-meme-how-these-TikTokers-n1243555.

Roth, Y. and Pickels, N. (2020, May 11). Updating our approach to misleading information. Twitter Blog. https://blog.twitter.com/en_us/topics/product/2020/updating-our-approach-to-misleading-information.

Salen, K. and Zimmerman, E. (2004). *Rules of play: Game design fundamentals*. MIT Press.

Salenger, M. [meredthsalenger]. (2020, March 02). "Real quick: How are Republicans like Donald ok with 2% of people dying from coronavirus as if 2% is not a very high number. But when you discuss a 2 cent wealth tax on people making over 50 million they freak out like it's the worst thing that could ever happened to them" [tweet]. https://twitter.com/meredthsalenger/status/1234337053.

Schellewald, A. (2021). Communicative forms on TikTok: Perspectives from digital ethnography. *International Journal of Communication, 15*, pp. 1437–1457.

Scheufele, D. A. and Krause, N. M. (2019). Science audiences, misinformation, and fake news. *Proceedings of the National Academy of Sciences, 116*(16), pp. 7662–7669. https://doi.org/10.1073/pnas.1805871115.

Schmitt, C. (2005). *Political theology: Four chapters on the concept of sovereignty.* University of Chicago Press.

Schwartz, O. (2018, December 4). Are Google and Facebook really suppressing conservative politics? *The Guardian.* https://www.theguardian.com/technology/2018/dec/04/google-facebook-anti-conservative-bias-claims.

Searles, S. (2020, August 4). Republican TikTok thinks "Red Kingdom" by Tech N9ne is their new hype song; We're laughing. *The Pitch.* https://www.thepitchkc.com/republican-tik-tok-thinks-red-kingdom-by-tech-n9ne-is-their-new-hype-song-were-laughing/.

Shane, T. (2020, December 1). Searching for the misinformation "twilight zone." Nieman Lab. https://www.niemanlab.org/2020/12/searching-for-the-misinformation-twilight-zone/.

Shao, C., Ciampaglia, G. L., Varol, O., Yang, K.-C., Flammini, A., and Menczer, F. (2018). The spread of low-credibility content by social bots. *Nature Communications*, 9(1), p. 4787. https://doi.org/10.1038/s41467-018-06930-7.

Shepherd, T., Harvey, A., Jordan, T., Srauy, S., and Miltner, K. (2015). Histories of hating. *Social Media + Society.* https://doi.org/10.1177/2056305115603997.

Shibutani, T. (1966). *Improvised news: A sociological study of rumor.* Ardent Media.

Shifman, L. (2012). An anatomy of a YouTube meme. *New Media & Society*, 14(2), pp. 187–203. https://doi.org/10.1177/1461444811412160.

Shirky, C. (2008). *Here comes everybody.* Penguin.

Silverman, C. (2016, November 16). This analysis shows how viral fake election news stories outperformed real news on Facebook. *Buzzfeed News.* https://www.buzzfeednews.com/article/craigsilverman/viral-fake-election-news-outperformed-real-news-on-facebook.

Silverman, C. and Alexander, L. (2016, November 3). How teens in the Balkans are duping Trump supporters with fake news. *Buzzfeed News.* https://www.buzzfeednews.com/article/craigsilverman/how-macedonia-became-a-global-hub-for-pro-trump-misinfo.

Skopeliti, C. and John, B. (2020, March 19). Coronavirus: How are the social media platforms responding to the "infodemic"? First Draft. https://firstdraftnews.org:443/latest/how-social-media-platforms-are-responding-to-the-coronavirus-infodemic/.

Smith Gale, S (2020, October 6). U.S. election 2020: TikTok gets pulled into the campaigns. *BBC News.* https://www.bbc.com/news/technology-54374710.

Smith, R., Cubbon, S. and Wardle, C. (2020, November 12). Under the surface: Covid-19 vaccine narratives, misinformation and data deficits on social media. First Draft. https://firstdraftnews.org/long-form-article/under-the-surface-covid-19-vaccine-narratives-misinformation-and-data-deficits-on-social-media/.

Sommer, W. (2018). Instagram is the alt-right's new favorite haven. *The Daily Beast.* https://www.thedailybeast.com/instagram-is-the-alt-rights-new-favorite-haven.

Sparktoro. (2021). Audience intelligence. https://sparktoro.com.

Stanley-Becker, I. (2020, August 1). How the Trump campaign came to court QAnon, the online conspiracy movement identified by the FBI as a violent threat. *Washington Post.* https://www.washingtonpost.com/politics/how-the-trump-campaign-came-to-court-qanon-the-online-conspiracy-movement-identified-by-the-fbi-as-a-violent-threat/2020/08/01/ddoea9b4-d1d4-11ea-9038-af089b63ac21_story.html.

Starbird, K. (2012). Crowdwork, crisis and convergence: How the connected crowd organizes information during mass disruption events [PhD].

Starbird, K. (2017). Examining the alternative media ecosystem through the production of alternative narratives of mass shooting events on Twitter. In *Proceedings of the 11th International AAAI Conference on Web and Social Media.* AAAI Press. http://faculty.washington.edu/kstarbi/Alt_Narratives_ICWSM17-CameraReady.pdf.

Starbird, K. (2020, April 27). How to cope with an infodemic. Brookings. https://www.brookings.edu/techstream/how-to-cope-with-an-infodemic/.

Starbird, K., Spiro, E., Edwards, I., Zhou, K., Maddock, J., and Narasimhan, S. (2016). Could this be true? I think so! Expressed uncertainty in online rumoring. In *Proceedings of the 2016 CHI Conference on Human Factors in Computing Systems,* pp. 360–371. https://doi.org/10.1145/2858036.2858551.

Sullivan, D. (2004, April 24) Google in controversy over top-tanking for anti-Jewish site. *Search Engine Watch.* https://www.searchenginewatch.com/2004/04/24/google-in-controversy-over-top-ranking-for-anti-jewish-site/.

Sunstein, C. R. (2001). *Echo chambers: Bush v. Gore, impeachment, and beyond.* Princeton University Press.

Sunstein, C. R. (2018). *#Republic: Divided democracy in the age of social media.* Princeton University Press. https://doi.org/10.2307/j.ctv8xnhtd

Systrom, K. (2014). 300 million Instagrammers sharing real life moments. Instagram Blog. https://about.instagram.com/blog/announcements/300-million-instagrammers-sharing-real-life-moments.

Tarkov, A. (2012, June 30). Journatic worker takes "This American Life" inside outsourced journalism. Poynter. https://www.poynter.org/reporting-editing/2012/journatic-staffer-takes-this-american-life-inside-outsourced-journalism/.

Tate, R. (2009, 19 Nov.). Twitter's new prompt: A linguist weighs in. *Gawker.* https://gawker.com/5408768/twitters-new-prompt-a-linguist-weighs-in.

Teitelbaum, B.R. (2020). *War for eternity: The return of traditionalism and the rise of the populist right.* Penguin.

Tiffany, K. (2020, August 18). How Instagram aesthetics repackage QAnon. *The Atlantic*. https://www.theatlantic.com/technology/archive/2020/08/how-instagram-aesthetics-repackage-qanon/615364/.

Trielli, D. and Diakopoulos, N. (2019). Search as news curator: The role of Google in shaping attention to news information. *Proceedings of the 2019 CHI Conference on Human Factors in Computing Systems – CHI '19*, 1–15. https://doi.org/10.1145/3290605.3300683.

Tuters, M. (2019). LARPing & liberal tears: Irony, idiocy & belief in the deep vernacular web. In M. Fielitz and N. Thurston (Eds.) *Post-digital cultures of the far right: Online actions and offline consequences in Europe and the U.S.* (pp. 37–48). Transcript.

Tuters, M. and Burton, A. (2021). The rebel yell: Toxic vox populism on YouTube. *Canadian Journal of Communication*. forthcoming.

Tuters, M. and Hagen, S. (2020). (((They))) rule: Memetic antagonism and nebulous othering on 4chan. *New Media & Society*, *22*(12), pp. 2218–2237. https://doi.org/10.1177/1461444819888746.

Tuters, M. and OILab (2020). Esoteric fascism online: 4chan and the Kali Yuga. In L.D. Valencia-García (Ed.), *Far-right revisionism and the end of history: Alt/histories* (pp. 287–303). Routledge.

Tuters, M., Jokubauskaitė, E., and Bach, D. (2018). Post-truth protest: How 4chan cooked up the Pizzagate bullshit. *M/C Journal*, *21*(3), Article 3. https://doi.org/10.5204/mcj.1422.

Twitter (2019a). Glorification of violence policy, Twitter Help Center. https://help.twitter.com/en/rules-and-policies/glorification-of-violence.

Twitter (2019b, October 15). World leaders on Twitter: Principles & approach. Twitter Blog. https://blog.twitter.com/en_us/topics/company/2019/worldleaders2019.

Twitter (2020a, February 7). Synthetic and manipulated media policy. Twitter. https://web.archive.org/web/20200207000218/https://help.twitter.com/en/rules-and-policies/manipulated-media.

Twitter (2020b, April). Coronavirus: Staying safe and informed on Twitter. Twitter Blog. https://blog.twitter.com/en_us/topics/company/2020/covid-19.

Twitter (2020c, May 11). Coronavirus: Staying safe and informed on Twitter. Twitter Blog. https://blog.twitter.com/en_us/topics/company/2020/covid-19.

Twitter (2020d, December 16). COVID-19 misleading information policy. Twitter. https://web.archive.org/web/20201216200114/https://help.twitter.com/en/rules-and-policies/medical-misinformation-policy.

Twitter (2021, January 8). Permanent suspension of @realDonaldTrump. Twitter Blog. https://blog.twitter.com/en_us/topics/company/2020/suspension.

Tynan, D. (2016, August 24) How Facebook powers money machines for obscure political "news" sites. *The Guardian*. https://www.theguardian.com/technology/2016/aug/24/facebook-clickbait-political-news-sites-us-election-trump.

UN DGC. (2020, March 31). UN tackles "infodemic" of misinformation and cyber-crime in COVID-19 crisis. UN Department of Global Communications. https://www.un.org/en/un-coronavirus-communications-team/un-tackling-'infodemic'-misinformation-and-cybercrime-covid-19.

Unkel, J. and Haim, M. (2019). Googling politics: Parties, sources, and issue owner-ships on Google in the 2017 German federal election campaign. *Social Science Computer Review, 39*(5), pp. 844–861. https://doi.org/10.1177/0894439319881634.

Urman, A. and Katz, S. (2020). What they do in the shadows: Examining the far-right networks on Telegram. *Information, Communication & Society*, 1–20. https://doi.org/10.1080/1369118X.2020.1803946.

Urquhart, C. (2013, January 12). Here comes the sun flash mob cheers Spanish unemployment office. *The Guardian.* https://www.theguardian.com/world/2013/jan/12/here-comes-the-sun-spanish-unemployment-office.

userleansbot. (n.d.). *List of political subreddits used by userleansbot.* Reddit. https://www.reddit.com/user/userleansbot/comments/cfzho2/list_of_political_subred-dits_used_ by_userleansbot/.

Vaidhyanathan, S. (2019, July 28). Why conservatives allege big tech is muzzling them. *The Atlantic.* https://www.theatlantic.com/ideas/archive/2019/07/conservatives-pretend-big-tech-biased-against-them/594916/.

Van Den Berg, E. (2019, July 30). Opnieuw misser bij Forum voor Democratie: Per-soonlijke advertentie Thierry Baudet offline gehaald. NPO3. https://www.npo3.nl/brandpuntplus/opnieuw-misser-bij-forum-voor-democratie-persoonlijke-advertentie-thierry-baudet-offline-gehaald.

Van der Linden, S., Panagopoulos, C. and Roozenbeek, J. (2020). You are fake news: Political bias in perceptions of fake news. *Media, Culture & Society, 42*(3). https://doi.org/10.1177/0163443720906992.

Van Driel, L. and Dumitrica, D. (2021). Selling brands while staying "authentic": The professionalization of Instagram influencers. *Convergence, 27*(1), pp. 66–84. https://doi.org/10.1177/1354856520902136.

Venturini, T. (2019) From fake to junk news: The data politics of online virality. In D. Bigo, E. Isin, and E. Ruppert (Eds.) *Data politics: Worlds, subjects, rights* (pp. 123–144). Routledge.

Venturini, T. and Latour, B. (2010). The social fabric: Digital footprints and quali-quantitative methods. *Proceedings of Futur En Seine 2009: The Digital Future of the City.* Futur en Seine 2009.

Vijay, D. and Gekker, A. (2021). Playing politics: How Sabarimala played out on TikTok. *American Behavioral Scientist, 65*(5), pp. 712–734. https://doi.org/10.1177/0002764221989769.

Vosoughi, S., Roy, D., and Aral, S. (2018). The spread of true and false news online. *Science, 359*(6380), pp. 1146–1151. https://doi.org/10.1126/science.aap9559.

Voué, P., De Smedt, T., and De Pauw, G. (2020). 4chan & 8chan embeddings. *ArXiv:2005.06946* [*Cs*]. http://arxiv.org/abs/2005.06946.

Wahl-Jorgensen, K. (2019). *Emotions, media and politics.* Polity.

Wakabayashi, D. (2018, September 5). Trump says Google is rigged, despite its denials. What do we know about how it works? *New York Times.* https://www.nytimes.com/2018/09/05/technology/google-trump-bias.html.

Wardle, C. (2016, November 18). 6 types of misinformation circulated this election season. *Columbia Journalism Review.* https://www.cjr.org/tow_center/6_types_election_fake_news.php.

Wardle, C. (2017, February 16). Fake news: It's complicated. First Draft. https://firstdraftnews.org/latest/fake-news-complicated/.

Warzel, C. (2021, November 11). Facebook's vast wasteland. *The Atlantic Monthly.* https://newsletters.theatlantic.com/galaxy-brain/618ad9942e822d00205a26b3/facebooks-vast-wasteland/.

Wendling, M. (2018). *Alt-Right: From 4chan to the White House.* Pluto Press.

Wikipedia contributors. (2020). Killian documents controversy. *Wikipedia: The Free Encyclopaedia.* https://en.wikipedia.org/w/index.php?title=Killian_documents_authenticity_issues&oldid=962589844.

Wilkinson, W.W. and Berry, S.D. (2020). Together they are Troy and Chase: Who supports demonetization of gay content on YouTube? *Psychology of Popular Media*, *9*(2). https://doi.org/10.1037/ppm0000228.

Willaert, T., Van Eecke, P., Beuls, K., and Steels, L. (2020). Building social media observatories for monitoring online opinion dynamics. *Social Media + Society*, *6*(2). https://doi.org/10.1177/2056305119898778.

Willaert, T., Van Eecke, P., Van Soest, J., and Beuls, K. (2021). A tool for tracking the propagation of words on Reddit. *Computational Communication Research*, *3*(1), pp. 117–132. https://doi.org/10.5117/CCR2021.1.005.WILL.

Woods, A. (2019). Cultural Marxism and the cathedral: Two alt-right perspectives on critical theory. In C.M. Battista and M.R. Sande (Eds.), *Critical theory and the humanities in the age of the alt-right* (pp. 39–59). Springer. https://doi.org/10.1007/978-3-030-18753-8_3.

Yong, E. (2020, April 29). Why the coronavirus is so confusing. *The Atlantic.* https://www.theatlantic.com/health/archive/2020/04/pandemic-confusing-uncertainty/610819/.

YouTube (2019, January 25). Continuing our work to improve recommendations on YouTube. YouTube Blog. https://blog.youtube/news-and-events/continuing-our-work-to-improve/.

YouTube (2020). COVID-19 medical misinformation policy—YouTube Help. https://support.google.com/youtube/answer/9891785?hl=en.

ytdl-org (2021, February 1). *Youtube-dl.* Youtube-Dl: Download Videos from YouTube (and More Sites). http://ytdl-org.github.io/youtube-dl/.

Zannettou, S., Caulfield, T., Blackburn, J., De Cristofaro, E., Sirivianos, M., Stringhini, G., and Suarez-Tangil, G. (2018). On the origins of memes by means of fringe web communities. *ArXiv:1805.12512 [Cs].* http://arxiv.org/abs/1805.12512.

Zannettou, S., Caulfield, T., De Cristofaro, E., Kourtelris, N., Leontiadis, I., Sirivianos, M., Stringhini, G., and Blackburn, J. (2017). The web centipede: Understanding how web communities influence each other through the lens of mainstream and alternative news sources. *Proceedings of the 2017 Internet Measurement Conference IMC'17* (pp. 405–417). ACM. https://doi.org/10.1145/3131365.3131390.

Zulli, D. and Zulli, D. J. (2020). Extending the internet meme: Conceptualizing technological mimesis and imitation publics on the TikTok platform. *New Media & Society.* https://doi.org/10.1177/1461444820983603.

Index

Page numbers in *italics* refer to figures and tables

Printed and bound by CPI Group (UK) Ltd, Croydon, CR0 4YY

23/04/2025

14661018-0001